Writing Baseball

THE SOUTHERN ILLINOIS UNIVERSITY PRESS SERIES

Bottom of the Ninth

Bottom
of the Ninth

Great Contemporary Baseball Short Stories

Edited and with an Introduction by

John McNally

With a Foreword by Richard Russo

SOUTHERN ILLINOIS UNIVERSITY PRESS

Carbondale and Edwardsville

Library of Congress Cataloging-in-Publication Data

Bottom of the ninth : great contemporary baseball short stories / edited and with an
introduction by John McNally ; with a foreword by Richard Russo.
p. cm.
Includes bibliographical references.
1. Baseball stories, American. I. McNally, John, 1965–
PS648.B37 B68 2003
813'.0108355—dc21
2002010548
ISBN 0-8093-2504-7 (cloth : alk. paper)
ISBN 0-8093-2505-5 (pbk. : alk. paper)

Printed on recycled paper. ♻

Writing Baseball Series Editor: Richard Peterson

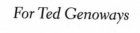

For Ted Genoways

Contents

Foreword

RICHARD RUSSO

Two things I try my best not to worry about are books and baseball. People are always asking me if I think there's a future for books, and it's hard not to take the question personally. After all, I write books and depend on their continued existence for my livelihood, and when someone asks me if I think they have a future, they're really asking if I think *I* have one. Which is why I reply with exaggerated confidence that *of course* there's a future for books; after all, I remind them, a book is a perfect thing. Books feel good in the hand, they smell good (even the ones that stink smell good), they travel well, they're relatively inexpensive for the pleasure and instruction they offer, and some even possess the power to change our lives. That they are preferable to movies, television, video games, the internet, and other technologies that appear to be cutting into their popularity is to me self-evident. As a professor friend of mine likes to say, after any new experience, "Well, here's one more thing that's not quite as good as a good book." Who could possibly disagree? Okay, the majority of our fellow humans, who vote their preference every evening after work, as it turns out. Nobody really *likes* television or ever feels better about themselves for wasting an evening in front of one, but passivity and relaxation seem to have become synonyms, so there we sit.

Just as a book is a self-evidently perfect thing, baseball is a perfect sport. I'm not talking about major-league baseball, which has been corrupted by greed, power, and celebrity. I'm talking about the game we used to play as boys (and, yes, as girls) when we slid our mitts over the handlebars of our bikes and peddled like mad, steering one-handed, our favorite bats resting on our shoulders, made half crazy by the possibility that we might arrive after the teams had been chosen, that the game would start without us, that we would miss our first ups. Like a book, baseball is relatively inexpensive, it travels well, it smells good (have you sniffed a baseball mitt recently? I recommend doing so), and it's powerfully instructive. Baseball is also designed to induce and embrace narrative. It's not slow, as its critics charge, just leisurely; its plots and subplots unfold richly, like a good novel, which is why baseball has found a place in our literature that's unparalleled by any other sport.

The great paradox of television (as well as many other technologies) is that things inside the box go fast, allowing things outside it (viewers) to go slow. People inside the television get to live life large, often at a dead run, while those outside barely register a pulse. It's no surprise, therefore, that television loves football and basketball, games played to a ticking clock, or that these sports have benefited from TV's pervasive influence. Still, that baseball should have lost some of its popularity to football and basketball doesn't trouble me particularly because these sports are played during baseball's off-season and appeal to different temperaments. Boys that prefer football to baseball *should* play football, in my view. Not everyone can be elegant. That baseball, the quintessential summer sport, should lose participants to *soccer*, however, is in every way untenable. Soccer—and let me be very clear about this—is what happens when parents get their way, and nothing troubles me more about today's youth than their willingness to let grown-ups organize their free time. Huck Finn had better sense, and so did Holden Caulfield. It's hard to imagine that children encouraged to play soccer will grow up any fonder of their parents than they'll be of the minivans used to transport them to their matches. I don't even like to think about the kind of nursing homes they put such parents in when the time comes. Worse, as we now know, children who are abused often turn out to be abusers, and it's not difficult to imagine soccer being passed on in this fashion from one sad generation to the next if the cycle isn't interrupted.

What's needed, clearly, is more books about baseball, and luckily you hold one in your hands. One of the very best things about the stories in this collection is that baseball has entered the imaginations of their authors so deeply as children that they are no longer able to separate it from other aspects of their adult lives. For these writers, baseball is like Catholicism or Zen, less a subject than a way of seeing and being; for them baseball gets all mixed up with politics (Jim Shepard's "Batting Against Castro"), memory (Philip F. Deaver's "Infield"), dreams (Leslie Pietrzyk's "What We All Want"), issues of justice (Ron Carlson's "Sunny Billy Day"), even race and class (Gordon Weaver's "Gold Moments and Victory Beer"). The astute reader will quickly note that most of these stories are not really *about* baseball, but baseball creeps into them, like King Charles's head into Mr. Dick's memoir in *David Copperfield*, refusing to be banished and yielding up a wealth of metaphor (Stuart Dybek's "Death of the Right Fielder"), fantasy (Ray Gonzalez's "Baseball"), psychological realism (Andre Dubus's "After the Game"), irony (David Carkeet's "The Greatest Slump of All Time"), tense human drama (Kurt Rheinheimer's "Umpire"), and brutally hard-won wisdom (Owen King's "Wonders"). To read this anthology is to understand how deeply ingrained baseball is in our culture. I'd put it up against any anthology of soccer stories you can name, if you can name one.

Acknowledgments

Thanks to all the fine folks at Southern Illinois University Press, with a special thanks to Karl Kageff and Kathy Kageff. Many thanks also to Richard Peterson, the series editor. My gratitude to Jim Harris and Eric T. Lindvall for their suggestions. Scott Smith again saves the day for taking care of ninth-inning projects. As with my previous anthologies, the authors played a major role in helping to secure permission or granting use of their stories. Special thanks to Jim Shepard, Carol Houck Smith, and Andre Dubus III. Once more, I'm indebted to my wife, Amy, for her help and support.

Introduction

By Chicago standards, I'm a traitor.

I grew up on the South Side of Chicago, an important distinction among those who follow baseball. Once this key piece of information comes to light, the person to whom I am speaking, if they know anything about baseball, will say, "So. You must be a Sox fan." How many times in my life have I heard this? Fifty? A hundred? I really don't know. A *lot*. Once, when I was a child and my parents took me as far away as Memphis, Tennessee, a kindly older man asked me what part of Chicago I was from, and when I told him, he said, "A Sox fan!" I suppose I could have lied to all of these people. I could have smiled and nodded. I could have said, "Of course! What else?" But, as I said, I am a traitor. The truth is that I have always liked the Cubs. You see, the Cubs are the North Side's team, and if you know anything about Chicago, you know that a great divide separates the South Side from the North Side. For starters, South Siders often align themselves with the working class. All of my friends' parents were laborers. Most belonged to the union. My father was a roofer; my mother worked in a factory. North Siders were sophisticates. They were white-collar; they had money. These were generalizations, of course, but there was truth to it, and the divide between the two was vast.

Did I understand all of these implications as a child? Did I comprehend the ramifications inherent to crossing that divide when I told people that I was a Cubs fan? I *felt* it—I could tell by the way folks looked at me when I admitted my allegiance—but, no, I didn't understand. Not fully, at least. I was a Cubs fan for reasons that had nothing to do with socioeconomics. I was a Cubs fan because I watched channel 9's WGN-TV more than any other station—WGN had the best children's programming and happened to be the station that televised the Cubs. The White Sox were televised on a UHF station, which, on our TV, was always fuzzy and required seemingly endless fiddling with the antenna. To cement my allegiance to the Cubs, my mother's friend Joan took me and her two boys to Wrigley Field one morning, making it a day of firsts—the first time I had ever been on the El; the first time I had ever seen the city from the perspective of a moving train; the first time I had ever attended a professional sporting event. I don't remember a lot about that particular game, but I do remember how much colder it was at Wrigley Field than where I lived, and I remember going home with a miniature baseball bat, a Cubs ball cap, and a Cubs pennant.

As an adult, my allegiance has continued. For me, the sum of a baseball team is more than just the game and its players. Being a Cubs fan was a full package deal. What came with it? For starters, there was Harry Caray, sometimes shirtless, sometimes drinking beer, but always belting "Take Me Out to the Ball Game." He was the kindly, albeit somewhat toasted, uncle we all wished we had. There was Wrigley Field itself, with its ivy-laced walls, so distinct that I could identify it from a split-second glimpse out of the corner of my eye while passing a TV screen. There were the apartment buildings alongside Wrigley, where people watched in lawn chairs from the rooftops, a freshly tapped keg nearby. There were the men with transistor radios who waited on Waveland Avenue for a home run, grown men with mitts whose glory it would be to catch a ball hit out of the park by the likes of Hank Aaron or, later, Jose Hernandez.

And there are more reasons. When I returned to Chicago in 1991, I moved to an apartment two blocks from Wrigley Field. By this time, the controversial night games had begun. Often, while leaving my apartment, I would look up and see floating lazily in the sky Shamu the whale, the blimp that filmed the overhead shots of Wrigley, and I knew that a Cubs game was in progress. Also that year, I frequently saw around my neighborhood a man known as Ronnie Woo Woo. He was a thin black man, maybe in his late forties, who always wore a regulation Chicago Cubs uniform. Every last detail of his uniform, from his cap to his shoes, was authentic. On the back of his jersey was stitched "Woo Woo." One time, on the El, a college girl asked, "Why *Woo Woo?*" He smiled at her and made the sound of a train whistle: *wooooo, wooooo*. This, apparently, was his signature sound during a ball game. She said, "So what do you do when baseball season is over?" He leaned forward and said, "I got a complete Chicago *Bears* uniform. The real thing. Helmet and all. It looks good, too. You should see me in it." Another time, while driving, I saw Woo Woo mowing a lawn. I don't know if it was his own lawn or somebody else's, but he was still decked out in full Chicago Cubs regalia.

What I'm getting at is this: I like the *aesthetics* of Wrigley Field. For a fiction writer, it has narrative energy that Comiskey Park (both the old Comiskey and the new one) never had for me. There is the game, sure, but then there is that which surrounds the game — the images, the minor characters, the setting. There is nothing more dull, to my mind, than a short story that documents a ball game. TV can do a much better job of bringing you play-by-play action than any short story could ever do. In his essay "On Writing," Raymond Carver quotes V. S. Pritchett's definition of a short story as "something glimpsed from the corner of the eye, in passing" (92). This is where watching a ball game and reading a story about baseball part ways. What TV can't bring you as well as the short story are the peripheries, the edges, the *glimpses*. This is what I've always loved about Wrigley Field: you see so much out of the corner of your eye.

The evolution of baseball coincided, more or less, with the evolution of the American short story. It comes as no surprise that the first short fiction in which baseball played a role didn't have much depth. According to scholar Cordelia Candelaria, "Except for sundry early poems, usually of a sternly didactic nature, the earliest baseball fiction was of a pulp variety, mostly intended for children" (15). Lacking depth and complexity, early baseball fiction failed to explore ambiguity — ambiguities of morality or of character — presenting instead baseball players who were rarely anything more than one-dimensional heroes. In his essay "Only Fairy Tales: Baseball Fiction's Short Game," Richard Peterson sums up baseball fiction's early agenda:

> Dime novels and series books had valorized baseball as a combative yet democratic game, worthy of becoming America's pastime because its heroes needed great skill, moral courage, and a clear vision not only to make the perfect pitch or get the game-

winning hit but to become successful members of American society. In early baseball fiction, a baseball hero also had to be a team
player and a moral paragon, so that his achievement on the field
and his rags-to-riches rise to fame validated baseball as the purest
expression of the American Dream. (78)

Another trend of late-nineteenth-century baseball fiction grew out of
what is known as the "local color movement," defined by scholar Walter
Blair as "the extensive portrayal in fiction of various sections of the country and their inhabitants" (124). Collectively, the local colorists helped to
create a mosaic of America, but this literary movement had its limitations.
When place becomes the primary focus of a story, characterization often
suffers. Most writings by the local colorists have long since been forgotten. In order to transcend the movement, as Mark Twain did in *The
Adventures of Huckleberry Finn*, the writers' stories or novels must be
"firmly rooted in minutely specific locales but both simultaneously and
primarily [be] concerned with the depths and nuances of the human condition" (Candelaria 16). Sadly, the vast majority of baseball fiction of the
local color variety did not achieve this standard. Not until Ring Lardner's
stories began to appear at the beginning of the twentieth century did baseball fiction transcend its genre and enter the realm of literature.

What was so special about Ring Lardner's stories? What was it that *he*
was doing that baseball story writers before him weren't doing? In a style
that combined vernacular speech, humor, and narrative realism, Ring
Lardner's baseball stories were the first to debunk baseball's mythologies,
letting some air out of the notion of the hero-player, the cumulative effect
of which were stories that "invite the celebration of baseball as a metaphor
for American life and an expression of the American Dream even as they
mock human nature" (Peterson 81). Or, as Candelaria puts it, "By presenting organized baseball starkly unadorned, Lardner helped reveal its
manifold texture, which had been veiled by the curtain of romance . . ."
(27). Where earlier baseball stories were formulaic in plot and populated
with one-dimensional characters, Ring Lardner, in such books as *You
Know Me Al*, did what all writers of literature do—he explored the ambiguity of morality through an individual's unique experience.

In *You Know Me Al*, that individual was Jack Keefe, a fictional rookie pitcher for the Chicago White Sox, who tells his story in a series of letters. Roger Kahn, author of the classic baseball book *The Boys of Summer*, describes Keefe as "vain, stingy, insensitive, gluttonous, selfpitying, a boob and a fourflusher" (137). And yet Keefe quickly became popular among readers. According to Ring Lardner biographer Donald Elder, Jack Keefe "is not very much worse than anyone else; he is real. He is not quite like yourself, but he bears a fatal resemblance to your friends" (Kahn 136).

Great fiction writers manage to do two things at once—that is, they achieve both universality and individuality simultaneously. Lardner did that. He created a character that readers could relate to, maybe even see something of themselves in; but he also created a character who provided the reader with a distinct—and fresh—vision of the world. It's often the originality of a character's *vision* that separates the important writers from the run-of-the-mill. Sadly, Lardner's popularity is no longer what it was in the 1920s—most of his books are out of print—but he will always be regarded as one of the seminal writers of the genre for giving readers a vision of baseball in fiction that they had not previously seen.

Thus began the slow rise of baseball fiction as literature, a rise that wouldn't really begin to soar until after World War II. Largely considered to be the first major postwar baseball novel was Bernard Malamud's *The Natural* in 1952, a landmark because, as Kahn notes, it's "the first book to suggest that tragic elements truly exist in baseball" (144). It was a landmark, too, because, as Kahn also suggests, Bernard Malamud, unlike Lardner, whose motives for writing were more financial than artistic, set out to write a great novel—and succeeded (145). Malamud's novel exhibited far more complexity of strategy and, as such, deeper levels of meaning than previous baseball novels. Candelaria writes, "Resembling Joyce's patterning of *Ulysses* upon the themes and plots of Homer's *Odyssey*, *The Natural* is built on a framework of allusion that deepens the story of a simple American sports hero, transforming it from the frivolous celebrity journalism of popular culture into an allegory of modern American life" (65).

A wave of serious (and seriocomic) baseball novels and stories followed the publication of *The Natural*, a wave that continues today. A comprehensive bibliography of such books would be several times thicker than this anthology, but among the highlights would be Mark Harris's *The Southpaw* (1953) and *Bang the Drum Slowly* (1956), Robert Coover's *The Universal Baseball Association, Inc., J. Henry Waugh, Prop.* (1968), Philip Roth's *The Great American Novel* (1973), Lamar Herrin's *The Río Loja Ringmaster* (1977), Eric Rolfe Greenberg's *The Celebrant* (1983), David Carkeet's *The Greatest Slump of All Time* (1984), Donald Hays's *The Dixie Association* (1984), and the many baseball books of W. P. Kinsella, including *Shoeless Joe* (1982), *The Thrill of the Grass* (1984), and *The Iowa Baseball Confederacy* (1986). Great baseball fiction continues to reinvent the genre, and every few years a new writer will appear on the literary landscape and leave his or her individual stamp.

Of note, too, are the novels and stories in which baseball merely reverberates, books that use baseball as a narrative thread, a significant image, or symbol. In his book *Home Games: Essays on Baseball Fiction*, John A. Lauricella examines the role of baseball in canonical work, claiming that "baseball allusions engage signature themes of American literature: versions of the American Dream, ethnic prejudice, city work and pastoral play, cultural identity, and the relationship of father and son, among others. Whatever their thematic import, baseball allusions retain a concern with 'home,' in various senses of that word" (9). The list of canonical works that use baseball is not insignificant. F. Scott Fitzgerald made use of the Black Sox Scandal of 1919 in *The Great Gatsby*. Babe Ruth and the 1928 New York Yankees play a pivotal role in William Faulkner's *The Sound and the Fury*. Throughout Ernest Hemingway's *The Old Man and the Sea*, "the great DiMaggio" is invoked. Baseball also plays roles in the works of Thomas Wolfe and James T. Farrell.

What is it about baseball, more so than any other sport, that takes hold of so many writers' imaginations and won't let go? Ironically, we need to look back at those characteristics that made for shoddy baseball fiction in the nineteenth century—among them the mythologizing of players, the romance of the game, the implicit bond between father and son. In the hands of lesser writers, such themes become didactic, strained, and unrealistic. But baseball is a dreamer's game, and in the hands of a talented dreamer-writer, a writer who understands the nature of cause and effect and who knows the difference between genuine sentiment and sentimentality, baseball's themes transcend the obvious and force us, the reader, to see the world anew.

My first impulse in compiling this anthology was to search out the little-known Ring Lardner baseball story, unearth a few lost classics by now-forgotten writers, and sprinkle into the mix some recent stories, but as I started reading through collections, asking for recommendations, and opening up submissions from the slush pile, I found that there were so many contemporary stories that haven't yet been collected in baseball anthologies. I was also surprised by the sheer number of well-known writers—like Andre Dubus, Ron Carlson, and Patricia Highsmith—who have to their credit one or two baseball stories. Before long, the anthology began to evolve into a collection made up solely of contemporary writers. While the oldest story here is Patricia Highsmith's "The Barbarians," first published in 1968, the majority have appeared within the past few years, the most recent being Owen King's story "Wonders," published in the May-June 2002 issue of *Book Magazine*.

Baseball stories come in all shapes and sizes, but one can't help but notice recurring themes and narrative strategies. Richard Peterson observes how "baseball stories are routinely played out on the fields of the grotesque, supernatural, or metaphysical" (73). This is certainly true of a handful of stories in *Bottom of the Ninth*. More than one story will find a character whose peak is behind him. Not infrequently, characters are haunted, often by what has eluded them, though sometimes, as in David Carkeet's story, by how *well* they're doing. In most literary fiction, a character's past informs the present, but in baseball stories, the past is often magnified, and frequently that past is reflected by a fraction of a second—a key play, a missed catch, a chance lost. Other stories in the book, however, may take the reader into otherwise unfamiliar baseball terrain, such as Highsmith's "The Barbarians," where a team of adult street players terrorizes everyone who lives in the apartment building next to where they play.

What do all of these stories share in common? For starters, they are populated with characters who, by and large, are driven, maybe even a little obsessed. A main character, the writer is told, should want something and want it intensely. This is what gives a story its narrative momentum. You'll find many characters here who want something and want it intensely, though *what* they want will shift from one story to the next.

In short story writing, the rule of thumb is that the closer to the *end* of the story that you can begin, the more intensity and immediacy you'll achieve—starting, as it were, in the bottom of the ninth. Since I have tried hard to veer away from stories that merely document play-by-play action, you'll find few *literal* bottom of the ninth moments here. But if you think of "bottom of the ninth" as a metaphor, you'll find plenty of characters who are at just such a juncture. In story after story, characters face moments when the stakes are high and the time to act is now. My hope is that you'll feel the same intensity and immediacy that these characters do.

Works Cited

Blair, Walter. *Native American Humor (1800–1900)*. New York: American Book, 1937.

Candelaria, Cordelia. *Seeking the Perfect Game: Baseball in American Literature*. New York: Greenwood, 1989.

Carver, Raymond. *Call If You Need Me: The Uncollected Fiction and Other Prose*. New York: Vintage, 2000.

Kahn, Roger. *Memories of Summer*. New York: Hyperion, 1997.

Lauricella, John A. *Home Games: Essays on Baseball Fiction*. Jefferson, NC: McFarland, 1999.

Peterson, Richard. *Extra Innings: Writing on Baseball*. Urbana: U of Illinois P, 2001.

Bottom of the Ninth

Batting Against Castro

JIM SHEPARD

In 1951 you couldn't get us to talk politics. Ballplayers then would just as soon talk bed-wetting as talk politics. Tweener Jordan brought up the H-bomb one seventh inning, sitting there tarring up his useless Louisville Slugger at the end of a Bataan Death March of a road trip when it was one hundred and four on the field and about nine of us in a row had just been tied in knots by Maglie and it looked like we weren't going to get anyone on base in the next five weeks except for those hit by pitches, at which point someone down the end of the bench told Tweener to put a lid on it, and he did, and that was the end of the H-bomb as far as the Philadelphia Phillies were concerned.

I was one or two frosties shy of outweighing my bat and wasn't exactly known as Mr. Heavy Hitter; in fact me and Charley Caddell, another Pinemaster from the Phabulous Phillies, were known far and wide as such banjo hitters that they called us—right to our faces, right during a game, like confidence or bucking up a teammate was for noolies and nose-droops—Flatt and Scruggs. Pick us a tune, boys, they'd say, our own team-mates, when it came time for the eighth and ninth spots in the order to save the day. And Charley and I would grab our lumber and shoot each other looks like we were the Splinter himself, misunderstood by everybody,

and up we'd go to the plate against your basic Newcombe or Erskine can-
non volleys. Less knowledgeable fans would cheer. The organist would
pump through the motions and the twenty-seven thousand who did show
up (PHILS WHACKED IN TWI-NIGHTER; SLUMP CONTINUES; LOCALS SEEK TO
SALVAGE LAST GAME OF HOME STAND) wouldn't say boo. Our runners
aboard would stand there like they were watching furniture movers. One
guy in our dugout would clap. A pigeon would set down in right field and
look around. Newcombe or Erskine would look in at us like litter was
blowing across their line of sight. They'd paint the corners with a few
unhittable ones just to let us know what a mismatch this was. Then
Charley would dink one to second. It wouldn't make a sound in the glove.
I'd strike out. And the fans would cuff their kids or scratch their rears and
cheer. It was like they were celebrating just how bad we could be.

I'd always come off the field looking at my bat, trademark up, like I
couldn't figure out what happened. You'd think by that point I would've.
I tended to be hitting about .143.

Whenever we were way down, in the 12-to-2 range, Charley played
them up, our sixth- or seventh- or, worse, ninth-inning Waterloos—tipped
his cap and did some minor posing—and for his trouble got showered
with whatever the box seats didn't feel like finishing: peanuts, beer, the
occasional hot-dog bun. On what was the last straw before this whole
Cuba thing, after we'd gone down one-two and killed a bases-loaded rally
for the second time that day, the boxes around the dugout got so bad that
Charley went back out and took a curtain call, like he'd clubbed a round-
tripper. The fans howled for parts of his body. The Dodgers across the way
laughed and pointed. In the time it took Charley to lift his cap and wave
someone caught him in the mouth with a metal whistle from a Cracker
Jack box and chipped a tooth.

"You stay on the pine," Skip said to him while he sat there trying to
wiggle the ivory in question. "I'm tired of your antics." Skip was our third-
year manager who'd been through it all, seen it all, and lost most of the
games along the way.

"What's the hoo-ha?" Charley wanted to know. "We're down eleven-
nothing."

Skip said that Charley reminded him of Dummy Hoy, the deaf-mute
who played for Cincinnati all those years ago. Skip was always saying

things like that. The first time he saw me shagging flies he said I was the picture of Skeeter Scalzi.

"Dummy Hoy batted .287 lifetime," Charley said. "I'll take that anytime."

The thing was, we were both good glove men. And this was the Phillies. If you could do anything right, you were worth at least a spot on the pine. After Robin Roberts, our big gun on the mound, it was Katie bar the door.

"We're twenty-three games back," Skip said. "This isn't the time for bush-league stunts."

It was late in the season, and Charley was still holding that tooth and in no mood for a gospel from Skip. He let fly with something in the abusive range, and I'm ashamed to say that I became a disruptive influence on the bench and backed him up.

Quicker than you could say Wally Pipp, we were on our way to Allentown for some Double A discipline.

Our ride out there was not what you'd call high-spirited. The Allentown bus ground gears and did ten, tops. It really worked over those switchbacks on the hills, to maximize the dust coming through the windows. Or you could shut the windows and bake muffins.

Charley was across the aisle, sorting through the paper. He'd looked homicidal from the bus station on.

"We work on our hitting, he's got to bring us back," I said. "Who else has he got?" Philadelphia's major-league franchise was at that point in pretty bad shape, with a lot of kids filling gaps left by the hospital patients.

Charley mentioned an activity involving Skip's mother. It colored the ears of the woman sitting in front of us.

It was then I suggested the winter leagues, Mexico or Cuba. "How about Guam?" Charley said. "How about the Yukon?" He hawked out the window.

Here was my thinking: The season was almost over in Allentown, which was also, by the way, in the cellar. We probably weren't going back up afterwards. That meant that starting October we either cooled our heels playing pepper in Pennsylvania, or we played winter ball. I was for Door Number Two.

Charley and me, we had to do something about our self-esteem. It got so I'd wince just to see my name in the sports pages—before I knew what it was about, just to see my name. Charley's full name was Charles Owen Caddell, and he carried a handsome suitcase around the National League that had his initials, c.o.c., in big letters near the handle. When asked what they stood for, he always said, "Can o' Corn."

Skip we didn't go to for fatherly support. Skip tended to be hard on the nonregulars, who he referred to as "you egg-sucking noodle-hanging gutter trash."

Older ballplayers talked about what it was like to lose it: the way your teammates would start giving you the look, the way you could see in their eyes, Three years ago he'd make that play, or He's lost a step going to the hole; the quickness isn't there. The difference was, Charley and me, we'd seen that look since we were twelve.

So Cuba seemed like the savvy move: a little seasoning, a little time in the sun, some senoritas, drinks with hats, maybe a curve-ball Charley *could* hit, a heater I could do more than foul off.

Charley took some convincing. He'd sit there in the Allentown dugout, riding the pine even in Allentown, whistling air through his chipped tooth and making faces at me. This Cuba thing was stupid, he'd say. He knew a guy played for the Athletics went down to Mexico or someplace, drank a cup of water with bugs in it that would've turned Dr. Salk's face white, and went belly-up between games of a doubleheader. "Shipped home in a box they had to *seal*," Charley said. He'd tell that story, and his tooth would whistle for emphasis.

But really what other choice did we have? Between us we had the money to get down there, and I knew a guy on the Pirates who was able to swing the connections. I finished the year batting .143 in the bigs and .167 in Allentown. Charley hit his weight and pulled off three errors in an inning his last game. When we left, our Allentown manager said, "Boys, I hope you hit the bigs again. Because we sure can't use you around here."

So down we went on the train and then the slow boat, accompanied the whole way by a catcher from the Yankees' system, a big bird from Minnesota named Ericksson. Ericksson was out of Triple A and apparently had a fan club there because he was so fat. I guess it had gotten so he couldn't field bunts. He said the Yankee brass was paying for this. They thought of it as a fat farm.

"The thing is, I'm not fat," he said. We were pulling out of some skeeter-and-water stop in central Florida. One guy sat on the train platform with his chin on his chest, asleep or dead. "That's the thing. What I am is big boned." He held up an arm and squeezed it the way you'd test a melon.

"I like having you in the window seat," Charley said, his Allentown hat down over his eyes. "Makes the whole trip shady."

Ericksson went on to talk about feet. This shortened the feel of the trip considerably. Ericksson speculated that the smallest feet in the history of the major leagues belonged to Art Herring, who wore a size three. Myril Hoag, apparently, wore one size four and one size four and a half.

We'd signed a deal with the Cienfuegos club: seven hundred a month and two-fifty for expenses. We also got a place on the beach, supposedly, and a woman to do the cleaning, though we had to pay her bus fare back and forth. It sounded a lot better than the Mexican League, which had teams with names like Coatzacoalcos. Forget the Mexican League, Charley'd said when I brought it up. Once I guess he'd heard some retreads from that circuit talking about the Scorpions, and he'd said, "They have a team with that name?" and they'd said no.

When Ericksson finished with feet he wanted to talk politics. Not only the whole Korean thing—truce negotiations, we're on a thirty-one-hour train ride with someone who wants to talk truce negotiations—but this whole thing with Cuba and other Latin American countries and Kremlin expansionism. Ericksson could get going on Kremlin expansionism. "Charley's not much on politics," I said, trying to turn off the spigot.

"You can talk politics if you want," Charley said from under his hat. "Talk politics. I got a degree. I can keep up. I got a B.S. from Schenectady." The B.S. stood for "Boots and Shoes," meaning he worked in a factory.

So there we were in Cuba. Standing on the dock, peering into the sun, dragging our big duffel bags like dogs that wouldn't cooperate.

We're standing there sweating on our bags and wondering where the team rep who's supposed to meet us is, and meanwhile a riot breaks out a block and a half away. We thought it was a block party at first. This skinny guy in a pleated white shirt and one of those cigar-ad pointed beards was racketing away at the crowd, which was yelling and carrying on. He was over six feet. He looked strong, wiry, but in terms of heft somewhere between flyweight and poster child. He was scoring big with some points he was making holding up a bolt of cloth. He said something that got them all going, and up he went onto their shoulders, and they paraded him around past the storefronts, everybody shouting "*Castro! Castro! Castro!*" which Charley and me figured was the guy's name. We were still sitting there in the sun like idiots. They circled around past us and stopped. They got quiet, and we looked at each other. The man of the hour was giving us his fearsome bandido look. He was tall. He was skinny. He was just a kid. He didn't look at all happy to see us.

He looked about ready to say something that was not a welcome when the *policia* waded in, swinging clubs like they were getting paid by the concussion. Which is when the riot started. The team rep showed up. We got hustled out of there.

We'd arrived, it turned out, a few weeks into the season. Cienfuegos was a game down in the loss column to its big rival, Marianao. Charley called it Marianne. Cuba took more than a little getting used to. There was the heat: one team we played had a stadium that sat in a kind of natural bowl that held in the sun and dust. The dust floated around you like a golden fog. It glittered. Water streamed down your face and back. Your glove dripped. One of our guys had trouble finding the plate, and while I stood there creeping in on the infield dirt, sweat actually puddled around my feet.

There were the fans: one night they pelted each other and the field with live snakes. They sang, endlessly. Every team in the *Liga de Baseball Cubana* had its own slogan, to be chanted during rallies, during seventh-inning stretches, or just when the crowd felt bored. The Elefantes' was "*El paso del elefante es lento pero aplastante.*" Neither of us knew Spanish, and by game two we knew our slogan by heart.

"What *is* that?" Charley finally asked Ericksson, who *habla*'d okay. "What are they saying?"

"The Elephant passes slowly," Ericksson said, "but it squashes."

There were the pranks: as the outsiders, Charley and me expected the standards—the shaving-cream-in-the-shoe, the multiple hotfoot—but even so never got tired of the bird-spider-in-the-cap, or the crushed-chilies-in-the-water-fountain. Many's the time, after such good-natured ribbing from our Latino teammates, we'd still be holding our ribs, toying with our bats, and wishing we could identify the particular jokester in question.

There was the travel: the bus trips to the other side of the island that seemed to take short careers. I figured Cuba, when I figured it at all, to be about the size of Long Island, but I was not close. During one of those trips Ericksson, the only guy still in a good mood, leaned over his seat back and gave me the bad news: if you laid Cuba over the eastern United States, he said, it'd stretch from New York to Chicago. Or something like that.

And from New York to Chicago the neighborhood would go right down the toilet, Charley said, next to me.

Sometimes we'd leave right after a game, I mean without showering, and that meant no matter how many open windows you were able to manage you smelled bad feet and armpit all the way back. On the mountain roads and switchbacks we counted roadside crosses and smashed guardrails on the hairpin turns. One time Charley, his head out the window to get any kind of air, looked way down into an arroyo and kept looking. I asked him what he could see down there. He said a glove and some bats.

And finally there was what Ericksson called a Real Lack of Perspective. He was talking, of course, about that famous South of the Border hotheadedness we'd all seen even in the bigs. In our first series against Marianao after Charley and I joined the team (the two of us went two for twenty-six, and we got swept; so much for gringos to the rescue), an argument at home plate—not about whether the guy was out, but about whether the tag had been too hard—brought out both managers, both benches, a blind batboy who felt around everyone's legs for the discarded lumber, a drunk who'd been sleeping under the stands, reporters, a photographer, a would-be beauty queen, the radio announcers, and a large number of interested spectators. I forget how it came out.

After we dropped a doubleheader in Havana our manager had a pot broken over his head. The pot held a plant, which he kept and replanted. After a win at home our starting third baseman was shot in the foot. We asked our manager, mostly through sign language, why. He said he didn't know why they picked the foot.

But it was more than that, too: On days off we'd sit in our hammocks

and look out our floor-to-ceiling windows and our screened patios and
smell our garden with its flowers with the colors from Mars and the breeze
with the sea in it. We'd feel like DiMaggio in his penthouse, as big league
as big league could get. We'd fish on the coral reefs for yellowtail and
mackerel, for shrimp and rock lobster. We'd cook it ourselves. Ericksson
started eating over, and he did great things with coconut and lime and
beer.

And our hitting began to improve.

One for five, one for four, two for five, two for five with two doubles:
the box scores were looking up and up, Spanish or not. One night we went
to an American restaurant in Havana, and on the place on the check for
comments I wrote, *I went 3 for 5 today.*

Cienfuegos went on a little streak: nine wins in a row, fourteen out
of fifteen. We caught and passed Marianao. Even Ericksson was slimming
down. He pounced on bunts and stomped around home plate like a man
killing bees before gunning runners out. We were on a winner.

Which is why politics, like it always does, had to stick its nose in. The
president of our tropical paradise, who reminded Charley more of Akim
Tamiroff than Harry Truman, was a guy named Batista who was not well
liked. This we could tell because when we said his name our teammates
would repeat it and then spit on the ground or our feet. We decided to
go easy on the political side of things and keep mum on the subject of our
opinions, which we mostly didn't have. Ericksson threatened periodically
to get us all into trouble or, worse, a discussion, except his Spanish didn't
always hold up, and the first time he tried to talk politics everyone agreed
with what he was saying and then brought him a bedpan.

Neither of us, as I said before, was much for the front of the newspaper, but you didn't have to be Mr. News to see that Cuba was about as bad
as it got in terms of who was running what: the payoffs got to the point
where we figured that guys getting sworn in for public office put their
hands out instead of up. We paid off local mailmen to get our mail. We
paid off traffic cops to get through intersections. It didn't seem like the
kind of thing that could go on forever, especially since most of the Cubans
on the island didn't get expense money.

So this Batista—"Akim" to Charley—wasn't doing a good job, and it
looked like your run-of-the-mill Cuban was hot about that. He kept most

of the money for himself and his pals. If you were on the outs and needed food or medicine it was your hard luck. And according to some of our teammates, when you went to jail—for whatever, for spitting on the sidewalk—bad things happened to you. Relatives wrote you off.

So there were a lot of protests, *demonstraciones*, that winter, and driving around town in cabs we always seemed to run into them, which meant trips out to eat or to pick up the paper might run half the day. It was the only nonfinable excuse for showing up late to the ballpark.

But then the demonstrations started at the games, in the stands. And guess who'd usually be leading them, in his little pleated shirt and orange-and-black Marianao cap? We'd be two or three innings in, and the crowd out along the third-base line would get up like the chorus in a Busby Berkeley musical and start singing and swaying back and forth, their arms in the air. They were not singing the team slogan. The first time it happened Batista himself was in the stands, surrounded by like forty bodyguards. He had his arms crossed and was staring over at Castro, who had his arms crossed and was staring back. Charley was at the plate, and I was on deck.

Charley walked over to me, bat still on his shoulder. I'm not sure anybody had called time. The pitcher was watching the crowd, too. "Now what is this?" Charley wanted to know.

I told him it could have been a religious thing, or somebody's birthday. He looked at me. "I mean like a national hero's, or something," I said.

He was still peering over at Castro's side of the crowd, swinging his bat to keep limber, experimenting with that chipped tooth whistle. "What're they saying?" he asked.

"It's in Spanish," I said.

Charley shook his head and then shot a look over to Batista on the first-base side. "Akim's gonna love this," he said. But Batista sat there like this happened all the time. The umpire straightened every inch of clothing behind his chest protector and then had enough and started signaling play to resume, so Charley got back into the batter's box, dug in, set himself, and unloaded big time on the next pitch and put it on a line without meaning to into the crowd on the third-base side. A whole side of the stands ducked, and a couple of people flailed and went down like they were shot. You could see people standing over them.

Castro in the meantime stood in the middle of this with his arms still

folded, like Peary at the Pole, or Admiral Whoever taking grapeshot across
the bow. You had to give him credit.

Charley stepped out of the box and surveyed the damage, cringing a
little. Behind him I could see Batista, his hands together over his head,
shaking them in congratulation.

"Wouldn't you know it," Charley said, still a little rueful. "I finally get
a hold of one and zing it foul."

"I hope nobody's dead over there," I said. I could see somebody holding up a hat and looking down, like that was all that was left. Castro was
still staring out over the field.

"Wouldn't that be our luck," Charley said, but he did look worried.

Charley ended up doubling, which the third-base side booed, and
then stealing third, which they booed even more. While he stood on the
bag brushing himself off and feeling quite the pepperpot, Castro stood up
and caught him flush on the back of the head with what looked like an
entire burrito of some sort. Mashed beans flew.

The crowd loved it. Castro sat back down, accepting congratulations
all around. Charley, when he recovered, made a move like he was going
into the stands, but no one in the stadium went for the bluff. So he just
stood there with his hands on his hips, the splattered third baseman pointing him out to the crowd and laughing. He stood there on third and
waited for me to bring him home so he could spike the catcher to death.
He had onions and probably some ground meat on his cap.

That particular Cold War crisis ended with my lining out, a rocket,
to short.

In the dugout afterwards I told Charley it had been that same guy,
Castro, from our first day on the dock. He said that that figured and that
he wanted to work on his bat control so he could kill the guy with a line
drive if he ever saw him in the stands again.

This Castro came up a lot. There was a guy on the team, a light-
hitting left fielder named Rafa, who used to lecture us in Spanish, very
worked up. Big supporter of Castro. You could see he was upset about
something. Ericksson and I would nod, like we'd given what he was on
about some serious thought, and were just about to weigh in on that very
subject. I'd usually end the meetings by giving him a thumbs-up and
heading out onto the field. Ericksson knew it was about politics so he was
interested. Charley had no patience for it on good days and hearing this

guy bring up Castro didn't help. Every so often he'd call across our lockers, "He wants to know if you want to meet his sister."

Finally Rafa took to bringing an interpreter, and he'd find us at dinners, waiting for buses, taking warm-ups, and up would come the two of them, Rafa and his interpreter, like this was sports day at the U.N. Rafa would rattle on while we went about our business, and then his interpreter would take over. His interpreter said things like, "This is not your tropical playground." He said things like, "The government of the United States will come to understand the Cuban people's right to self-determination." He said things like, "The people will rise up and crush the octopus of the north."

"He means the Yankees, Ericksson," Charley said.

Ericksson meanwhile had that big Nordic brow all furrowed, ready to talk politics.

You could see Rafa thought he was getting through. He went off on a real rip, and when he finished the interpreter said only, "The poverty of the people in our Cuba is very bad."

Ericksson hunkered down and said, "And the people think Batista's the problem?"

"Lack of money's the problem," Charley said. The interpreter gave him the kind of look the hotel porter gives you when you show up with seventeen bags. Charley made a face back at him as if to say, Am I right or wrong?

"The poverty of the people is very bad," the interpreter said again. He was stubborn. He didn't have to tell us: on one road trip we saw a town, like a used-car lot, of whole families, big families, living in abandoned cars. Somebody had a cradle thing worked out for a baby in an overturned fender.

"What do you want from us?" Charley asked.

"You are supporting the corrupt system," the interpreter said. Rafa hadn't spoken and started talking excitedly, probably asking what'd just been said.

Charley took some cuts and snorted. "Guy's probably been changing everything Rafa wanted to say," he said.

We started joking that poor Rafa'd only been trying to talk about how to hit a curve. They both gave up on us, and walked off. Ericksson followed them.

"Dag Hammarskjöld," Charley said, watching him go. When he saw my face he said, "I read the papers."

But this Castro guy set the tone for the other ballparks. The demonstrations continued more or less the same way (without the burrito) for the last two weeks of the season, and with three games left we found ourselves with a two-game lead on Marianao, and we finished the season guess where against guess who.

This was a big deal to the fans because Marianao had no imports, no Americans, on their team. Even though they had about seven guys with big-league talent, to the Cubans this was David and Goliath stuff. Big America vs. Little Cuba, and our poor Rafa found himself playing for Big America.

So we lost the first two games, by ridiculous scores, scores like 18–5 and 16–1. The kind of scores where you're playing out the string after the third inning. Marianao was charged up and we weren't. Most of the Cuban guys on our team, as you'd figure, were a little confused. They were all trying—money was involved here—but the focus wasn't exactly there. In the first game we came unraveled after Rafa dropped a pop-up that went seven thousand feet up into the sun, and in the second we were just wiped out by a fat forty-five-year-old pitcher that people said when he had his control and some sleep the night before was unbeatable.

Castro and Batista were at both games. During the seventh-inning stretch of the second game, with Marianao now tied for first place, Castro led the third-base side in a Spanish version of "Take Me Out to the Ball Game."

They jeered us—Ericksson, Charley and me—every time we came up. And the more we let it get to us, the worse we did. Ericksson was pressing, I was pressing, Charley was pressing. So we let each other down. But what made it worse was with every roar after one of our strikeouts, with every stadium-shaking celebration after a ball went through our legs, we felt like we were letting America down, like some poor guy on an infantry charge who can't even hold up the flag, dragging it along the ground. It got to us.

When Charley was up, I could hear him talking to himself: "The kid can still hit. Ball was in on him, but he got that bat head out in front."

When I was up, I could hear the chatter from Charley: "Gotta have this one. This is where we need you, big guy."

On Friday Charley made the last out. On Saturday I did. On Saturday night we went to the local bar that seemed the safest and got paralyzed. Ericksson stayed home, resting up for the rubber match.

Our Cuban skipper had a clubhouse meeting before the last game. It was hard to have a clear-the-air meeting when some of the teammates didn't understand the language, and were half paralyzed with hangovers besides, but they went on with it anyway, pointing at us every so often. I got the feeling the suggestion was that the Americans be benched for the sake of morale.

To our Cuban skipper's credit, and because he was more contrary than anything else, he penciled us in.

Just to stick it in Marianao's ear, he penciled us into the 1-2-3 spots in the order. The game started around three in the afternoon. It was one of the worst hangovers I'd ever had. I walked out into the Cuban sun, the first to carry the hopes of Cienfuegos and America to the plate, and decided that as a punishment I'd been struck blind. The crowd chanted, "The Elephant passes slowly, but it squashes." I struck out, though I have only the umpire's say-so on that.

Charley struck out too. Back on the bench he squinted like someone looking into car headlights. "It was a good pitch," he said. "I mean it sounded like a good pitch. I didn't see it."

But Ericksson, champion of clean living, stroked one out. It put the lid on some of the celebrating in the stands. We were a little too hungover to go real crazy when he got back to the dugout, but I think he understood.

Everybody, in fact, was hitting but us. A couple guys behind Ericksson including Rafa put together some doubles, and we had a 3–0 lead which stood up all the way to the bottom of the inning, when Marianao batted around and through its lineup and our starter and went into the top of the second leading 6–3.

Our guys kept hitting, and so did their guys. At the end of seven we'd gone through four pitchers and Marianao five, Charlie and I were regaining use of our limbs, and the score was Cuba 11, Land of the Free 9. We got another run on a passed ball. In the ninth we came up one run down with the sun setting in our eyes over the center-field fence and yours truly leading off. The crowd was howling like something I'd never heard before. Castro had everybody up on the third-base side and pointing at me. Their arms moved together like they were working some kind of hex. Marianao's pitcher — by now the sixth — was the forty-five-year-old fat guy who'd worked the day before. The bags under his eyes were bigger than mine. He snapped off three nasty curves, and I beat one into the ground and ran down the first-base line with the jeering following me the whole way.

He broke one off on Charley, too, and Charley grounded to first. The noise was solid, a wall. Everyone was waving Cuban flags.

I leaned close to Charley's ear in the dugout. "You gotta lay off those," I said.

"I never noticed anything wrong with my ability to pull the ball on an outside pitch," he said.

"Then you're the only one in Cuba who hasn't," I said.

But in the middle of this local party with two strikes on him Ericksson hit his second dinger, probably the first time he'd had two in a game since Pony League. He took his time on his home-run trot, all slimmed-down two hundred sixty pounds of him, and at the end he did a somersault and landed on home plate with both feet.

For the Marianao crowd it was like the Marines had landed. When the ball left his bat the crowd noise got higher and higher pitched and then just stopped and strangled. You could hear Ericksson breathing hard as he came back to the bench. You could hear the pop of the umpire's new ball in the pitcher's glove.

"The Elephant passes slowly, but it squashes," Charley sang, from his end of the bench.

That sent us into extra innings, a lot of extra innings. It got dark. Nobody scored. Charley struck out with the bases loaded in the sixteenth, and when he came back to the bench someone had poured beer on the dugout roof and it was dripping through onto his head. He sat there under it. He said, "I deserve it," and I said, "Yes, you do."

The Marianao skipper overmanaged and ran out of pitchers. He had an outfielder come in and fling a few, and the poor guy walked our eighth and ninth hitters with pitches in the dirt, off the backstop, into the seats. I was up. There was a conference on the mound that included some fans and a vendor. Then there was a roar, and I followed everyone's eyes and saw Castro up and moving through the seats to the field. Someone threw him a glove.

He crossed to the mound, and the Marianao skipper watched him come and then handed him the ball when he got there like his relief ace had just come in from the pen. Castro took the outfielder's hat for himself, but that was about it for a uniform. The tails of his pleated shirt hung out. His pants looked like Rudolph Valentino's. He was wearing dress shoes.

I turned to the ump. "Is this an exhibition at this point?" I said. He said something in Spanish that I assumed was "You're in a world of trouble now."

The crowd, which had screamed itself out hours ago, got its second wind. Hurricanes, dust devils, sandstorms in the Sahara—I don't know what the sound was like. When you opened your mouth it came and took your words away.

I looked over at Batista, who was sitting on his hands. How long was this guy going to last if he couldn't even police the national pastime?

Castro toed the rubber, worked the ball in his hand, and stared at me like he hated everyone I'd ever been associated with.

He was right-handed. He fussed with his cap. He had a windmill delivery. I figured, Let him have his fun, and he wound up and cut loose with a fastball behind my head.

The crowd reacted like he'd struck me out. I got out of the dirt and did the pro brush-off, taking time with all parts of my uniform. Then I stood in again, and he broke a pretty fair curve in by my knees, and down I went again.

What was I supposed to do? Take one for the team? Take one for the country? Get a hit, and never leave the stadium alive? He came back with his fastball high, and I thought, Enough of this, and tomahawked it foul. We glared at each other. He came back with a change-up—had this guy pitched somewhere, for somebody?—again way inside, and I thought, Forget it, and took it on the hip. The umpire waved me to first, and the crowd screamed about it like we were cheating.

I stood on first. The bases were now loaded for Charley. You could see the Marianao skipper wanted Castro off the mound, but what could he do?

Charley steps to the plate, and it's like the fans had been holding back on the real noisemaking up to this point. There are trumpets, cowbells, police whistles, sirens, and the godawful noise of someone by the foul pole banging two frying pans together. The attention seems to unnerve Charley. I'm trying to give him the old thumbs-up from first, but he's locked in on Castro, frozen in his stance. The end of his bat's making little circles in the air. Castro gave it the old windmill and whipped a curve past his chin. Charley bailed out and stood in again. The next pitch was a curve, too, which fooled him completely. He'd been waiting on the fastball. He started to swing, realized it was a curve breaking in on him, and ducked away to save his life. The ball hit his bat anyway. It dribbled out toward Castro. Charley gaped at it and then took off for first. I took off for second. The crowd shrieked. Ten thousand people, one shriek. All Castro had to do was gun it to first and they were out of the inning. He threw it into right field.

Pandemonium. Our eighth and ninth hitters scored. The ball skipped away from the right fielder. I kept running. The catcher'd gone down to first to back up the throw. I rounded third like Man o' War, Charley not far behind me, the fans spilling out onto the field and coming at us like a wave we were beating to shore. One kid's face was a flash of spite under a Yankee hat, a woman with long scars on her neck was grabbing for my arm. And there was Castro blocking the plate, dress shoes wide apart, Valentino pants crouched and ready, his face scared and full of hate like I was the entire North American continent bearing down on him.

Death of the Right Fielder

STUART DYBEK

After too many balls went out and never came back we went out to check. It was a long walk—he always played deep. Finally we saw him, from the distance resembling the towel we sometimes threw down for second base.

It's hard to tell how long he'd been lying there, sprawled on his face. Had he been playing infield his presence, or lack of it, would, of course, have been noticed immediately. The infield demands communication—the constant, reassuring chatter of team play. But he was remote, clearly an outfielder (the temptation is to say out*sider*). The infield is for wise-crackers, pepper-pots, gum-poppers; the outfield is for loners, onlookers, brooders who would rather study clover and swat gnats than holler. People could pretty much be divided between infielders and outfielders. Not that one always has a choice. He didn't necessarily choose right field so much as accepted it.

There were several theories as to what killed him. From the start the most popular was that he'd been shot. Perhaps from a passing car, possibly by that gang calling themselves the Jokers who played 16 inch softball on the concrete diamond with painted bases in the center of the housing project, or by the Latin Lords who didn't play sports period. Or maybe some pervert with a telescopic sight from a bedroom window, or a mad sniper from a water tower, or a terrorist with a silencer from the expressway overpass, or maybe it was an accident, a stray slug from a robbery, or shoot-out, or assassination attempt miles away.

No matter who pulled the trigger it seemed more plausible to ascribe his death to a bullet than to natural causes like say a heart attack. Young deaths are never natural; they're all violent. Not that kids don't die of heart attacks. But he never seemed the type. Sure, he was quiet, but not the quiet of someone always listening for the heart murmur his family had repeatedly warned him about since he was old enough to play. Nor could it have been leukemia. He wasn't a talented enough athlete to die of that. He'd have been playing center, not right, if leukemia were going to get him.

The shooting theory was better, even though there wasn't a mark on him. Couldn't it have been, as some argued, a high powered bullet traveling with such velocity that its hole fuses behind it? Still, not everyone was satisfied. Other theories were formulated, rumors became legends over the years: he'd had an allergic reaction to a bee sting, been struck by a single bolt of lightning from a freak, instantaneous electrical storm, ingested too strong a dose of insecticide from the grass blades he chewed on, sonic waves, radiation, pollution, etc. And a few of us liked to think it was simply that chasing a sinking liner, diving to make a shoe-string catch, he broke his neck.

There *was* a ball in the webbing of his mitt when we turned him over. His mitt had been pinned under his body and was coated with an almost luminescent gray film. There was the same gray on his black, hightop gym shoes, as if he'd been running through lime, and along the bill of his baseball cap—the blue felt one with the red C which he always denied stood for the Chicago Cubs. He may have been a loner, but he didn't want to be identified with a loser. He lacked the sense of humor for that, lacked the perverse pride that sticking for losers season after season breeds, and the love. He was just an ordinary guy, .250 at the plate, and we stood above him not knowing what to do next. By then the guys from the other outfield positions had trotted over. Someone, the shortstop probably, suggested team prayer. Then no one could think of a team prayer. So we all just stood there silently bowing our heads, pretending to pray while the shadows moved darkly across the outfield grass. After a while, the entire diamond was swallowed and the field lights came on.

In the bluish squint of those lights he didn't look like someone we'd once known—nothing looked quite right—and we hurriedly scratched a shallow grave, covered him over, and stamped it down as much as possible so that the next right fielder, whoever he'd be, wouldn't trip. It could be just such a juvenile, seemingly trivial stumble that would ruin a great career before it had begun, or hamper it years later the way Mantle's was hampered by bum knees. One can never be sure the kid beside him isn't another Roberto Clemente; and who can ever know how many potential Great Ones have gone down in the obscurity of their neighborhoods? And so, in the catcher's phrase, we "buried the grave" rather then contribute to any further tragedy. In all likelihood the next right fielder, whoever he'd be, would be clumsy too, and if there was a mound to trip over he'd find it and break *his* neck, and soon right field would get the reputation as haunted, a kind of sandlot Bermuda Triangle, inhabited by phantoms calling for ghostly fly balls, where no one but the most desperate outcasts, already on the verge of suicide, would be willing to play.

Still, despite our efforts, we couldn't totally disguise it. A fresh grave is stubborn. Its outline remained visible—a scuffed baldspot that might have been confused for an aberrant pitcher's mound except for the bat jammed in the earth with the mitt and blue cap fit over it. Perhaps we didn't want to eradicate it completely—a part of us was resting there. Perhaps we wanted the new right fielder, whoever he'd be, to notice and wonder about who played there before him, realizing he was now the only link between past and future that mattered. A monument, epitaph, flowers wouldn't necessary.

As for us, we walked back, but by then it was too late—getting on to supper, getting on to the end of summer vacation, time for other things, college, careers, settling down and raising a family. Past thirty-five the talk starts about being over the hill, about a graying Hoyt Wilhelm in his forties still fanning them with the knuckler as if it's some kind of miracle, about Pete Rose still going in head-first at thirty-seven beating the odds. And maybe the talk is right. One remembers Mays, forty and a Met, dropping that can-of-corn fly in the '71 Series, all that grace stripped away and with it the conviction, leaving a man confused and apologetic about the boy in him. It's sad to admit it ends so soon, but everyone knows those were the lucky ones. Most guys are washed up by seventeen.

Umpire

KURT RHEINHEIMER

The town of Blueston sits on a little flat piece of flood plain confined by the river at one edge and by the abrupt start of Cullhat Mountain at the other. It is a foundry town that had its best days in the forties and fifties, when the hot waste water ran freely down into the river, and gawky steel forms rolled away on big flatcars headed north. The weeds around the foundry offices are as tall as the men who once worked in the thick wooden chairs inside, and reach up as if to look into the high, wavy-glassed windows, each of which has a trim arc of on-end brick above it. On a summer day in Blueston the heat builds along the river in the mid-day hours and then rises to collect—late in the afternoon—in a little low spot between the flat and the first quick rise of the mountain. It is on this little scoop of land, amid a few small and poorly kept houses and a thin line of rock road that runs up the mountain, that Callis Field is located. It sits with its back to the town, and in 1937, when the diamond was laid out, either nobody had the power to hit the ball more than 284 feet into the thick air to right, or someone just stuck the plate down somewhere and forgot to think about the fact that the start of the mountain was going to dictate that the right field line would be unnaturally short.

Reid hates the field because of the heat. The whole league is hot, but this field seems to draw it and hold it, so densely that the dust doesn't rise right on a slide. The outfield—in deep left-center—is damp even in dry spells, and downright mushy in the spring. As Reid brushes the plate in preparation for the start of the game he watches the red-orange dust as it hangs low to the ground, clinging to his shoes more thoroughly than dry dust would. He comes up from the plate, kicking the heels of his shoes against his shin guards, and allows himself a furtive glance up into the stands, just behind the plate. There is no sign of Ellen, as he knew there wouldn't be—it is too early—and there are no more than twenty-five people on the long rows of two-plank, deep blue benches that make up the "box seats" behind the plate. Above those seats, in a home-made-looking booth, are the two guys from WBLS, already barking out information to their vast audience. Reid likes to see them up there because they are a consolation to him. They broadcast rookie league baseball—Class D, it used to be called—to a town of 16,000 people over an AM station way down at one end of the dial. And all this while anyone who is really interested in the game can come out to Callis Field, pay hardly anything, and see the game in person. The WBLS guys are seven million miles from the big league broadcast booth they dream about at night, especially with all the ex-players bouncing in front of men like these, who probably decided at age ten they were going to be broadcasters. The two men up behind Reid are farther from their hope than Reid is from a big league plate with an inside chest protector and real meal money.

Kammler, a big square man of German descent who is thirty-three years old, will work the bases. He comes slowly in toward Reid as they wait for the Blueston Braves to hit the field. "Anything in those shadows out there deep, cover me," he says to Reid, as if Reid doesn't know to do it. "Right," Reid says. "Foul pops by the screen, you watch the runners," he tells Kammler. "Right," Kammler barks back. "No lip and keep it quick." He turns his big body then, claps his hands together twice, and jogs out toward first. Reid doesn't like Kammler because he is too old to be working for $57 a game—$3700 for the whole summer, for Christ's sake—in a hot-town rookie league. Reid has already told himself that this is it for him. This is his third year in the Southern Mountains League—made up of a bunch of little towns you never heard of in Tennessee, Virginia, North

Carolina and West Virginia—and he will turn twenty-five in the winter. A year of umpire school and three years at the bottom are more than enough. Either he gets an offer to move up after this season, or he goes back to Fremont, Nebraska, to play softball and drive into Omaha every day to work full time for his brother, who is a lawyer.

Kammler is clapping his hands again, trying to get the Braves onto the field. He has told Reid that in his eleven years of umpiring, the teams have gotten slower and slower to come out, as if they want to make you stand there so everybody gets a good look at you—to let the crowd warm up its collective hatred of umpires. At last the Blueston first baseman breaks out of the dugout. "Number fourteen," the radio/PA team barks into Reid's neck, "the first baseman, Cary Banders." He stretches out the end of the name. "Banderrrzzz," it comes out, as if to cover for the small applause generated by the crowd. The other players follow by position, each with an elephantine syllable at the end of his name.

The Blueston catcher is a short, squat kid named Lucas. They signed him out of a junior college after they'd already run through three other catchers with broken fingers and pulled hamstrings. You can take one look at Pat Lucas and know he is going no place whatsoever. He reminds Reid of catchers in Little League. The fat kid, basically, who is dumb enough to sit back there and scream and holler and sweat his brains out. Lucas is that red-faced kid grown up a little, and he is so surprised, so damned amazed to be in professional baseball that he has lost all perspective on the fact that he really is still that red-faced fat kid. As Reid settles in behind the plate, Lucas is already shouting out orders to his infielders, who are casually picking up grounders and ignoring the catcher completely.

"Gonna call them strikes when they're strikes, balls when they're balls," Reid tells the pudgy red neck beneath him. "Anything you don't like has already been called and won't be called again. Stay down there to give me a good look and everything will be fine." Reid used to give this little soft-voiced talk to all the catchers, but has let it go as the summers have worn on and his reputation has begun to precede him. But Pat Lucas needs it. And as Reid speaks, the neck gets redder. Reid sighs deeply, motioning the leadoff man for Prestonburg into the box. Another night of listening to gripes on everything up to a half foot off the plate.

Ellen Childress is Reid's entire version of the collective girl-in-every-town dream of the Southern Mountains League. There are two or three players in the league—tall, statuesque young men out of colleges—who will have you believe they've long since accomplished the feat. Reid weighs the factors of girls' love for baseball players against the size and conservatism of the towns, and he doubts it. If anybody has done it, he suspects it might be some runty little infielder with a whole lot to prove. It is Reid's opinion that the farther up into these hills you get, the ropier the women are..Or else fat. No middle ground between the lean, hard-armed girls with freckles and straight, no-color hair, and the ones who grew up round. Ellen, he tells himself, is almost an exception. Her hair is dark brown, and she fills out the back of a pair of Levi's the way a girl is supposed to. Smooth and full, but not too full. Ellen has a daughter who is ten and a son who is nine, and they come to the games on some nights, and stay at their grandmother's on others, when Ellen comes by herself. Henry Childress, Reid learned one soft summer night, left the county when the children were six and five, with a woman who has since made the local paper on two separate occasions for flimflam schemes on the Amtrak train that comes through Blueston at three in the morning without stopping. So Ellen has raised the kids by herself and taught fourth grade at Blueston Elementary and, as she tells it, had no inclination at all to have anything to do with another man from her home town. Reid tells himself that before he came along she was well on her way into the process of shriveling up into a dried vine and turning in her femininity in return for martyrized motherhood. If she brings the kids she's there by eight, and if not a little later, staying to talk with her mother before heading to the park.

"Like hell," the beef-necked catcher squawks. "It wasn't even on the black."

Reid easily resists the temptation to agree—the pitch was indeed four inches *off* the black—as the Prestonburg leadoff man trots down to first with a walk. Reid feels heat at his own neck. Already there are voices behind him. "Yeah, get them off to a good start, ump," says one. "Just keep it on your shoulder," comes another, ostensibly talking to the second hitter. "He'll send you on down to first too." Reid thinks often about levels of intimidation in different leagues. He has decided that it is worst in these little one-show towns where people have nothing to do with their anger except spit it out at an umpire on a baseball field. So they sit, ten or twelve feet away, and rip him to pieces. In the major league cities, Reid's logic goes on, there are a few major league hecklers, to be sure, but at least they are farther away, and held there by something more substantial than the thin, undulating chicken wire that separates Reid from the locals in this town. They will gain strength as their numbers increase through the innings. And as their volume increases so too does their daring, as they prod each other on to greater insults, in the manner of children trying to get each other into trouble in a classroom.

The second Prestonburg hitter, mercifully, pops out on a 3-1 pitch that was a ball, and Reid is spared the crowd's momentum being built more rapidly than it needs to be. But as the Blueston team comes to bat in their half of the first, he is aware that the town's biggest voice—a man Reid has shouted at through the chicken wire—has arrived. He is a middle-aged, roly-poly man with hair worn in a flat-top. There is no drinking in Callis Field, and so the flat-top and his buddies have to step outside the park every inning or so for a nip—a situation which gives Reid a small break, but which also tends to build the level of comment and to destroy their notion of the flow of the game just enough to allow them to make mistakes of judgment—condensing batting orders, confusing hitters and situations just enough to be able to berate Reid for something that is not quite related to the actual progress of the game.

The level of pitching in the Southern Mountains League has gone up a notch or two this season. The consensus among the umpires is that these things go in cycles, while the hitters of course attribute it to a corps of umpires which favors pitching over hitting. On this night Reid is particularly impressed. The Prestonburg team is using a small left-hander who nibbles at the corners and fields like a cat when they try to bunt on him. He is a college graduate, and about twelve steps ahead of the league in guile and craft. Reid is sure he will move up fast—perhaps before the season is over. And Blueston is using a tall right-hander who is just out of high school—of the type who will walk the bases full and strike out the side in the same inning. By the end of the fourth inning each team has no runs and one hit, and Reid feels the game settling into a pitcher's duel— so long as neither team has a fielding lapse and the tall right-hander doesn't lose the plate.

After the fifth Reid brushes off the plate even though it is clean, and stares openly up into the stands to look for Ellen, having conquered the temptation at the end of each of the last two innings. "Don't look up here for help," the flat-top screams immediately. "There ain't no eye doctor up here." Reid feels his face warm. He has left his mask on to cover his eyes, but a good umpire baiter does not let any opportunity slip by. Reid waits, expecting—dreading—the first comment on why he is really looking up there. Somehow, through dumb luck or perhaps respect for a school teacher in a small town, or maybe just plain stupidity, his big talkers have never mentioned her. And again, as he settles in to start the sixth, they have let him look and made no mention. They are staying with the eyesight theme, their favorite. "You realize he does see well enough to find the plate to dust it off, anyway," someone yells, to general laughter. Reid misses Ellen behind him. In her silence through the jeers she helps him absorb, allows him to remain stoic when he would rather not. Her absence annoys him to a degree that he knows it should not. He has no claim on her. One of her kids could be sick. Or her mother maybe. Or maybe a PTA meeting. No, not in summer. Reid has traveled through six ratty little mountain towns to have Ellen sit behind him for these three games, and now he is finally here and she is not.

In the top of the sixth the big right-hander walks the first two batters. The pitches are all high, and there is not much static from behind. The Blueston manager, a no-hit shortstop who made it to the big leagues for a cup of coffee years ago, trots to the mound and tilts his head back to talk to his pitcher. The kid nods, hands on hips, and the manager trots back. No delay. No casual shot at Reid. No nothing. Reid goes back to his crouch and calls a ball high. "Wait till it gets there," comes a voice from behind. The next two pitches are also high, and down along the right field line people are moving around in the Blueston bullpen. As Reid calls a strike on the next pitch, with some protest from the Prestonburg bench, he feels a strap snap on his left shin guard. It is one of the criss-crossing straps which hold the shin guard in place, and the feeling of looseness annoys Reid immediately and deeply. He has always associated umpiring with tight control. And especially when you are as little as he is, you need a feeling of total firmness and containedness—a secure possession of the game. And the sloppiness at the inside of his left knee—the shin guard will not fall, but will slip slightly until the arch of his foot stops it—is just enough to compromise Reid's feel of control. If things do not feel right you can't do the job right—you don't have the same confidence, and if you don't have the confidence you don't have conviction, and if you don't have conviction people are all over you. Especially if you are small. Reid begins immediately to try to discount the annoyance, to equate it with a lingering drizzle. It is there, and must be dealt with, but it cannot become your whole focus. He cannot stop and fix the strap because it has torn away on the sewn side, and even if he could repair it he would have to endure the complete attention of the crowd while he stopped to work on it. So he has no choice but to deal with the irritation. He reminds himself of other umpiring problems. Guys working with diarrhea. Broken toes. Alone, for God's sake, with a hostile crowd. He glances out at Kammler who is bent, hands on knees, just behind the mound, and is glad he is there.

The hitter walks, loading the bases and putting the potential go-ahead run at third. The Prestonburg catcher—David Harkness—is the batter. He is a tall, strong kid who almost never complains about a call. He is perhaps Reid's favorite player in the league, with a good chance to move up, though Reid has never seen anyone run more slowly on a baseball field. His stride to the plate brings increased chatter from the Prestonburg bench. The first pitch to him is on the corner and Reid shoots up his right arm. "Christ, I didn't know there was called strikes on visiting teams in this town, did you?" comes a voice from behind Reid. "That's the first one tonight, isn't it?" David Harkness steps out briefly—as strong a registering of disagreement as he is likely to make. The next two pitches are high. There are a few shouts from the crowd to take the pitcher out. Reid expects the manager to do just that. But he does not, and the kid comes in with a good pitch that Harkness taps weakly toward short. The drawn-in shortstop, in his eagerness to come home and cut off the run with a force, bobbles the ball momentarily. Pat Lucas is screaming "Home! Home! Home!" as loudly as he can. The shortstop guns the ball in, and Pat Lucas, in his eagerness to get the ball to first for the double play, pulls his foot off the plate far too soon. He has taken a full step before he catches the ball, and Reid has no choice but to call the runner safe at the plate. As Kammler calls Harkness out at first, Pat Lucas is throwing his mask at Reid's shins and jumping up and down. The little manager comes out in a hurry, and the chicken wire behind Reid is suddenly a maze of voices and faces. "We had him by a goddamn week," Pat Lucas is screaming again and again as he shoves at his manager's chest to try to get through him to Reid. "You're so goddamn short you can't see to make the call." The manager is pushing at Pat Lucas, trying to keep him from getting kicked out of the game. He doesn't have another catcher. In the infield all is quiet. No one has come in to join the protest because they all know Reid made the call. But at the fence there is pandemonium. "It's a force out, you blind ass-hole." "You never read the rule book? You don't need a tag on that play." "Can you believe this? Guy throws just the pitch he wants, and then a bush ump goes and blows it for him. Could be the difference for that kid on the mound out there." The voices are blended and irrational—too close to Reid. The manager still has not said a word to him, to Reid's relief. The call was so clear as to be indisputable, and the silence confirms that the manager knows it too. But the crowd and Pat Lucas are of one blind mentality. By now they are talking about where Reid stays in Blueston—a line of taunt that frightens him slightly. He hopes against knowledge that Ellen is back there, hearing all of this—but he knows she is not. She would be able to tell him if the threats are real or just the idle blather of half-drunk, small town fans from where she grew up.

At last Pat Lucas is calmed and the game resumes. Reid expects an under-the-breath barrage as the catcher settles in, but instead there is total silence. No infield directions, no hum-babe-shoot-it to the pitcher, and not a word to Reid. Maybe the boy has realized that he was wrong. Or, more likely, he has decided to pout because no one took up for him except the crazy fans. Reid hitches the shin guard and settles back to the game. Behind him now the taunts are no longer as consistent. He has come to realize, in his three years, that there is an optimum pace to umpire bait-ing, and it takes the right kind of game, the right levels of alcohol, and the right kind of weather to have it go just right. There is a certain pace and momentum to be built. When there is one huge explosion, it often kills the momentum for the rest of the game. Reid hopes it will go that way, instead of this being just a lull before another roar.

"He could've went to a Japanese ump school," comes the first distinct voice when things are calm, and after Reid has called strike two on the next Prestonburg hitter. "I'm not too sure they have force outs over in Yaga-shaki." There is general laughter, and the hitter pops meekly to second.

The Prestonburg right fielder steps in, twitching his neck and back muscles. "Nah, I doubt it was Japan where he learned," comes another voice. "He didn't meet the height requirements over there." Louder laughter. The batter fouls the next pitch high and toward the screen. Reid jumps out of the way of the catcher and comes back to watch the attempt. The ball falls just on the crowd side of the chicken wire screen, scattering his baiters momentarily. Reid steals a futile glance for Ellen.

"Get up there where you belong," comes a voice.

And when Reid is back in position behind the catcher, "I think he started out in the Three-I League." A pause, while the first pitch comes in. Then the same voice, with the punch line. "You think he would have made it out of there with at least one eye left." Explosive laughter. They use that one game after game. The hitter swings at the next pitch and lines the ball hard toward left field. The Blueston left fielder gets a good jump on the ball and dives for the short hop. But Kammler, running out from behind the pitcher's mound, throws up his thumb immediately and forcefully. Reid looks down, and adjusts the shin guard. The Prestonburg manager, once a pitcher for the old Washington Senators, takes off for Kammler from his third base coaching box. The two Prestonburg baserunners are right behind him, swarming all over the square umpire. Reid could have predicted it. One big rhubarb generally means one more big rhubarb. Kammler walks away from his accusers—out toward center field as the Blueston Braves trot in, some with open grins on their faces. "You just plain totally blew it," Reid can hear the Prestonburg manager shouting. "He trapped it and you took it away from us. Get help. Go ask. You blew it—maybe he saw it." Kammler walks away as Reid thinks of a time in Clairsburg when a rookie ump named Pelouge, of all things, reversed a call of tagging up too soon, that Reid had made. Reid was so mad he couldn't see, and Pelouge made enough similar calls to be out of baseball within two months after that one.

The manager and the runners have moved Kammler out into the short right field corner now, and he has turned to head in toward the plate—along the first base line. He is leading them to me, Reid cannot help but think, but halfway down the line Kammler turns back across the infield. Reid is grateful, and knows that he should start out to break it up, even though Kammler did not help him with the call at the plate. But before Reid starts out, the manager gives up on Kammler and comes in toward Reid, his arms in the air even as he takes his first step. "You gonna let that crap stand?" he says to Reid when he is still forty feet away. "Are you the home plate umpire? Are you?" He is building momentum as he comes in. Reid spreads his legs slightly and folds his arms across his chest, feeling the pounding of his heart. He is, of course, trapped. He can go talk to Kammler, tell him he saw the play differently, back the older man down, and then face the Blueston team and fans, as well as having to establish where the baserunners should be. And risk the wrath of Kammler. Or, he can stonewall for Kammler, and face the loss of some respect from the old pitcher, who knows full well that Reid is a good umpire, and that he cannot desert another ump. Reid has always known that umpiring is the ultimate no-win situation—you call them right and nobody notices—or some drunken fool convinces the crowd that you haven't called them right—and you make one mistake and it hangs there forever. No praise for doing it right and all kinds of hell for one mistake. But this situation is even worse. Reid not only cannot win, he cannot escape with full self-respect intact. If you second-guess another ump you quickly become an outcast among your peers, who are as patient as the devil himself in waiting for their opportunity to hang you out to dry. And if you allow one bad call to stand, a manager will never let you live it down, even though he knows you had no choice but to do what you did.

"Leaving shit like that lay around on the field doesn't get you any closer to the majors, son," the old pitcher is saying to Reid now, calm and almost polite as he stands in front of Reid and goes for the jugular. Reid tells him the call has been made and the inning is over. "There's no real purpose served," the manager goes on, as if Reid had not spoken. "It leaves a big brown ugly spot on the outfield and in your record. You don't think somebody from the league's not up there? You have a chance, son, and the guys that make the majors don't pass those chances up."

Reid turns away, hating the line the manager is taking with him, because it is the perfect blend of fatherliness and con. He starts up the first base line, seeing his own instant replay of the short-hop catch in left. Kammler, still out behind second, does not move. He is smoothing the infield dirt with the toe of his shoe. "One call like that sticks with the guy," the manager is saying now. "You eat one here and you'll be eating them the rest of your short umpiring life." Reid knows he is right. And that Kammler is not worth protecting. It is only Kammler's connection with the other umpires in the league that holds Reid back. "Nestor Chylak had a call almost exactly like that one time," the manager all but coos into Reid's ear. "It's tough, I know." Reid realizes that he has changed his own course, and is headed out toward Kammler. He tells himself that it is only a coincidence, but the drumming of his heart at his neck tells him otherwise. He thinks of the fact that he is doing this godforsaken, impossible job for $3700 a summer—that he is out here in the sticky dust and tobacco juice night after night for practically nothing. There is no justice in having to handle two full teams of highly unreasonable men for $57 a night. He wonders what federal mediators make, sitting in air-conditioned offices with people who do not curse them. He straightens, looks at Kammler, pushing the murmuring of the manager's voice out of his head.

"You okay?" he says to Kammler.

Kammler looks up, feigning surprise. "I hit that little dip there, behind short, as he went for it. Could've bounced my head a little." He looks down again, at his infield dirt.

Jesus Christ, Reid thinks above the renewed protests of the Prestonburg manager, he's caving in like a mud dam. Why the hell didn't he do something himself? Why stand out there like some kind of Kraut statue and hope it will all go away, or that the other guy will handle it? Reid fights the intense heat in his face—made of both pity and anger for Kammler—and asks him if he saw the play as a trap.

"Could've been," Kammler says, this time not even raising his head. And all at once Reid is ready. His hatred for Kammler becomes complete, as does his realization that the game is totally his to handle. All of this mingles with his need to see justice prevail. There is simply no call to be an umpire if you aren't after justice, in every sense of the word. Reid remembers that from umpiring school. And he hears his own words to others as he explains why he is a bush league umpire—the courts may get prostituted by plea-bargaining and the inequalities of social station, but on a baseball field, and maybe nowhere else in the world except on a baseball field, there is only one answer. You are either safe or out. There is no second degree safe or involuntary out or any of that crap. Reid starts to go to Kammler, to at least put on the appearance of having conferred and reached a mutual decision. But in his distaste for the older man he turns away and starts toward the plate. He motions for the Blueston manager, who is already running toward him, having read Reid's body as it moves resolutely toward change. "Oh no," he is screaming. "Oh no you don't. Oh no, oh no, oh no. This isn't the Pony League, you little runt, where the daddies talk you into the calls. This is goddamn professional baseball. There is money on the line here, you little runt. This isn't fucking Sunday afternoon slow pitch." Reid tells him to shut up, which has no effect whatsoever, and so Reid begins his explanation in a soft voice, into the rantings.

"The infield umpire and I have conferred," he begins, "and have agreed that the ball was trapped, as we all saw. Therefore, the batter will be at first, the runner at third will come home, and the runner at second will advance to third. There are two outs. Blueston will take the field." He turns to walk away, hoisting his chest protector into place and pulling his mask down over his face.

"Like hell we will," the Blueston manager is screaming. "Like hell. I won't play another goddamn second with you out there making it up as you go along. What's the goddamn sense?"

Reid sets himself behind the plate, as if it might be a haven from the chaos around him. Behind him, at last, the baiters have caught on to what is happening, and are warming to the task. "Look at God out there in the ump uniform," somebody—a female—is screaming. "He runs the world. Reverses history. Walks on water." And then, with the license and encouragement provided by the female voice, the men begin to curse Reid unmercifully. He is a runty motherfucker and they'll run him out of the league and the state. He couldn't umpire with binoculars strapped to his face. Where did he leave his guts? There is a place in Russia for him and other traitors and yellow bellies. Why didn't his mother ever teach him not to make up stories? How much is Prestonburg paying him to screw over the home team? How long have he and the Prestonburg manager been queering around together? His ass is grass. They could find better umpires at the state hospital. And on and on.

Reid stands unmoving, suddenly lifted above it all with a vision of a headline in a newspaper about an umpire being beaten to death in some obscure southern town on a hot summer night. With a "Sixty Minutes" crew doing a follow-up investigation. Reid can see the reporter standing in left field, pointing down to the spot where the short-hop catch was made. Reid turns toward the Blueston dugout. "If Blueston is not on the field in thirty seconds," he says just loudly enough to be heard, "then we will have a forfeit. It makes no difference to me. This is my game to call and I will call it correctly." He aims his comments toward the old short-stop, who is the only person on the field who is his own height. "You saw him short-hop it, same as I did."

"Go to hell," the manager says. "Don't tell me what I saw. You don't go around undoing a baseball game. You want to go back to the second when you blew that 2-2 pitch to my cleanup hitter? Maybe we should go back to the first when you called two strikes in a row on pitches that were down at the shoe tops. Huh, what do you think?"

Reid says nothing, refusing to give the manager anything to use for fuel. Reid can see that he is calming slightly, can see that the manager knows the umpire is right, and is now doing no more than going through the obligatory motions of winding down, so that his team does not lose respect. "Look, if you're going to change one, you have to do it right away," he is saying now, almost as if giving Reid advice. "You don't walk around the field for twenty damn minutes getting your nerve up." He is shooting both arms up in the air as he talks. But his words are now much softer than his gestures. "These are kids out here. They have to know what to expect. You can't be surprising them all goddamn night." He is heading for the dugout. "Baseball isn't supposed to have trick endings," he says over his shoulder, and then looks ahead to the dugout. "Get the hell out there," he screams at his bench, and the softened din behind Reid erupts again. Someone is hitting one of the support poles with something—a bat per-haps—and the noise is deep, hollow and awful. Reid can feel it go through his head. For the first time he wonders if there is a cop in the place. Or anyone who has some sense, some perspective. "Give them twelve outs this inning, ump. What the hell's the difference?" the tirade begins, and deteriorates from there.

At last, when some order is restored and the baserunners are in posi-tion, and Pat Lucas has greeted Reid by going through an extended imi-tation of someone throwing up, the PA man behind Reid asks the crowd for its attention. "The Blueston Braves are playing this game under protest." Reid starts to spin around, knowing that the announcer has made it up. But he checks himself, repeats his order to play ball, and hitches the shin guard, all at once aware that through the whole hellish sequence he forgot it, and survived with the looseness. He allows the pitcher six warm-ups and they are ready to go. The Prestonburg hitter settles in and Reid tells himself to block out the crowd and get back to the game. The big Blueston pitcher goes into his windup and throws. And just as Reid starts to move his right arm up to call the pitch a strike, he suddenly realizes that Pat Lucas is not going to catch the ball. The fat red neck is falling off to one side of the plate, as if in collapse. Reid realizes that the ball will hit him at the precise moment that it does indeed hit him—high on his upper left thigh. He buckles as the pain registers, immediately grateful for the cup and the fact that the slight break of the ball at the end and his own beginnings of an attempt to jump have spared his genitals. He is aware of cheers from behind the plate as his face hits the soft red dirt of Callis Field. He raises himself back to one knee almost immediately, to watch the field. He is trying to decide if the ball is dead or in play. It has rolled up the first base line, as though he has bunted it with his thigh. Of course it is a live ball. And the runner from third has broken for the plate. The Blueston first baseman scoops the ball with his glove and in the same motion flips it to Pat Lucas, who has raised himself to one knee also, bumping Reid as he does. Lucas takes the throw, whirls and waits for the runner, who realizes he will be out, and therefore barrels into Pat Lucas as hard as he can. Pat Lucas tumbles back through the batter's box but holds on to the ball, and while Reid gives the out call from his kneeling position, Lucas goes after the runner with his mask. Both benches empty immediately, and for one brief moment, when he realizes he cannot yet stand, Reid imagines himself being crushed to death by two groups of sweaty young men fighting over a chunk of rubber set down into the ground at the far edge of some little no-name, no-count town. He has had dreams like that—when there are nine pitchers instead of one, and he has to call all the pitches at one time. As he tries to stand, Reid sees Kamm-ler arriving at the plate. He does not come to Reid, but goes to the fight, which is already being broken up by both managers and some of the play-ers. The crowd is at the screen, and as the fight subsides Reid wonders what has kept them from breaking onto the field. Finally, as players begin to straggle back to dugouts, the Blueston manager comes to check on Reid. "Leave him down there," comes from the crowd, several times. Reid accepts the manager's hand and pulls himself to a tentative standing position. As he tries to put weight on the leg, Reid hears the manager saying that the fat catcher will never play again for the Blueston Braves. Reid has to fight off the urge to tell the manager that it is Reid's decision on who gets kicked out of a game, and then nods and moves to dust off the plate. "Aw, the little blind guy hurt hisself," comes from behind him. Reid straightens, turns—now not caring what they say—and searches openly for Ellen.

As if to frame the events of the inning—as if to put them into glaring focus—the rest of the game ebbs away peacefully. In their half of the eighth the home team goes in order. In the top of the ninth Prestonburg gets a runner to second with one out but strands him. In the bottom of the ninth, with the crowd thinning and the throbbing in Reid's leg building, the Blueston leadoff man hits a long drive to left that just clears the fence, making the score 2–1, Prestonburg. "Hey ump," comes from a remaining baiter, "you realize the score is now one-nothing us? Do you, you blind cripple?" Another Blueston runner reaches with one out, but the last two hitters strike out against the little left-hander, and the game ends.

As the teams and the umpires head across the field to the clubhouse beyond the outfield fence, Reid walks alone, trying to minimize the limp, while Kammler talks to the Prestonburg pitching coach, and others walk in little clumps of three or four—motioning, pointing, gesturing—recapping the game. For all but Reid, perhaps, it is no more than one game in the Southern Mountains League schedule, now ready to be tucked away into the records. Another little pile of statistics that will find their way into the *Sporting News* and little newspapers here and there around the country. Reid watches Pat Lucas, perhaps the only other person walking alone on the field, and allows himself one brief moment of feeling sorry for the red-necked fat kid, whose baseball career will consist of these few games in a rookie league. Back in his hometown—Reid pictures him being from a dying coal town in Pennsylvania—he will brag about the time he took an umpire out with a fastball and got the runner at the plate on the same play. Reid has been a part of the forming of one boy's legend and claim to fame. Reid envisions Pat Lucas as a drunk, semi-toothless man of forty, going to the same bar every day to see if there might be someone who has not heard the story of the catcher and the ump and the play at the plate.

Reid decides that Ellen has met someone new since the last time he was in town, and she has decided that the easiest way to let him down is to just not come back. Reid views this speculation with a calculated calm, as if the events of the evening need a cap—to be sure that he can maintain in the face of total adversity. Near the gate in the deepest part of center field he catches sight of someone running along the fence. He glances up and sees the flat-top baiter moving at bouncing-gut top speed toward the opened gate. He is carrying a bat, and Reid understands immediately what is happening. Ahead of him, the players have not seen the man, and Reid does not call out to them. He brings his chest protector up into his left hand, and prepares to protect himself once again.

"You lousy motherfucking asshole," the man screams as he comes through the gate, and the screams alert those in front of Reid. "You got no reason to pick on Blueston. This is a championship town and you are screwing it all up. And you aren't going to do it anymore."

As the man nears Reid three or four players move in and tackle him easily, and as he lies on the ground Reid sees tears in his eyes. Reid sees the face as if it is being presented to him in a slowed-down pace—almost as if he can see what will happen a fraction of a second before it does. In the eyes Reid sees a boy who grew up in the town and who has perhaps never been out of it, a man who probably held one of the jobs that aren't there any more. As the players rise and move the man back outside of the field, a policeman arrives from out of nowhere, so far as Reid can tell, and the drunken fan, now crying freely, is led passively away. Reid waves toward the players as they look back at him just before re-forming their clusters.

In the umpire's showers—they have separate stalls in only two of the Southern Mountains League towns—Kammler is off-hand, nearly jovial. "Good goddamn thing we don't get one of those every night," he says over the opaque divider. Reid is not sure whether he means the blown call or the game as a whole. He does not ask. "How's the leg?" Kammler goes on. "It's all right," Reid says. Actually, it is a deep, red-purple color, and is raised in the shape of a large male breast. He has tried to touch it to gauge the depth of the injury, but has not been able to. Toward the bottom half of the circle are stitch imprints, almost as perfectly distinct as on a baseball. Reid moves the leg constantly in the shower, trying to keep the swelling and tightening from becoming too severe.

"At least I get the plate tomorrow night," Kammler is saying. "Save you some bending."

"Right," Reid says. He is not sure he will be able to walk, much less run into the outfield to cover fly balls. For one brief moment he considers walking out. He could get in his car and start for Fremont, as soon as he is dry and dressed. He could be there in twenty hours, and walk into Dr. Branch's office and have him look at the leg. He wonders what keeps him here—what real reason there is to stay. With sabotaging catchers and no-show women, he can think of none. But he pushes the thought aside as quickly as it occurred to him, amid new visions of a league commendation as a result of his handling of the game. But of course there was no one from the league in the stands, and so his only hope is that something will come from one of the managers, who don't tend to think past the next day's pitcher, a cold beer, and payday, so far as Reid can tell.

He touches his upper thigh as lightly as he can with a towel, while Kammler is still in the shower, singing Garth Brooks songs in a voice that is as bad as his umpiring. Kammler, who teaches junior high school history in the off-season, once told Reid over four or five beers that he still thought he could be a pretty fair MOR country singer if he put his mind to it. Reid almost laughs aloud as he remembers this through the pain in his leg. He pulls a yellow pullover down onto his chest, and then steps to the mirror to look at the bruise again. It is bright and large and alive, more riveting than the clump of his sex next to it. He knows he should go to the hospital. The only real benefit that the league offers is that if you are injured in a game they take care of it. Reid doubts he will go, and decides to admire his thinness in the mirror, the hang of the yellow shirt at his waist, the sturdy look of his legs. He grimaces as he bends his left leg to pull up his underwear, and then repeats the pain with dark blue slacks. He slips his sockless feet into cordovan penny loafers, throws his baseball clothing into the laundry cart, and puts his soap and shampoo into his bag. He combs his hair back so that it will dry light and full as it falls back forward, and tells Kammler he'll see him back at the hotel or something.

"You want to wait?" Kammler says, sounding almost offended. Reid is not sure why Kammler wants him to wait. They have not spent an evening together since their first three or four games together. Reid wonders if the older man is offering protection from the bat wielder. Or is just lonely himself, or if he perhaps is looking for a way to apologize for the blown play.

"I think I'll go ahead," Reid says. Outside he decides to be wary, but sees nothing. There are only four or five cars on the forlorn rock lot just outside of Callis Field, and the moon-tinted expanse of space away from the cars appears to be empty, without threat. Reid walks even more slowly now, allowing himself the knowledge that the leg may really need attention. He doesn't know a doctor in Blueston, but is sure that there is one associated with the Braves. He pictures the doctor refusing to treat him, berating him for bad calls, and telling him to see an eye specialist. He is all the way to his car before he realizes that the front tires are flat. He throws his bag against the hood of the car—a six-year-old Toyota Corona he inherited from his father—and then winces as he tries to stoop to see if the tires have been cut or just deflated. He holds his bad leg out straight behind him as he bends to look. Halfway down he comes up again and spins around, fists formed.

"No," she cries, as if already hit. "It's me."

"Jesus," he says, "don't sneak up . . ."

"I'm sorry." She is moon-lit, damp-looking. A plain, thin white blouse allows her tan to show through, even at night. The blouse is tucked into newish blue jeans. Several fingers of one hand are stuck down to the second knuckle in a tight front pocket as she narrows her shoulders as a part of an apology. "I guess I really did want to surprise you though. I saw you and Fred Southmire . . ."

"Who?"

"The guy with the bat. I'm sorry I'm so late, Lenny, but Michael has a fever and kept crying, and I really get worried over a fever in summer. I kept trying to leave and Mom kept telling me to. What happened to your leg?"

"I got hit," Reid says, "with a fastball. And now my goddamn tires are flat. How come I didn't see you when you saw this Fred guy?"

"I was on my way in from out here, and then I stopped and decided to let you go ahead and shower. I though it might embarrass you to have the girl show up right after this guy tries to club you. I have my car, Len." She motions toward her car, an old red Impala that Reid, in his pain and anger, failed to recognize. "I'll get Triple A to come out for you." She touches his arm lightly now, as if sensing that he needs to be approached tentatively.

"Just let me look at the tires," he says. She pulls more strongly at his arm. "It's okay, Lenny, it's okay. They'll fix it. And we'll get Southmire to pay for it. He's always sorry the next day, and he's one of the few still on at the foundry, so he can handle it. And he will." She guides him away from the Toyota, taking his bag. She moves her arm around his waist, as if to help support the bad leg. Reid conquers a momentary urge to limp more severely, to lean into her. As they move toward her car the first breeze of the night hits the back of his neck.

His body moves in sympathetic motions with hers as she moves him toward the driver's side of her car. He has always driven when they are in a car, and the injured leg will not keep him from doing it now, especially since the car is an automatic. At the wheel, as he turns and looks back over his right shoulder to back the car out, she slides herself in beneath his arm, and brings her own arm across his stomach as she pushes her head to his chest in a soft, quick hug of sympathy and apology.

On the empty little road toward town Reid glances back at Callis Field. The mountain behind it is silhouetted by the moonlight, and the angles of the gates and walls around the field are softened by the light and the huge dark mountain behind them. On down the road, the town is still distant enough to be unspecific—to be made of a spread of lights that are yet so small as to be mistaken for reflections of the stars. The tall foundry buildings at the western end of town reach up into the night as if in competition with the mountains for the light of the moon. As Reid drives with Ellen next to him, the town is somehow transformed. Covered with night, it takes on the little-town virtues she talks about so often, and which excited Reid when he first got out a map to see where his new Southern Mountains League job would take him. With her narrow shoulders beneath his arm, he is able to allow her to embody the feel and spirit of the sweet southern town he had expected to find. It is the feel of the shoulders that overtakes him as he aims the car along the last ridge before the road turns to pass the flat-roofed restaurants and bars that signal the beginning of downtown. The dull throb of his leg is all at once no more than evidence that he has done his work for the day and done it well, and has earned this drive into the night. He is poised just then—still high above the harshness of the town, and at the first soft edge of love for the woman.

The World's Foremost Fungo Hitter Watches Bugs Bunny in the Spartanburg, South Carolina Days Inn

JOSH RUSSELL

for Vance Bourjaily

"Who's gettin footyprints all over mah desert?" an Arab-garbed Yosemite Sam asks his camel. My roomie, nineteen-year-old shortstop Bobby Lester from Opelousas, Louisiana, is dead drunk and asleep in his clothes—save for one lizard boot he managed to yank off before passing out—asleep in what had been my choice of bed. His snoring is loud and he belches as he dreams, his gut filled with Dr Pepper and gin. We'd been in a bar with the rest of the team celebrating our win over the Greenville Braves and the first time he ordered the mix of bar brand and soda pop, the bartender, unable to believe someone would drink such a thing, made Lester repeat himself three times. Dr Pepper and *gin.*

In our room he's lit by the TV and his babyface looks even younger in the weird light. I've found a station on the cable box that seems to be playing nothing but old Bugs Bunny cartoons, and the walls and Bobby are glowing in vivid reds, blues and oranges. There'll be three or four different cartoons, then a commercial for a nine-hundred sex line, then more cartoons.

I'm stone sober and awake, like always. It'll be daylight before I'll be able to sleep. Even then I'll get my usual two or three hours, then be up and at it. When I was Lester's age I too drank nightly, crashed at three and woke groggy at nine to wolf down a doughnut-and-Folger's continental breakfast before staggering to the bus to sleep again, dozing through hamlet after hamlet. After fifteen years in the minors, the thought of hours and hours of booze-induced sleep is as foreign to me as the dream I once had of starting in the majors.

The cartoon changes from the one with Bugs as a bullfighter, to the one in which he and Elmer Fudd do a version of *The Barber of Seville*. From my gear bag I get a new fungo bat and a roll of cloth tape. While I tape up the new stick I watch Bugs shave Elmer. With the help of some fertilizer in the place of tonic, flowers sprout along Fudd's bald scalp. Once I have two long tape strips along the barrel, I fetch three cans of tennis balls, my bottle of mineral water, and my orange terrycloth cap with the logos of the dozen-plus clubs I've played for snaking around its crown, a hatband of angry birds, ominous natives and homicidal insects.

When I pull the tab on the first can, there's a lovely rush of air and smell of trapped rubber. After I have all the cans open I line the balls up along the foot of my second-choice bed. I take one and bounce it on the bat the way you'd bounce a ball on a tennis racket. I'm watching a scissors-wielding Elmer running after Bugs when Lester sits bolt upright and says, "Momma?"

"Wrong," I tell him, "Elmer Fudd."

He plops back into his pillows, belches, and starts to snore again. I let the ball fall past the bat and hit the floor where it rebounds weakly off the carpet. When it hops up, I slap it with enough backspin that it curls straight up above my head, then falls into my wheelhouse. I take a Reggie swing, all butt twist and toes off the ground, and hammer the ball into the drapes. Eight swings later I'm out of ammo.

Collecting the balls, I can see out the sliding glass door. A yellow bulb perched high atop a pole glazes the pool and the patio doors of all the other rooms. Lester is making so much noise I'm sure he's going to be sick.

I have two balls going, juggling them on the bat, when an editorial comes on. It has to do with some local issue—garbage service price hikes or cuts, it's hard to tell which—and out of the corner of my eye I watch a dude wearing a wide tie tell it like it is, surprised not to see women in underwear telling me to call them. It ends and the station's number comes on screen. I dial it, snug the phone between my chin and shoulder, and add a third ball into the halo I have spinning. After seven rings a woman answers. She says simply "Hello" and for a moment I think I have the wrong number.

"Is this the TV station?"

"Sure it is," she says.

"Good," I say. On the screen Bugs is pestering a construction worker. I get a fourth and a fifth ball into the circle.

"What do you want?" she asks, and I realize I haven't said anything for a good twenty seconds.

"I was just watching the cartoons and I thought I'd call to say I liked them. A lot. I like them very much."

"That's good to hear." Her voice noticeably brightens. "Are you new in town? Never seen the show before? 'Midnight Menagerie'?"

"I'm a baseball player," I tell her. "I'm up at the Days Inn. We beat Greenville today. Play them tomorrow and I assume we'll beat them again."

"I see," she says. "Hold on. Watch."

Bobby sits up again. "Leelee? *Leelee?*" he whispers.

"Your girl's not here," I tell him.

"Leelee?" he says again.

I one-hand my bat, keeping the balls going, and toss an empty tennis ball can at him. It rings off the headboard and he snuggles back down into the nest he's made of the comforter. When I look back at the TV Bugs is playing baseball. Big square-jawed guys in gray uniforms drill balls at him, stomp him as he slides into second.

The voice comes back on the phone. "For you, 'Baseball Bugs,' 1946."

"I've never seen this one before."

"One of the best of the post-war ones. Warner Brothers got so muddled down in the anti-Japanese and anti-German propaganda stuff it was hard for them to get back to really good *funny* ones."

"I see."

Lester sits up and yells "Leelee!" at the top of his lungs. A ball to the ear shuts him up, a second off a cheekbone makes him cover his face with a pillow.

"So what position do you play?"

"All of them. I've played every position." There's a long pause, long enough for me to tell I've stumped her. Maybe she thinks I'm not really a ballplayer, thinks I'm some pervert with a thing for Daffy Duck. "I'm a utility player," I explain. "I do whatever needs to be done."

"What's your name?"

"Chapel, Ken Chapel."

There's a pause. On the screen thunder cracks and lightning flashes. Elmer Fudd is in a horned helmet. She's plugged in *The Rabbit of Seville* again. "I'm Sherry James and I've never heard of you," she finally admits.

"Glad to meet you." I have the three remaining balls plonking rhythmically back and forth.

"So what do you do best? There must be one thing you do better."

"I am," I tell her, "the world's foremost fungo hitter." There's another pause and in the silence Bobby moans, Elmer sings "Kill the wabbit," and the balls make their hollow-against-wood sound.

"A fungo hitter?"

"I can do magic with a bat and ball," I say, hamming like mad. "There was an article about me in *Sports Illustrated* three weeks ago." That's true. A reporter came and watched me hit, send flies three hundred feet down a foul line to land kicking up lime. I quote from the article: "A virtuoso of the inconsequential long ball, a maestro of the meaningless perfectly placed 'tweener.'"

"What you do doesn't matter?" she interrupts.

Bobby sits up, points a wavering finger at my head. "Sick lid, chief," he says, then laughs.

I cover the phone with my cheek, aim the bat at him like a gun, ring of green balls still spinning. "Yo, hambone, shut up. I'm on the fucking *phone.*" I hear Sherry clear her throat. What can I say? I want to ask her to meet me somewhere, the Waffle House across the parking lot, poolside to share a Coke. I could leave passes for her at the gate, chat with her from the dugout. I want to make the chance that she's there programming cartoons in the middle of the night into something, some chance connection between the two of us that'll blossom into something, anything.

"Was there really an article about you?"

I'm hurt. "Why would I tell you that if there wasn't?"

"Listen, let me interview you? If it's good enough they might want me to come down to the game and do it with a crew, get a bit for the six o'clock sports spot. I need something like this, OK?"

"Sure," I say. The line goes quiet and I can hear faint noises on her end. I get four more balls into the air, have seven going, then catch a glimpse of myself in the surface of the sliding glass door, startle myself with my own reflection and lose all the balls. I'm on my hands and knees pulling them out from under the bed and the dresser when she comes back on.

"OK, I'm taping." Her voice rises; she enunciates each word cleanly. "I'm talking to Ken..."

"Chapel."

"The foremost hitter of . . ."

"The world's foremost fungo hitter."

"Right. Now, Ken, could you tell me your lifetime batting average?"

I tune my voice to the fake tone she's using, try to play along. "Well, Sherry, I'm not too sure. I believe it's around two-thirteen. It was two-o-seven at the close of last season, but I've done quite well for myself this time around."

"Do you hit a lot of home runs?" There's concern in her voice.

"No, Sherry, I don't. I've hit two this year and that's two more than I hit last year." Using my bat like a putter, I send a ball into the open mouth of Bobby's removed snakeskin Justin.

"I see," she says.

"Yes," I answer. I hear what is obviously the click of a tape recorder being turned off.

"Pardon me, Ken, if this sounds rude, but why was there an article about you?"

"Fungo."

"Fungo?"

"The practice of tossing a ball up and hitting it as it descends through the strike zone." I do this as I narrate the act. The ball ricochets of the wall, comes back at me and I hit it away again. It lodges in a pleated lampshade.

"And you're good at this?"

"The best in the world according to *S.I.*, and I'd assume they'd know."

"It's just that, well, that sounds dull, Ken. I doubt they'll want me to interview you."

On the TV a cartoon Humphrey Bogart is demanding that Elmer Fudd bring him a cooked rabbit. Elmer's sweating huge pearls of perspiration. I start to dribble three balls, their voice-like patter is good for me.

"Sherry," I start, "I'm thirty-three years old and I'll never make it. I've had so many cups of coffee, so many one game stints, that I know I'll never make it. What I have is what I have. I can do things with a ball and a fungo bat that no one else is able to do. I can hit balls straight up. When I went up with Houston in '79 I nailed the roof of the Dome, the *roof* of the *Dome*."

Even with the bat sweet against my fingers and the balls turning smoothly, my voice starts to shake. "I can hit knuckle balls—understand, I don't mean that if someone pitches me a knuckle ball I can hit it, what I mean is I can tweak a ball so it twitches like a spastic butterfly." I stop and listen for her response. The line is dead; she's hung up.

I get the balls I fired at him from beside Lester's bed, find a couple under an armchair, pluck the one from the lampshade, shake the last from Bobby's boot, then feed all nine into a spinning hoop. Looking into the chartreuse universe I think how much I want to be home in Gainesville hitting flies out across the high school soccer field behind my house for my half-pitbull-half–Jack Russell terrier, Rodney, to chase.

Lester sits up and looks at me, looks at the balls moving in the air; his head bobs as he follows their flight. "Huh," he says. "My, my."

Wonders

OWEN KING

Game 1

The best contact wasn't like contact at all, it was like swinging straight through, and the baseball was only an echo of the bat's motion. The game was so hard, but that moment was so easy—the ball flew, Eckstein ran, and there was no chance they were going to catch him. The rest of the time, moment to moment, Eckstein generally felt out of sorts, jumpy and clumsy, like a man who has only just been awakened by a sharp noise. Playing was the only part of his life that had ever felt completely natural. Except tonight. Tonight, even the notion of knocking a true one and watching it fly, even that didn't soothe him. He had made a real mess of matters and didn't want to so much as tighten his laces, let alone take a swing.

Eckstein, the second baseman for the Coney Island Wonders, was sitting out that night's game against the Hoboken Gentlemen. He told Gordy Wheelock, the manager, that he was sick, a sour gut. "You better have a couple of seltzers, kid," Wheelock had groused. "I ain't here to rub your tummy." But Wheelock wasn't about to take any chances with a talent like Eckstein, the best hitter they had—the old man gave him the night off. The kid was surely headed for the big-league club, and sooner than later.

So now Eckstein slumped on the bench, watching the game from under the low bill of his cap. He tried not to think about what a sorry human being he was, but it was hard to ignore the tiny steel teeth grinding his insides. And on top of it all, the heckler in the left-field grandstand was giving an earful to Burnham, the Negro who played left for Coney Island.

The left fielder's name was Cleatus "Woodpecker" Burnham, and he stood at his position with a placid look, as if he did not hear the heckler. Of course, he would have had to be deaf not to hear.

"You're horrible, Burnham," bayed the heckler. "Not only do you look like you got struck by lightning, you play like it, too." The heckler was a spindly creature with a patchy black fungus of beard.

"A big damn wind oughtta come along and blow you back to Africa. Not a typhoon, *a ty-coon.*" There were a few guffaws, and the heckler bowed to the people around him.

The top half of the seventh ended, and the Wonders trotted off the field for the seventh inning stretch. The groundskeeper came out to rake around the base paths and tamp down the pitcher's mound.

Meanwhile, the seventh inning stretch entertainment, two attractions from the freak show, the Backwards Man and Jenny Two Heads, raced miniature tricycles in the outfield while the organist played "Don't Fence Me In."

Woodpecker sat down next to Eckstein. The bench creaked. He was the oldest guy on the team and pretty well past it. There weren't any other Negroes in the Hudson League; strictly, it was against the rules; but Coney Island had an entertainment exemption for special attractions. The previous season, they had used the exemption on a weight-lifting dwarf from Baltimore, but he had been a drunk and caused trouble in the clubhouse. So this season, they had brought in Woodpecker for the special attraction, a Negro who could play baseball.

Woodpecker apparently used to be a hell of a hitter. Sometimes he could still turn on a ball and knock it a good distance, but his average wasn't much. In the outfield, he was flat-footed and seemed to move through thick mud.

They called him Woodpecker because he was always chewing on a homemade toothpick. He had a carving knife that he kept on his person at all times and used to chip shards from whatever was around. There were hundreds of jagged bites in the dugout bench, like a beaver had been at it.

Some of the guys liked to have some sport with him. One time, Pelky, the third baseman, asked Woodpecker to autograph a watermelon. The Negro had been decent about it, too, signed "Woodpecker Burnham" real big and clear, and now Pelky kept it on the top shelf of his locker wearing a Wonders hat and with a toothpick sticking from its skin.

He was a different bird, but Eckstein liked him. He could always have a talk with Woodpecker about the pictures. Almost any time he went to the Odeon, when he looked up to the balcony, Woodpecker would be sitting in the front row, hunched over the railing, toothpick dangling from the front of his lip. Eckstein liked to pick the left fielder's brain sometimes, go over the latest film with him, and try to get at it a little.

The heckler's incessant screaming made Eckstein wince. Every game he was out there, every game shrieking at Woodpecker like a dime ticket gave him the right.

The second baseman watched as his teammate turned an old broken Louisville Slugger over a few times on his knee before selecting a spot high up on the barrel, and with a flash of the knife blade cut away a neat toothpick. Woodpecker spit his old toothpick on the ground and inserted the new.

In the outfield, beneath the flare of the light stanchions, the Backwards Man tumbled from his tricycle. He stood up, confused, and ran in the opposite direction, away from the finish line. The freak handlers hurried to correct him, but it was difficult to get the attention of the Backwards Man; his cross-eyed peanut of a head was set on his neck looking over his spine.

"You get a good one?" Eckstein asked him.

Woodpecker shrugged. He rolled the pick around in his mouth, seeming to taste it. "It ain't too fine," he said.

"That son of a bitch out in the bleachers never shuts up, does he?"

"I don't listen to him none," said Woodpecker. He scratched his belly, rubbing his long black fingers, their tips whitish, over the soft bulge of flesh.

"You see anything good lately? At the Odeon?"

"I seen the new one. It's pretty good. Got some vampires."

"Much killing?"

"Some."

"Girls?"

"Just one. She don't show much," said Woodpecker. "Little leg. No thigh."

Eckstein nodded gravely. Woodpecker cut a pick from the Louisville Slugger and gave it to him. To the second baseman, the pick tasted like dust, but wanting to be polite, he chewed diligently.

When the seventh inning stretch was over, the freak handlers guided the Backwards Man and Jenny Two Heads off the field. One of Jenny Two Heads' heads was asleep. This head, the bald one, was rarely awake and never spoke, but the other head stuck its tongue out at the Backwards Man.

Batting in the bottom half of the inning, Woodpecker slapped a hit in the right field gap but got thrown out lumbering into second base.

"You fat bastard," screamed the heckler. "Move your lead ass!"

Woodpecker appeared not to notice him and jogged back to the dugout still nibbling on the pin of Louisville oak.

In the ninth, Wheelock told Eckstein to "tie up his guts, put em in a bow," because he was pinch-hitting. Watching him, Eckstein could see that the pitcher was clearly tired, the zip gone off his fast one and just spin on his curve. He figured on banging one, no problem. But as he swung, his feet slipped in the batter's box and the ball dribbled to the mound. The pitcher pounced. A snap throw to the second baseman and over to first. Double play.

"C'mon, Eckstein," wailed the heckler. "What, are you a nigger now, too? *C'mon.*"

The crowd—families on holiday, the boys in yarmulkes and short pants, working men with no wives, and the seven or eight Negroes standing outside with their fingers in the right field fencing—sighed and began to file out, heading home or back to the boardwalk. The scoreboard operator put up the final score: Hoboken Gentlemen 4, Coney Island Wonders 3.

Eckstein went and sat back down in the dugout. The other players, Woodpecker included, departed. The scoreboard operator replaced the digit placards for each inning with the advertisement boards for Red Giraffe Extra-Long Hotdogs. There was a series of cranking noises, as one after another, the switches were thrown on the three light pylons that towered over the field. As the filaments cooled, the night filled in around the banks of lightbulbs and turned the grass black.

After the game, Eckstein walked to the Odeon. Lillian scowled at his nickel and let him in for free.

The movie playing was called *Black Mansion*. Despite his low mood, sitting down in the theater, he felt somewhat cheered. You couldn't do much better than a vampire picture.

It started off with two hobos, Gooch and McMasters, riding on a boxcar. The two of them jump off to get something to eat in this little South Dakota town. What they don't know is the town is under the control of a horde of vampires who live in a mansion on the highest hill in town. To placate this enclave of bloodsuckers, the townspeople lure fellows like these hobos up to the house at night, promising free chow and a place to sleep. Which is exactly what happens, except McMasters has a crucifix from his uncle, a priest, and he always wears it, even though he stopped believing in God when his kid sister died of polio. McMasters uses the crucifix to ward off the vampires and escape, but Gooch gets trapped.

It was around this point in the film that Lillian sat down beside him.

"The town's being run by vampires," Eckstein whispered excitedly to her. "But this rough old hobo made a break for it."

"What a lot of trash," said Lillian.

McMasters raises hell in the town, trying to get together a posse to storm the mansion, but the people are all vampire bootlickers. The only one who will help him is the mayor's daughter, Kelly-Anne. McMasters sneaks back into the mansion while Kelly-Anne sets up dynamite, and he makes her promise on his kid sister's soul that she'll set off the whole load in thirty minutes if he doesn't come out. Inside, McMasters kills the king vampire by stabbing him in the heart with a chair leg. But he takes so long that Kelly-Anne has to set off the dynamite, and she's brokenhearted, because she realizes that she loved the lug, never mind all his tough talk. That's just before he digs out of the rubble with his crucifix, and the townspeople throw a big party as a way of saying thanks for saving them from a life of servitude to the black mansion vampires.

Throughout the movie, Lillian made small, sighing noises of dissatisfaction, but Eckstein hardly noticed—he was dazed and tingly from the movie. It was the sort of picture a person could maybe see two or three times and still not get sick of. His favorite part was when McMasters pushed over the huge vampire throne and trapped the screeching, squealing bloodsucker underneath. The hobo had torn off a throne leg—the foot shaped like a bear's claw—and stabbed into the vampire's black heart.

While he waited for Lillian to close up the theater, Eckstein paced the curb, kicking at pebbles. The tingly feeling had worn off, and he was guilty again. After what he'd done, Eckstein figured he deserved the same fate as Gooch. He shivered, thinking of the moment in the film when the vampire family surrounded the unlucky hobo, moving in slowly, slowly, hunching over the man and lifting their capes, shrouding the cringing figure, seeming to melt down the wall, until they became one dark undulating mass, a living shadow.

That was the one part Eckstein maybe hadn't liked so much.

Down the arcade, a barker was running a quarter pitching game against a brick wall. There was a beat cop standing by, collecting bets in a cigar box. A bum with a guitar slung over his back walked in the gutter, collecting cigarette butts and warbling to himself. A Model T clattered over cobblestones. The big wheel at the top of Luna Park blinked green and white, green and white, green and white.

Lillian came outside and started to draw down the steel shutter. He went to help her, but she told him to get out of the way. The metal sheet clanked down, and she locked it. "I'm hungry," she said.

They walked in silence down the street to the diner around the corner. Her heels clicked on the sidewalk. Lillian was a big girl, heavy around the hips. Her face was perfectly round, cute in a babyish way; she usually smelled strongly of talcum. But tonight they walked too far apart for Eckstein to catch even a whiff.

Taking a booth in the back, Lillian let the waitress pour their coffee and move away before she said, "I know what you want to ask and the answer is no. It didn't come. That's nine weeks, buddy boy."

She stared at him hard, and he looked out the window.

That first night, back in April, she'd seen him at a game. Her face had been flushed when she leaned over the grandstand railing and handed him a ticket for that night's show. The film turned out to be a love picture, about a beautiful girl with amnesia and a millionaire playboy. Eckstein had never got to see how it turned out, though. "I'm bored," Lillian had said after a while, tugging him through the side door and up the stairs to the dark closet where the movies came from.

Steam crawled out of a cracked manhole cover in the middle of the street. Eckstein thought of the vampires.

The waitress came over. Lillian ordered a steak, a potato, and strawberry pie. Eckstein ordered coffee.

"It was an accident," Eckstein blurted. "And you knew what you were doing—"

"—It's all your fault. I was just sweet on you, and I get this." She blinked several times and rubbed at the corners of her eyes.

It had been his first time, that night in the projection room. "Don't do it inside me," she told him. There was hardly space for them both in the tiny room. The reflection of the movie, flickering out of the cannon-like lens, covered the walls in a backwash of black-and-white. "Don't do what?" asked Eckstein. A moment later he had groaned, and spent himself.

The ecstatic moment was cut off by Lillian's frantic shoving. Eckstein tumbled backward into a shelf of movie reels. She said he was an idiot, that he must be from outer space not to know any better. Eckstein said he hadn't been thinking, that was all. And it was the only time they had ever done it; she barely let him kiss her since. One desperate evening, willing to do anything for another taste, he had offered to marry her, whether she was pregnant or not. "That's a laugh," Lillian had said. "My family'd love you, a ballplayer with a Jew name."

"I ain't a Jew," said Eckstein. "I'm German."

"Sure," sneered Lillian, "Sure." There was a pause. Then, Eckstein blurted that he loved her, purely loved her. Lillian's eyes had widened, gathering him up, and Eckstein felt her looking deep inside him. His throat caught, and he let a nervous breath. Her eyes had narrowed. "You're a monster," Lillian had finally said very quietly. The memory made him more ashamed, and he thought again that he deserved Gooch's fate, to be eaten by vampires.

"I'm gonna lose my job," she said, and began to cry.

The waitress brought the food. Lillian's face was flushed, streaked with tear tracks. "Did I ask for gravy?" she snapped at the waitress. "And what about napkins? Don't I look like someone who needs a napkin?"

He walked Lillian home, to the apartment she shared with three other girls in a women's boardinghouse on Mermaid Avenue.

"After you're done work tomorrow, I'll get it taken care of," said Eckstein. Lillian began crying again and hit him weakly with her purse. "Bring a change of clothes," said Eckstein, because he felt like he needed to say something more, something to reassure her that he was in control, and he heard once that it was something a girl ought to do in a situation like this one.

That night, Eckstein felt so terrible he told his roommate, Bobby Pelky, the Wonders' third baseman.

"It ain't no big problem," said the third baseman.

Now that it was out, Eckstein regretted having spoken. Saying the words aloud only made it more plain. He was guilty—the truth was as bright as a lamp.

He tried to change the subject: "I saw the new picture at the Odeon, the vampire one."

Pelky stood up and shadowboxed a combination by the window. He was wiry, sneaky fast. Sometimes he had trouble with the inside pitch. Pelky was a good third baseman. "I've had some big problems. This one here is just tiny."

"I'll go with you to see it if you want," said Eckstein.

"You got the money?" asked Pelky. He went to the mirror and flexed his bicep. An ink mustang reared across the skin.

"I got twenty," sighed Eckstein.

Pelky snorted. "You wanna scare off the stork you're gonna need at least forty, maybe fifty."

Eckstein shrugged.

"You know where to go?" Pelky went to his nightstand, got his wallet, and fished out three or four dollars.

"Yeah," said Eckstein, "sure, I heard."

"Good. Then all we gotta do is get you some more dough." The third baseman sashayed across the floor with an invisible dance partner. His white drawstring boxer shorts were loose around his hips, and the cleft of his pale buttocks was visible. "That's a snap: we'll take up a collection." He stopped in mid-dance step and threw a wild punch at the air.

Pelky dropped the bills on Eckstein's night table. "There's a start for you—so when are you gonna teach me how to clear out that inside snapper?"

Eckstein sagged in his bed. He reached out from beneath the covers, touched the bills with a finger, and took back his hand. "You're still crowding the plate," said the second baseman. "You ought to back off—and your bat's too big. Use a smaller bat."

"A smaller bat—I'll have to give it some consideration. Takes a big one to really knock it far—," said Pelky, then added, "Say, you oughtta wipe that frown right off. This ain't no problem. This is tiny."

Game 2

In the third inning, as Woodpecker was camping under a high fly ball, the heckler threw a bottle. The bottle struck Woodpecker in the side of the head, and he fell face first on the turf. "Stone-hands-nigger!" screeched the heckler. He ran up the grandstand and then down the runway out of the park before anyone could stop him.

A couple of the guys on the team propped Woodpecker up and helped him off the field. Eckstein was appalled at the web of blood at the left fielder's temple, staining the rim of his cap, and dripping down to the collar of his pin-striped uniform. "Son of a bitch is heavy as hell," complained Pelky.

After a few minutes, when the new left fielder was warmed up, the game resumed.

Eckstein had hoped playing would take his mind off Lillian and what they were going to do—to *undo*. But the bad thoughts were impossible to stop: he imagined Lillian obscenely sprawled on a wooden table, crying and screaming, and blood splashing from all directions. When he finally forced the image out of his head his mind jumped to Gooch's death in *Black Mansion*. Except that instead of Gooch, Eckstein was the one who was sliding down the wall and the vampires were lifting their capes like nets and slowly closing in.

Near the end, when the tuberculosis had got into her head, Eckstein's mother, a washerwoman who had raised him alone, had whispered, "I should have got you taken care of. Now look at me." And that was where his thoughts finally settled.

By the seventh inning stretch, along with going hitless in three at bats, Eckstein had also made two errors.

"You're garbage today," barked Wheelock. "Nobody throw out Eckstein. He's garbage but nobody throw him out. You hear me? No matter how damn much Eckstein looks like a damn piece of trash sitting in a dugout full of baseball players, nobody throw him out. If I find that little son of a bitch in my clubhouse trashcan, I don't know what I might do, I just might not be accountable."

Eckstein spat on the ground but didn't say anything.

During the seventh inning stretch, Jenny Two Heads and the Backwards Man raced across the outfield on pogo sticks. The organist played "The Music Goes 'Round and 'Round" with maniacal energy while another two freaks, the Purple Girl and Three-Ton Timmy, added squeaking vocals and tuneless trumpet, respectively. The Backwards Man fell over again in a crashing heap on the grass, pretzeled around his pogo stick, and had to be led away, the small eyes in his dainty head rolling wildly while the crowd howled. Jenny Two Heads took a bow; the head that was awake licked the ear of the bald head that was asleep, but the bald head did not respond. Rippling, the crowd cheered and stomped. A cart transported Three-Ton Timmy out the service gate in right field. The Purple Girl blushed green at the catcalls that fell down and around her.

In his last at bat, Eckstein got hit in the hip by a pitch. It stung, and he hobbled to first. "Fuck you," he said to the Hoboken pitcher on his way to first.

Final score: Hoboken Gentlemen 9, Coney Island Wonders 1.

Going from one locker to another in the clubhouse, Pelky asked each player for a donation. "There's a dollar minimum," he said. To the shortchangers, the third baseman said, "You Jew—when'd seventy-five cents turn into a dollar?" There weren't many complaints. Even Gordy Wheelock, after a head shake in Eckstein's direction, gave two dollars.

For his own part, Eckstein sat and bit his nails. Then he fled to the showers and stayed beneath the hot spray until his skin felt as though it were shrinking around his bones.

When he returned, Pelky was harassing Woodpecker.

His head wrapped with a bag of ice, Woodpecker lay stretched out on a bench. Swollen and meaty-looking, the flesh around his right eye, close to the point of impact, glistened with oil. A shard of red wood, clearly cut from the locker room bench of the same color, pointed from his mouth.

"A dime ain't going to cut the mustard, nigger," said Pelky. "And don't offer me no freebies with your sister or your mother." The lanky third baseman stood above the prone man with his fists clenched.

"It's all I got," said Woodpecker. "I was only going to get a sandwich."

"You don't need a sandwich, you fat bastard, you need one dollar."

The black-skinned man turned his head away and looked at the wall.

Pelky slammed his fist into his teammate's soft belly. Woodpecker let out a gasp. Pelky slapped the toothpick out of his mouth. A couple of guys shifted uncomfortably, but nobody got up.

"I didn't think Jews could come out as spades, but what do you know." Pelky made a feint, and Woodpecker flinched, curling on the table. "You better have five dollars tomorrow."

Towel around his waist, Eckstein had frozen up. It was a small dirty room, humid from the showers. The men sat on stools in front of their lockers. They were mostly naked, their bodies pale suits, faces and arms brown from the sun. Woodpecker, also naked, was a black smudge in the middle of them, chest rising and falling, the ice pack in a turban around his head. Pelky slowly scratched his exposed genitals before turning away to go and take donations from the last couple of guys on the team.

The miasma—sweat, mildew, liniment, tobacco—of the locker room filled Eckstein's nose, and he felt like vomiting.

When the second baseman was dressing, Pelky came over and, with a tight grimace, pressed a wad of bills into the his hand. "That's thirty, not counting the spade's five." Pelky threw his arm around Eckstein's shoulder and pulled him into a huddle. "It's a little short, but I figure they ain't the kind to turn down a decent amount of dough."

"Thanks," whispered Eckstein. "I owe you."

"No problem," said Pelky with a grin and roughly pinched his roommate's nipple.

He went to the movies, hoping to find a mistake. Once, in a cowboy picture, he saw the fender of a Ford sticking out from around the back of a building. The movies were full of mistakes, and usually such carelessness irritated the second baseman—it was like coming up too soon on a ground ball and letting it trickle between your legs—but tonight Eckstein felt that he needed proof that it was all make-believe, that *Black Mansion* wasn't true.

But there was no proof.

The hobo's eyes seemed to swell from his head as the monsters closed around him. Tiptoeing forward, nearer, nearer still, the vampires' capes followed across the floor, oozing and curling like living animals. White-faced, black tongues expectantly licking their black lips, they did not bare their teeth, but the shape of them—tiny swords beneath the flesh—was visible at the skin of their tight, ghastly cheeks. Gooch moaned repeatedly. Capes and shadows enveloped his body.

There *were* vampires: undead creatures who sucked the blood of the living.

In the lavatory, Eckstein splashed water on his face. When he pissed, the crackling of the ice in the urinal made him shiver.

Eckstein thought maybe he didn't like the movies anymore. He went outside to walk around until the theater closed and Lillian got out. He strolled down to the boardwalk.

The weekend crowd was thick and boisterous. Children chased each other. Tinkling piano keys echoed from the dance hall. Two drunks wrestled feebly with each other, arm-locked and lurching while passersby stepped around them. A man pulled a giggling girl into an alley. Eckstein unbuttoned his shirt a couple of buttons, and pushed his hat back on his head in a way that felt good. He let the flow of the crowd carry him to the end of the boardwalk. There were colored lights and barkers hollering out the latest attractions. Eckstein bought a pop. The vendor recognized him. "Is it a slump?" the man asked, meaning the last couple of games. "No," said Eckstein, "just giving Hoboken a break. We'll put the wood to 'em tomorrow, I believe." He tipped his hat to the vendor, and the vendor tipped his red-striped paper cap in return. Eckstein found a baseball tossing game. One ball after another he fired through the dangling hoops, while the operator smoked a cigarette. "Get outta here, ringer," said the operator. "No prize for you."

Woodpecker sat on a curb, carving toothpicks from a chunk of driftwood laid across his knees. They saw each other at the same moment, and Woodpecker waved his teammate over and nodded for him to sit down. Eckstein felt a burn of embarrassment in his cheeks.

At his feet, Woodpecker had a little pile of new toothpicks. He flicked at the grey chunk of wood with his pocket knife, popping loose another fragment of wood. Then he studied his work, the uneven cuts and shelves, and nodded with satisfaction. "Good wood," he said.

"I bet," said Eckstein, just to say something.

"I got that five dollars," said Woodpecker.

"No, it's okay. I don't need it," said Eckstein. "I'm sorry about Pelky, he was just trying to help me out and—well, he got too hot."

"It don't bother me," said Woodpecker. He took out a bill and pressed it into Eckstein's shirt pocket. The Negro twirled his toothpick around his mouth and sucked at it.

The sounds of the boardwalk were distant and faint. Reflecting off the night clouds, the big wheel splashed green and white, green and white, green and white.

Lillian would be closing up soon.

"I owe you," said Eckstein, and looked down at the street. "I guess I oughtta scoot."

"You see that movie?" asked Woodpecker.

"Yeah," said Eckstein, "it scared the heck out of me."

"Looked real, didn't they, them vampires?"

"Heck," said Eckstein.

"That's right," said Woodpecker, "that's right."

Lillian avoided Eckstein's eyes as they walked from the theater. He slouched along beside her. Frequently pretending to scratch an itch at his nose, he dabbed at his eyes, which were teary. Moving away from the boardwalk, the houses on Surf Avenue narrowed, the slats peeled and grew scabby, the lawns wilted; indistinct mounds of garbage lay in the gutters, and the air was rotten with the smell of fish. The howling of two fighting dogs startled him. "Dammit," he cursed, and Lillian did not scold him.

When they reached the alleyway, Eckstein was nauseated at the sight of the makeshift street sign, a broken scrap of crating nailed to a burnt-out lamppost, painted in chipped black letters: Wretch Lane. Lillian hiccuped and began to sob.

He went to touch her, but she curled her shoulder away from him. "Someday I'm going to have beautiful babies," she said thickly, her voice rising and breaking with the hiccups. "You'll just be a used-up ballplayer in some jerkwater town."

There was an empty bottle lying in the street. Eckstein went and got it, then hurled it as far as he could, over the rooftops on the opposite side of the road.

She stopped crying, and he held her purse while she applied fresh makeup, using her compact and the light of the moon.

He offered her his hand, and she took it. Their palms suctioned with sweat.

At the end of the alleyway, they emerged into a small courtyard littered with trash. A twisted unicycle was propped up against one wall. There was an animal cage, big enough to hold a lion, pushed up against another wall. Something very large lay in it, unmoving or dead. The courtyard belonged to a darkened, sagging house; the shutters were battened; a porch leaned before it, giving access to two doors, one black, one red.

"It's the red door we want," said Eckstein.

He knocked hesitantly while Lillian waited at the bottom of the stairs, holding her elbows. Eckstein's eyes had dried out very suddenly. He found himself blinking rapidly, shifting from one foot to another.

After a minute, the second baseman heard steps, a slinking, one-two-*shhh*, one-two-*shhh*. His hands clenched.

The door opened. "You come for a screw?" asked the Purple Girl sleepily. "It's after hours. It's extra now." Her skin was bruised-looking in the moonlight. For some reason she held a broom, which had been dragging behind her, which accounted for the *shhh*-noise.

Eckstein couldn't speak. He blinked and looked at the broom.

The Purple Girl followed his gaze. She stared at the broom as well. "Sometimes, I just feel like sweeping," she said finally. "I can start sweeping at almost any time."

"Oh," said Eckstein.

"You come for a screw?" she asked again. She took the broom and brushed it over Eckstein's shoes. The Purple Girl wore a white nightgown, and her skin peered blackly through the material. Eckstein felt a fearful stirring of arousal.

"We need the surgeon," he blurted.

The Purple Girl looked out over his shoulder, spotted Lillian, and wrinkled her nose. "Follow me," she said. She turned and swept away down the hall.

Eckstein signaled to Lillian. She hurried to him, grasping his hand. Inside, at the end of the hall, a light had appeared, and the Purple Girl had vanished.

They followed, heading for the light. A naked bulb hanging above an open basement door. There was more light at the bottom of a set of wooden stairs. Lillian clenched Eckstein's hand. They went down the stairs.

"You'll have to wait til he's done munchin'," said Jenny Two Heads' wakeful head. The two-headed freak was standing beside the table that was placed in the middle of the dim, dirt-floored room. Sitting in a chair that was turned away from the table, his body facing the wall, the Backwards Man opened and closed his mouth obediently as Jenny fed him, spooning soup to his lips.

Somewhere in the darkness at the far end of the basement, the Purple Girl was sweeping, *shhh-shhh-shhh*, but she was not visible.

"Munch, munch," said the Backwards Man in a tiny voice that was like air whistling through a cracked window. His hands rubbed his thighs happily, while his head ate soup behind his back.

"He can't feed hisself," said Jenny, "The fuckin' idiot." Her sleeping head, the bald one, lolled at her shoulder, sickeningly.

"Munch, munch, munch," squeaked the Backwards Man.

Eckstein and Lillian stood without speaking, their hands squeezed numb together.

When the feeding was done, Jenny Two Heads took the Backwards Man upstairs.

She returned with a large dusty jar and a lamp. She set these things on the floor beside the table. "You get your ass up there," Jenny ordered Lillian. "And you gimme the money."

Lillian went to the table and climbed awkwardly onto it. She began to cry softly again.

Eckstein gave the freak the money.

"Wad it worth it?" Jenny cackled and stuffed the bills between her breasts.

He squatted, hoping that it would be easier to breathe at floor level. It wasn't.

Eckstein noticed something move inside the jar. He wiped a hand across the film of dust. Slithery things, oily worms, it looked like, made him fall back with surprise.

"What are those for?" he asked.

"They eat it," said Jenny Two Heads. "That's they job."

He stood by the table and held Lillian's hand. The freak flipped up Lillian's dress, and with a savage swipe, tore away the girl's underwear. "You won't want 'em after this, honey," she said.

Jenny raised up the lamp and set it on the table between Lillian's legs. From a drawer she took out a pince-nez and two instruments — a battered spoon and a probe with a thin hook at the end.

"First things first," she said, adjusting the eyeglasses and setting the probe down close by. Jenny leaned over with the spoon and studied the girl's private parts. "Wider," the freak growled and slapped the girl's heavy pale thigh.

Lillian moaned and stretched herself open.

Eckstein thought of a baseball, clean and white, soaring into a high, bright night, soaring farther than any other baseball before it. He thought of it still rising, of the droplets of dewy air sliding over it, and then of its long, grand descent, *plunk* into Sheepshead Bay, down, down, sinking down, and settling gracefully into the silt, between stands of waving seaweed. For a moment, thinking all this, he was away from the basement, and he was fine, as fine as he had ever been, or ever could be.

With a snort, Jenny Two Heads straightened. The bald head suddenly lifted, its eyes opened, and it burped. Just as abruptly, the head shut its eyes and fell back, and cracked on her shoulder.

Shhh-shhh-shhh, went the Purple Girl's broom in the dark.

"She's dead in there. Black and dead. Rotten fruit. They ain't no babies ever comin' from there. Rotten fruit. Fuck all you want, and there won't never be any." Jenny removed the money from between its breasts. "You can have half back."

When they got outside, Lillian ran away from him, scrambling through the courtyard and down Wretch Lane.

The massive thing in the cage called pitifully to Eckstein as he passed. "Please don't let them make me eat any more. They won't let me stop. They keep feeding me. Please. I'm not hungry. I haven't been hungry in years. Please. Make them stop. Make them stop."

Game 3

The first pitch came to him in black and white, and the slump was over; Eckstein saw the white ball as a black spot and the colored world around it as a blank mat. He swung and the ball rocketed off the barrel of the lumber club, straight up the middle of the diamond. It ricocheted off the ankle of the Hoboken pitcher and squirted into foul territory. By the time the third baseman tracked it down, Eckstein had trotted into second. The pitcher was helped off the field, and a reliever was brought in.

In his next at bat, the kid drove the ball on a flat arc, hissing through the air and not stopping until it boomed off the scoreboard. He dug into second with another, a double. Eckstein stood on the base and ground his teeth.

"You knocked that one," said Gordy Wheelock when Eckstein returned to the dugout. "That was a frozen rope."

"Stick it up your ass," said Eckstein.

Toeing into the batter's box for his third at bat, Eckstein was able to see the fear in the Hoboken pitcher's face. The pitcher's cheeks glistened with sweat; the pitcher bit his lip and took off his cap, brushed his hand through his hair. Eckstein watched the man fiddle and waited patiently. When the pitcher finally did throw, the kid hit the baseball up and away, over the scoreboard, where it bounced off the cobblestones of Neptune Avenue.

The Wonders were winning 7 to 1 by the time the seventh inning stretch rolled around. The kid had batted in all the runs but one.

On the bench, Woodpecker offered Eckstein a pick. "Good wood," he said. "It's fine—real piney."

The second baseman grunted no.

Woodpecker looked Eckstein over and shook his head. "You ain't exactly here, is you?"

"No," Eckstein shook his head. He thought of the two heads, peering inside Lillian, into the core of her. He thought of the worms in the jar, hungrily squirming over each other. Maybe his mother had been lucky after all—maybe there were worse things even than Eckstein. "No, I don't guess I am."

There was no race in the outfield today. Instead, the cart with Three-Ton Timmy unloaded the giant freak in right field. He sat there like a small mountain. The Purple Girl, the Backwards Man, and Jenny Two Heads ran circles around him. Three-Ton Timmy roared and made feeble grabs at them, as if he wanted to devour them. The organist played "The Moten Swing."

The Purple Girl blew kisses to the crowd on her way off the field and flipped her skirt good-bye.

With one out in the ninth, a Hoboken batter hit a high fly into the area of shallow left field. Woodpecker got a bead on it, tracking the ball as it drifted into foul territory, heading for the grandstand. He stumbled against the wall, straining to catch the ball as it fell about two rows back. At that moment, a hand reached from the crowd and plucked Woodpecker's cap from his head.

"Got your hat, nigger!" The heckler jumped up and down in the aisle of the grandstand, waving the cap.

Woodpecker stood by the wall but made no move.

Eckstein bolted. "Come on, you bastards," he yelled at the rest of the Wonders' infield. Pelky and several of the others looked around at each other, shrugged, then jogged after him.

The heckler swatted the cap across Woodpecker's face. "Down, boy!" he cried. "Sit, boy!"

Woodpecker's head snapped back.

Eckstein reached the wall and vaulted over it.

The heckler turned, dropped the hat, and started running up the grandstand stairs.

Four more Wonders pushed past Woodpecker, pouring over the wall. The black man watched them go. A spectator handed him back his hat.

"Thank you, sir," said Woodpecker.

Eckstein caught the heckler just in front of the exit. He jumped onto the man's back and rode him to the cement floor. "Niggers! Niggers!" the man yelled.

But Eckstein's fist stopped the man's mouth. The first blow split his lip, the second made something in the heckler's face snap. The heckler crumpled to the ground. Eckstein grabbed the man by his hair and slammed his head against the ground. Blood spurted onto the cement. Twice more he banged the man's face against the cement.

Eckstein stepped back. He looked at his bloody right fist. There was a white chip imbedded in his knuckle. The heckler was moaning and making sucking noises, trying to find air. "Well," said Eckstein, half to himself and half to the heckler, "well, you asked for it." Eckstein stepped back, sore hand cradled against belly and staining his jersey with blood. He felt sorry and strange.

The other Wonders had gathered in a loose circle. They began to close in, nearer, nearer still. Pelky delivered the first kick. The heckler made a shocked gurgling noise. They all started kicking him.

What We All Want

LESLIE PIETRZYK

W e came here because of Fernando. Everyone knew what had happened to Fernando Valenzuela, how he'd pitched for the L.A. Dodgers in the 1980s until his wondrous arm collapsed. Then he disappeared. Several years later a scout from the Baltimore Orioles found him pitching here in Mexico, striking out batters like it was as easy as drinking water. Want to try it again? the scout asked him. He did. The arm was back. In '93 he was a starting pitcher for the Orioles.

If it could happen to Fernando. . . . I sat in the stands and watched them each think it. Luis Torres, Manuel Ramirez, all the rest, and especially my husband, Lee. During batting practice, during warm-ups, during a game, the words rose from the dusty field: Then it could happen to me.

Why not? In baseball it's a way of life, not a question.

It was Lee's birthday. What do you do in Oaxaca, Mexico, when your husband turns thirty? I bought a baseball piñata and filled it with foil-wrapped chocolates that looked like baseballs that my sister Fed-Exed from Dallas. I woke up early and hung the piñata where it would sway in the breeze coming through the balcony. While I waited for Lee I watched the women in the plaza below pull the coverings off the booths where all day they sold brightly colored weavings or plastic bags of fruit slices while their children splashed in the fountain. At night the men came by to collect the money and escort their families back to the villages in the mountains.

Lee came in after he finished shaving; there was a tissue dot on his cheek, and he still looked sleepy. His neck popped when he stretched.

"Happy birthday," I said, pointing to the piñata.

He didn't even look. "Jenny, I'm not doing this," he said.

"All you do is hit it with the bat," I said.

He shook his head. "It's not my birthday," and he walked out. I heard his feet thump down the stairs of our rooming house, I heard Señora Martinez call out good morning, I heard Señora Martinez's daughter ask in awkward English if he wanted juice for breakfast. He didn't answer, just more footsteps until I looked out the balcony and saw him walking across the plaza, not slowing as the women called after him to buy their weavings, their embroidered blouses, their flowers, their fruit, and finally he broke into a jog and turned the corner out of my sight.

I picked up the bat, gave the piñata one good whack, and candy showered down, rolled across the wooden floor. So now it was just a mess to sweep up.

Lee pitched that night, and his slider was sending down batters. I sat where I always sat, with the wives. Only two others made every game the way I did: Ruth from South Carolina and Tanya from Phoenix. We were the only American wives. *Las gringas*, we called ourselves, but we only saw each other at the games. We'd never think to meet for coffee or shopping or anything like that. They were younger than I was, just as their husbands were younger than mine. Mexican League baseball was a matter of filling out the year for these husbands, getting in some practice before heading to the States for single-A ball in the spring, and on to double-A, triple-A, the majors. It was simple as climbing stairs. To hear Ruth and Tanya talk, their husbands had contracts that promised "1-2-3." Phil had been on the "Hot Prospect" list, and Randall's batting average in last year's College World Series was .402.

But when Ruth and Tanya started going on about "just a matter of time" and "when he gets to the majors" and comparing how many Corvettes they'd buy or on which beach they'd build their vacation houses, I wanted to jump in with, "Don't count your chickens." But saying anything that sounded like good advice got me one of those looks: "There she goes again, talking like an old lady." So I let them go on about the leather coats and diamond earrings and all the rest.

Ruth said, "Lee's looking good tonight. Isn't he?" We were sitting only two rows off the field, but Ruth was watching home plate through binoculars. She'd asked me to teach her how to call pitches. "Wasn't that a ball?" she asked, as the umpire gestured a strike.

I said, "Caught the corner."

"You always say that," she said.

"Because that's what always happens," I said. "Because Lee's some kind of pitcher."

I took the binoculars so I wouldn't see Tanya and Ruth give each other that look they had, "If he's so good, why's he down here at thirty years old?"

I studied my husband's face through the binoculars. He used to practice glaring in the mirror until his face ached because someone once told him he looked too nice to be a pitcher. Lee and I met at our fathers' company picnic, and after the softball game was over, he took me aside to teach me how to throw. "You throw like a girl," he said. I said, "Because I *am* a girl," and he leaned over and kissed me with lips that tasted like mustard. We were fifteen. He said, "Someday I'm going to pitch in the World Series." He said it just like that, like someone had shown him it would be that way, and later, when the local sports reporters talked about Lee's authority on the mound, I knew what they meant.

"I miss hot dogs," Tanya said. "Sitting in a bleacher makes me want to eat hot dogs."

I said, "When Lee was pitching for the Prince William Cannons, they sold grilled hot dogs over by right field. They'd bring them to the guys in the dugout."

"The Cannons? That's single-A?" Ruth asked.

"You're getting to be a real baseball wife," I said.

"What charity are you going to work for when Randall gets to the majors?" Ruth asked Tanya. "I'm doing March of Dimes."

"It's better to do something local," Tanya said. "You know, set up a foundation. Then you can actually be in charge of instead of just showing up at luncheons and celebrity auctions."

Ruth nodded. "Suppose so." She took the binoculars from me.

Tanya said, "Anti-drug stuff is usually a good bet. Or some kind of stay in school program."

Ruth said, "Can I do stay in school when Phil didn't really graduate? Does GED count as graduating?"

Tanya said, "Sure."

Ruth said, "Was that a slider?"

"Fastball," I said.

Tanya said, "Wasn't it Lee's birthday coming up?"

"No," I said.

"Thought you went and got some special piñata or something?"

"Wedding anniversary," I said.

"How many years?" Ruth asked. "Pitch was outside."

She was about to repeat her question, so I said, "You're right about the pitch."

She wasn't, but she smiled and high-fived with Tanya. "I'm getting there," Ruth said. "Just a matter of time."

That night in bed, Lee said, "The piñata was great. Sorry I was a jerk."

"Thirty's tough," I said.

He said, "Never thought I'd spend my thirtieth birthday in fucking Mexico."

"Fernando did," and I didn't know when the hell Fernando's birthday was, but couldn't it have been during the Mexican League season? Why not? "He turned thirty when he was down here pitching. There was a big party for him at the hotel, and everyone was drinking tequila and making toasts and all the pretty girls lined up to kiss him, and the next day he went out and pitched a ten-inning no-hitter."

There was a pause. I thought there was a chance I convinced him. Then he said, "God, I love you for saying that."

I leaned over and kissed him, kissed his ear, his neck, but he rolled away from me, sat up and looked towards the open window, tapped his bare feet on the floor. In the dark like this he didn't look any age at all.

"I was good today," he said. "The plate was all mine."

I agreed, sat up and kissed his hard, bare shoulder.

"Fuck," he said. "Thirty years old, and I've never paid a mortgage. Got no kids. What do I have? Nothing."

I said, "It's going to work out this time; it really is."

"I'm the oldest guy on the team," he said. "I never told you. Everywhere I go now, I'm the oldest. Know what that's like? Pitchers like me are even old in the majors. And here I am playing down in bumfuck Mexico, no contract."

"Age is in your head. Everyone was saying you looked great tonight. I know it will be your year."

"What makes you so sure?"

"Nothing makes me sure," I said. "Just being sure makes me sure."

"That doesn't make any sense."

"Why should it?" I asked. "Why should any of it?" and I was thinking of Fernando, discovered, discarded, discovered again, the way his eyes rolled up to the heavens with every pitch he threw as if to say, Why not? I said, "You tell me what makes sense about baseball."

Outside I heard a group of drunk men singing badly, the chatter of the women packing up their goods for the night. It could have been what I heard outside our windows all the other nights that were like this one: trucks criss-crossing the interstate, neighbors squabbling over the last beer, someone's bug zapper.

Because you know it happens this way doesn't make it easy. Because you know that your fastball will drop from 92 mph to 89 and then down to 85, 84, even 80, even lower, doesn't make you any less afraid. I wanted Lee to think I understood that.

"What makes sense about baseball?" he repeated. I watched the glow of the clock while I rubbed my palm in tight circles along his back. Finally he laughed. "Designated hitter rule, for one thing," and I laughed, too. So it would be all right. So he was thirty, and we were in Mexico, and it would be his year. It just had to be.

The next morning I was hurrying through the plaza on my morning walk, trying to ignore the calls of the women urging me to buy their things. I looked down at the sidewalk as I passed, shaking my head, but one woman jogged alongside me, tugging my arm harder and harder until I stopped. I smiled, shook my head. "No, thank you," I said. "*No gracias.* No."

She didn't smile back, instead reeled off a string of words. The only ones I recognized were "*su marido*" and "*mi marido,*" which meant "your husband" and "my husband."

"*No comprendo*," I said.

She extended her hand as if for a handshake, but then she curled in her lower fingers, leaving only the index finger pointing at me. She triggered downwards with her thumb and said, "Bang-bang." Her son toddled up and clutched at her skirt, poked his thumb in his mouth.

I pulled some pesos out of my pocket, handed her the bills. Sometimes that was just quickest.

She tucked them into a pouch tied to her waist but said very slowly, "*Su marido* buy bang-bang. Buy." There was more then, in Spanish, that I didn't understand but she watched me as if I should. Then there was silence.

I shook my head. "My husband wouldn't buy a gun. Why would he need a gun?"

But she didn't follow the words in English, and she pointed her finger at me and twitched her thumb. "Bang-bang," she said. Her son thought it was funny and screamed, "Bang-bang-bang!" pointing his finger first at me, then at his own face. She slapped his hand away and glared at me before picking up her son and lugging him back to her booth of embroidered blouses.

When I asked Lee that night, he said, "I felt sorry for the guy. He needed the money." Maybe there was something about my face because he added, "Of course I threw away the gun, Jenny. Why would I want a gun?"

But afterwards I couldn't sleep; there was too much moonlight sneaking through the curtains or the blankets were too hot or something, and I got out of bed and went into the bathroom where we kept our suitcases shoved behind the door, and there was a hard small lump in the zippered side pocket of Lee's duffel bag—a gun. It fit easily into my hand, and I knelt on the cool tile floor tilting it to catch the light from the bare bulb hanging off the ceiling. I thought about wanting something so much, this much. Then I slipped the gun back in the duffel bag, zipped it shut.

I heard a rustling behind me, but I didn't turn around or move my head. Looking up, I saw Lee's hand wrapped around the door jamb.

"I want it to happen for us so bad, baby," he whispered. "Is that crazy?"

"Not when you want it," I said.

Even though I threw away the gun the next morning, it wasn't really gone.

When Lee's record got to 5–1, they started calling him *Señor Poncho*—
Mr. Strikeout. "This is where it starts," Tanya told me. "He gets a nickname, people talk so there's a buzz, and next thing is he's got himself a
contract."

Ruth said, "Lee made it up to Triple-A once or twice already, didn't
he?"

I nodded. Three times, actually.

"And then what happened?" she asked. "How'd he end up all the way
back down here?"

Tanya said, "What matters now is he's got a nickname, right, Jenny?
Right, *Señora Poncho?*" and she smiled the kind of smile you save for
someone you don't care much about.

I said to Ruth, "Same old story. Injuries, bad luck, bad manager. It
could happen to anyone."

"Oh sure, I know," but Ruth was twisting in her seat to wave at someone a couple rows behind us, had forgotten we were having this conversation.

"Lee was on the 'Hot Prospect' list," I said. "Same as Phil."

"Don't worry, Jenny," Tanya said. "Next time we all meet, it'll be at
the World Series."

"Or the All-Star Game," Ruth said. "Isn't that better?"

"No," Tanya and I said together.

Ruth said, "Hey, I'm new to all this. Cut me a break."

Tanya pointed to the opposition pitcher taking his warm-up pitches
on the field. "See how he flips his glove like that? That tells the catcher
he's throwing a curve ball next. Right, Jenny?"

"Right." Lee told me that when I was fifteen. These girls would have
been, what, three and seven, something like that?

"Gees, I'll never learn it all," Ruth said.

"Sure you will," Tanya said. "Before long you'll know as much about
baseball as Jenny does."

"Like knowing baseball does us any good," I said, and something must
have been wrong with the way I said it, or the way they thought I meant
it, because they looked away quick. The pitcher flipped his glove again.
Once you knew to watch for that, you couldn't not notice.

Ruth said, "What's that supposed to mean?"

I shrugged. "Doesn't really matter what we know or don't know. We're just the wives. All we're supposed to do is believe them every time they tell us this is their year."

Ruth said to Tanya, "What's with her lately?" and she pressed the binoculars to her face.

Tanya said, "Come on, guys, we've only got two more weeks to go," and she bought us *paletas*—popsicles—from the boy tramping up and down the aisles.

After a short pause, Tanya said, "It's no hot dog."

"Phil wants nine children," Ruth said. The *paleta* had stained her tongue red. "He comes from a big family."

"Nine!" Tanya said. "Get busy, girl!"

"As soon as we get back home," Ruth said. "Then I start popping them out. That's the plan."

Tanya shook her head. "Two's as many as I plan to handle, and Randall knows it. You're brave."

"Or stupid. Phil's already got the names lined up," Ruth said. "He wants six boys and three girls. He says that—"

I interrupted: "What about you? What do you want?"

Ruth set the binoculars in her lap. "Why, Jenny," she said. "Same as what we all want." She pulled off her cap and shook her hair. She was pretty enough that a man could forget she was smart. That was maybe the smartest thing about her.

The bat cracked, rousing the crowd. Our first baseman Luis Torres had sent another one sailing straight out over center field, way over the fence. A swarm of kids raced to find the ball. The outfielders didn't bother to move; they'd recognized the sound, what it meant. So did I. An entire stadium collectively looking at their scorecards and thinking, I'll have to remember this guy. That's how it happens. It's not your first home run or tenth or even thirtieth. It's simply that one hit on that one day or that one pitch on that one day. I'd seen it happen to other guys on other teams— guys whose names everyone knows now. It's better than a nickname. Better than a buzz. It's what you wait for all your life, that pitch, that hit. That moment.

The manager stalked to the mound, and the pitcher handed him the ball and slunk into the dugout. A new pitcher trotted out, but it was too late. Luis Torres had been marked for the future.

"He's good," Ruth said, picking up the binoculars to follow Luis's path around the bases. "Right?"

Tanya nodded. "This is his first year."

"He's only seventeen," I said.

"Think the scout came to check him out?" Ruth asked.

I pretended to watch the new pitcher throw his warm-up pitches. He wasn't like Lee; he had no tricks, just the fastball making a lot of noise in the catcher's mitt. I guessed 93, 94 maybe. What you throw when you can muscle your way through an inning rather than having to rely on finesse.

Tanya collected our *paleta* sticks and wrappers and went to find a trash can, to go to the bathroom.

Ruth repeated, "Think the scout came to check him out?" A ball game is never really quiet, but that's how it felt just then, all quiet with only the sound of the ball smacking the catcher's mitt too hard, too fast.

Finally I said, "There are no scouts here, Ruth."

She looked at me, and with Tanya gone, it was clear that Ruth didn't much like me, that she called me "stuck-up" or something like that. She handed me the binoculars, pointed towards the third base line.

Through the binoculars I saw a man trying to control his three sons while flirting with two pretty girls sitting behind him. The kids were swatting each other with their baseball caps. I saw the boy selling two *paletas* to a fat man wearing a Chicago Bulls T-shirt that had faded to pink in the armpits. I was about to challenge Ruth when I looked again and saw an American man sitting next to the father. There was no reason to think he was a scout. There was no reason to think he wasn't. He didn't fit into the usual Oaxaca categories: tourist, burned-out hippie, Peace Corps dropout, stray journalist. And there was something so unobtrusive about him. Yet when he glanced at the game in progress, his eyes narrowed to a tight squint that pulled in each detail, if a batting stance should be opened up or which corner of the bag was stepped on rounding second.

Ruth nudged me. "That was a fastball, and it was inside."

I watched the scout light up a cigarette, smile as the littlest boy whacked him with a baseball cap. The father apologized, and the two girls giggled behind their hands, tossed back their hair. The scout smiled at them, too, said something that made them laugh and clutch at each other's arms.

Ruth murmured, "Fastball. Too low."

One girl whispered in the other's ear, and the scout made a goofy face that got the little boys laughing. He waved over the *paleta* boy, and the boy pulled popsicles out of his box one after the other as the scout pointed first to the little boys, then to the girls, next to the father, and finally to himself. Hurry up, I wanted to scream, there isn't all the time in the world, but the scout counted out his money slowly, fumbling some coins, and the boy couldn't find the proper change, so the scout took one more *paleta* which he handed to the fat man in the Chicago Bulls shirt.

"Do you mind?" Ruth said, and I returned the binoculars because the batter had been hit by a pitch and now Phil was up and I knew because she'd told us plenty of times that she liked to watch his butt when he batted.

I didn't want it to be like I was just someone else coming up to him after the game. That wasn't the way to get these guys to listen. So I waited, and then I went to the hotel where I figured he'd be staying, the fanciest hotel in Oaxaca, the famous one where Pancho Villa once slept. I didn't have to ask around or even look hard; he was in the bar, sitting alone at a table that looked onto the courtyard garden. A half-finished margarita was on the table, an overflowing ashtray, a section of an English-language newspaper that hadn't been opened, an unlit candle. Two waiters were in the back, whispering to the bartender, but otherwise we were alone.

I stepped in front of his view, smiled. "Mind if I join you?" It was a line I'd heard plenty of people say in the movies, usually those heart-of-gold hookers you know will be redeemed before the final credits.

He didn't say yes right away, just picked up his drink and tinkled the ice in the glass. He said, "The ice is okay in the hotel, right? Or am I going to spend all day tomorrow regretting this margarita?"

"The hotel purifies its water," I said.

"So regretting the margaritas depends on how many I have." He smiled at me, then held out his hand. "Chuck Dunbar."

I shook his hand, sat down. "My name's Jenny."

"There's a name I haven't heard for a while," he said. "Seems like most Jennys turned into Jennifers somewhere along the line." He gestured a "two more" flip of his wrist to the waiter without asking what I wanted.

"Thank you," I said. My lipstick felt too thick, and I tried to lick some of it off.

"Expense account," he said. "Thank my company," and to make sure there was no mistake, I asked who he worked for, and he said, "No business talk, okay? Meetings are for business. Bars are for booze and broads and old baseball stories." It was the kind of line he liked to say, to throw around a word like "broads."

The waiter brought two margaritas and a small bowl of shelled peanuts. Chuck popped a handful of peanuts into his mouth. "Peanuts are my weakness," he said. "I'll put these away in ten minutes. My ex-wife was a peanut farmer's daughter and that kept us together longer than anything else. Nothing beats good Georgia peanuts."

So I took a few from the bowl. They tasted stale. I said, "How do you like Oaxaca?"

"Thing about this hotel is I could be anywhere," he said. "Know what I mean?"

I nodded.

"Course who says that's all bad?" he said. "Knowing what to expect."

"Do you travel a lot?" I asked.

"Some," he said.

There was a silence. I watched him look me over the way he'd look at any prospect, trying to whittle all of me down to three or four quick, perfect words. Good hitter, weak on defense. Throws heat, no endurance. It was what he did, what he was paid for.

I licked the salt from the rim of my glass. I wanted to explain to him, to the waiters, to the bartender that I'd never done anything like this before.

I cleared my throat, looked away, said, "Have you eaten any *molé* yet? Oaxaca is famous for it."

He kept watching me, and I went on: "They call Oaxaca the land of seven *molés*, and each kind tastes different. There's a restaurant where you can get—"

He interrupted: "Honey, I know you're married, so why don't you tell me straight up what this is about."

"Is being married a problem?" I asked, looking down at my left hand. The rings were in my pocket.

"Depends on what exactly we're talking about," he said, putting more peanuts in his mouth, chewing quickly. "What are *you* talking about?"

"I don't know what you mean," I said.

"This about baseball?" he asked. "Or something else?"

"Why would I want to talk about baseball?" and I leaned forward, smiled, set my hand on top of his. The skin felt hard, thick.

"I didn't get to where I got by not being able to see what's going on between each and every line," he said, slipping his hand out from under mine. "Show me an eighteen-year-old kid, and I gotta know exactly how long that hot arm of his'll stay hot. I gotta know his knee's not giving out anytime soon. Gotta figure out what's lucky streak and what's long-haul talent the club can use. Above all, I gotta know all this within five minutes of watching the kid on the field. So don't insult me. Which one of those guys out there're you married to?"

"Lee Dupree," I said.

"Well, Mrs. Dupree, now we're getting somewhere." He took all that remained of the peanuts and shoved them in his mouth, crunched noisily. "Lee Dupree. I remember seeing him go up against Rickey Dawson in the Carolina League finals couple years back. Hell of a game. But I thought by now he'd—how old is he? Thirty-one? Thirty-two? I'd've guessed he'd've settled down by now, started selling insurance, coaching his son's Little League team."

I shook my head.

"They can't all make it, Mrs. Dupree. Least he got close. Got some stories to tell his kids. Any kids, Mrs. Dupree?"

"Not yet."

He finished his drink in two swallows, swiped his mouth with the back of his hand, traced his finger around the rim of his glass to knock all the salt onto the table. I knew exactly what sex with him would be like.

"How long are you going to be down here?" I asked.

"I'm leaving after tomorrow's game," he said. "It's my granddaughter's first Christmas."

"Stay one more day to see Lee pitch."

"I saw what I came to see," he said.

"He's 5 and 1," I said.

He shook his head. "Didn't come here looking for a pitcher."

"Don't insult me," I said. "Everyone's always looking for a pitcher."

He waved for the bill, and the waiter trotted over. "Can you read this?" he asked, handing it to me. "Too damn dark in here." The waiter quickly bent and lit the candle on the table.

"It's right," I said.

He signed the check and pulled some pesos from his pocket, threw them on the table for the waiter. It was way too many.

"Nice meeting you, Mrs. Dupree," he said.

"They call him *Señor Poncho*," I said. "Mister Strikeout. He's good."

"You're a nice lady," he said, patting my shoulder. "But I've got to shove off now," and he picked up his unread newspaper, turned to walk away.

I quickly looked around. No one else had entered the bar. I stood up and pulled my shirt off over the top of my head. "Mr. Dunbar," I called, and he turned. "One more day."

The waiters in the back were suddenly silent. I tossed my shirt at him; he caught it underhanded, held it away from his body.

"Why not?" I said, and I unhooked my bra. I'd changed into the blue one that fastened in the front, the one Lee liked best.

He looked at my shirt in his hand, then shook it out and sort of folded it, the awkward way a man folds clothes, and he draped it over the chair back nearest to where he stood. He looked at my breasts, and I could feel him wanting to reach out and grab them the way he'd done with the peanuts, and he stepped closer. In a low voice he said, "Don't embarrass yourself like this, Mrs. Dupree."

"Who's embarrassed?"

"I know you've never done anything like this before," he said. "You'll wake up tomorrow and be sorry."

"Not if the day after you're watching Lee pitch a game," I said. I cupped my hands around my breasts, brushed my fingers against the nipples so they stiffened. Maybe I threw like a girl. Maybe it didn't matter how much I knew about baseball because the fact was I'd never be out there on the field. But this I could do.

I watched his eyes watch my hands. It was too easy. I said, "Should we go to your room?"

He said, "Lord knows I'm no saint, but this isn't right."

I stepped closer and picked up one of his hands, placed it between my breasts. His fingers were cold. I felt callouses in different places than the callouses on Lee's hands, and I almost backed away. Instead I leaned in to kiss him; he ducked aside so all I got was air.

He said, "Don't take this the wrong way."

I looked down at his hand between my breasts, at the uneven, broken nails; the knuckles thickened from years of getting cracked; the way the veins protruded.

"This isn't what you really want," he said.

"You don't know what I want," I said. "I want Lee to have a chance."

He spoke quietly, as if explaining something to a child. "He already had his chance. Now don't do this to yourself. Please."

Something behind me caught his attention. Reflected in the mirror behind the bar I saw the other side of the courtyard where the two Mexican girls from the afternoon's game leaned up against a stone pillar. Short skirts, high heels, bright red lipstick, flowers in their hair. What you wear on a date. What you wear when you're young and beautiful and you think maybe you're in love. What I wore when Lee took me to the movies the first time.

"You're too smart for this kind of thing, Mrs. Dupree." His voice was almost too scratchy, like he tried to talk a certain way he thought he should talk.

"What do you mean, too smart?" I said. "How do you know how smart I am?"

"You're a classy, intelligent lady," he said. "Something like this is beneath you." He slid his hand up to my shoulder, patted it, thought I didn't see him wave to the girls. They smiled and waved back before they stepped out of my view. Then he smoothed his hair, shoved his hands into his pockets.

"I'm too old," I said. "That's what you mean."

"Now, Mrs. Dupree," and I could see he was afraid I was going to cry. "Now, now," he said. "You're a beautiful woman. I know your husband loves you." He picked up my shirt, held it to me. "Go ahead and put this back on."

I slapped him as hard as I could. His cheek was spongy and I would've liked to hit him again, it felt that good.

He nodded. "No one has to know about this," he said. "You just want
to help your husband. I respect that," and he made nudging motions with
my shirt, trying to get me to take it from his hand.

"How old are you?" I asked.

He looked embarrassed, dropped my shirt on the table in front of me.
"I'm meeting Luis Torres for dinner," he said. "And I'm already late."

"How old?"

He sighed. "Forty-five, fifty, give or take. More like give."

I nodded.

He said, "I get offers all the time. I'd have to be Superman to keep up."

"Or an 18-year-old," I said.

"Bingo," he said. The silence that followed was finally broken by the
sound of the two girls giggling. He shook my hand hard as if I were any
prospect, said, "Good-bye, Mrs. Dupree. And good luck."

I hate when people say that. There's no way to feel after hearing it but
pathetic.

As if he could read my mind, he turned at the archway out to the lobby
and called, "Don't you know luck is what you want most in baseball?" The
two girls stepped out of the shadows. He draped his arms around their
shoulders as the three of them left.

I waited for Lee at the cafe where we were meeting for a late dinner. The
plaza was busy; people were crowding in from the villages for market day
tomorrow where they'd sell and buy special items for Christmas, visit
family members, light a candle at the church, leave a request for St. Jude.
I sipped my hot chocolate, tried to look a certain way so people wouldn't
stare, wouldn't think they could approach to sell me cheap souvenirs. I'd
never been in a place long enough to fit in. That came from following
Lee around. I could have been like some of the wives—just stopping
somewhere and saying, "This is it," and buying a house there. Someone
like Tanya I imagined picking a place on the map, saying to Randall,
"Here." Someone like Tanya wouldn't go long without her house, her children, her career, the things she wanted. Unlike me, she always knew what
to say, when to say it.

Lee slid into the seat next to me, put his hand on mine on the table,
said, "Chuck Dunbar's here from the Angels." He pushed his other hand

through his hair, squinted as if he were looking into the sun. A waiter
brought us two menus that we didn't open.

"He was at the game," I said.

Lee shook his head. "Remember when it was me they'd come out to
see?"

"Maybe it was you," I said. "Maybe it was the famous *Señor Poncho*
who brought the scout down to Mexico."

"Don't."

There was a long silence. The waiter started to walk over, but something in our faces made him back off. Lee folded his arms tightly together
as if he were holding all the pieces of himself.

There should have been something better to say. I said, "Why not? It
could be you."

The church bell rang, and I glanced at my watch. Nine o'clock.

"What do you want for Christmas?" he asked.

"What?"

"Isn't it almost Christmas?"

"Three days," I said.

"So what do you want?"

What do we all want for Christmas? Peace? Love? Hope? Understanding? Enough faith to get through another year? What do we get?
Sweaters and jewelry. I looked at Lee's face, at the squint lines burrowed
deep, at where the freckles used to be before they faded, at the lips he
licked every time he threw a slider. It's not that he looked tired, but he definitely looked scuffed, like your first glove, the one you learned to play
catch with. The lucky one you can't bear to throw away.

"So, Jenny, what do you want?" he asked again.

I was ready to say it. Give it up, let's go home, get a job selling insurance — we'll buy a house and have a baby. We're not getting any younger.
Life's too short. Blah, blah, blah. They were words I'd been practicing
since I left the hotel.

Lee sat back in his chair as if he knew what I was about to say. His face
closed up. He could've been thinking anything.

The moment stretched longer and longer. I thought about that gun
in my hand, thought about what had made Lee buy it. Thought about
what if Chuck Dunbar had said yes. Was there really a time when I

wouldn't have believed these kinds of things could happen? When a place like Mexico was only a haze in the distance?

The words were right there: Let's give up. But I said, "What I want for Christmas is . . . a moose head."

"A moose head? That's the craziest damn thing I ever heard."

"That's exactly why I want it," I said. "A big one."

"But why a moose head?"

I shook my head, smiled, giggled. "Why not?"

"Why not?" he repeated. "What's that supposed to mean?"

"I don't know." I was laughing now. "But you better find one. It's all I want." I didn't know what I was going to do if he didn't laugh soon. It was all so ridiculous, just a game you played with bats and balls, a game for children.

He smiled. "Okay, Jenny. I'll get you a moose head."

"The biggest one you can find."

"I'll do it," he said, starting to laugh. "I swear I will."

"Remember—it has to be really, really big."

"It'll be the biggest damn moose head you ever saw."

We were both laughing hard now, and I accidentally knocked my hot chocolate onto the ground. That made us grab each other and laugh even harder, so hard the tears finally came, and the waiter hurried to sweep away the broken pieces of the mug, rolling his eyes as he moved his broom across the mess, looking for all the world like Fernando on the mound, about to put one right over the plate.

The Bigs

DAVID JAUSS

I am a baseball player. I come here from the Dominican Republic the home of Juan Marichal because baseball can't make you the same much of money in the Dominican League. That is why I live in the U S of A and play baseball for the Arkansas Travelers which are a team in the Texas League but live in Arkansas. The Arkansas Travelers are a team which is called a Double A team, meaning not so good as Triple A or Major Leagues—what everybody call The Bigs. Everybody here want to make it to The Bigs. There is no Bigs in the Dominican Republic and that is why I am living here so miserable and now that my family leave me I am more miserable ever than before. The only time I smile is after when I win a big game or if I forget for some minute and think my little Angelita is waiting at home for me to kiss her for goodnight. But tonight I am more miserable than I think a dead man because Coach he suspend me off the team and all because they leave me.

I love baseball. I love to pitch the ball. When I am the pitcher everybody depend of me, if I just stand there and hold the ball nobody do nothing. When I throw the ball everything happen. It is a good feeling but not the same as love which is something I have too much of I think. My heart it feel like it is in shreds each time when I think about Angelita and her

black braids. And Pilar. I can not even say her name now without wanting to cry. Pilar is so beautiful, sometimes when I was in her I could not
breathe right. When I think about her gone and Angelita with her I want
to be on the mound throwing hard like Juan Marichal who come from
Santo Domingo the same like me. I am a starter so I pitch the ball each
four days, no more, and the rest of the time it go by so slow. I want I could
pitch the ball each night if I will not tear my shoulder which is what I do
at St. Peterburg my year of being a rookie when I try to show off I have
stuff. Now my shoulder it hurt when I think about Pilar and Angelita so
I try not to think about them when I am pitching the ball. But most of
the time it is of no use because I think about them anyway. That is why I
get in such big trouble tonight, I think of them when I should be thinking curve ball or slider, down or up.

The nights they are the most bad. I have dreams. Jackie say I grind my
teeth when my dreams get so bad and when I wake up I am all wet with
sweating and scared. Jackie try to make me all right then but it never work.
She hug me and kiss me and say it only is a dream. Then I tell her what I
dream and she say what it mean like a *curandera*. Some times I dream
Pilar is opening her legs for Antonio who was sent back to Santo Domingo
for weak field and no hit. Other times I dream I am pitching the ball when
Angelita run out on the field with her arms reaching out for me but I don't
see her before it is too late and I have already throw the ball and it hit her
in the face and make her be dead. To me the dreams mean I love Pilar
and Angelita so much my heart want to die. Twice I almost buy a gun and
shoot my head. But Jackie say a gun is dumb, she say my dreams mean I
should get married again and show Pilar some thing or two. She tell me
to stop being a Mr. Sadface. That's what she call me when she try to make
me smile. I know she want to marry with me by these signs but I don't want
to marry with her, I want her to go away and leave me to be alone.

Pilar take Angelita back to the Dominican Republic because she
don't care about The Bigs. She don't care about Juan Marichal or the Hall
of Fame or driving a car with electric windows. She miss her mama and
papa and the pacaya grove in her yard in Santo Domingo. When she look
at the photographs of home that was when she would start crying and then
a minute later yell at me for taking her to the U S of A. She don't understand English so good and no one except Antonio who play second base
like a hole in his glove also speak Spanish. And she don't understand base-

ball too. To her it make no sense, to her it is crazy to pitch a ball that no one can hit it. She say to watch a game if no one hit the ball is no fun so I should make the batter to hit some home runs. She say Why you keep everybody from having fun, you think the fans pay so much of money to see pop-ups. She is a woman and she think like a woman. Still I did not suspect her to leave me. The trouble I am in tonight is all because she leave me. I try to tell Coach so he understand but still he suspend me off the team maybe for good. He have a wife who never leave and no kids.

The day Pilar go I pitch six and two-third no-score innings against the Shreveport Captains which are a team too in the Texas League, East Division. Then my arm it get sore and Coach say to get a shower and ice my shoulder up. I think now my shoulder ache because Pilar and Angelita are going that same minute. It was a sign but I don't see it then because I am wondering if Parisi will lose my win for me like usual, the rag arm. But this time he is lucky and I don't lose my win but because I am worrying so hard I miss the sign. God give all of us signs like a manager so we know what He want us to do. But now I don't know what to do. I don't see any signs. I think maybe God is mad with me and I am scared.

The night Pilar and Angelita leave I am halfway to almost home when all of a sudden I know what my sore arm mean and I drive fast with my foot down on the floor and run through red lights one after each other and squeal into the parking lot like a madman. I go up the curb and almost into the swimming pool next by the apartment manager's office I am so much scared they have left me. And when I open the door Pilar and Angelita are gone and I can not find them everywhere. I look in the kitchen and living room and both bedrooms even behind the shower curtain but they are so gone I can feel how they are not there. I sit down on the bathroom floor and look at the shower curtain which Pilar buy when Angelita pull the other one down. She buy it because there is parrots on it like in our country and palm trees. I am so much sad I want to hold this curtain against me tight.

I did not think she would leave, I think only she talk about it. But now I see she mean what she say. After when I get up from the bathroom floor I go back in the kitchen and find what I did not see at first, a note sticked on the refrigerator door with a yellow smiling face magnet. It say in Spanish If you don't make The Bigs come to home and be a family again. I sit down then and put my big dumb head in my hands and cry. Mr. Sadface.

I don't know why I stayed in Little Rock. I should have went to Santo Domingo that same minute. Maybe there is something wrong with inside of me that make me stay. Maybe I don't love Pilar and Angelita like I think so. Maybe I want to hurt them like they do me. Or maybe I don't want to be like Antonio and go back to home the same I left, a worthless nothing. When I go back I want to be like Juan Marichal who is a Hall of Fame pitcher with more strikeouts than dogs in Santo Domingo. I want World Series rings on all my fingers and a car so big it have a TV in it and a bar. But I want more my Pilar and Angelita I think. Why I did not go back I am not sure but maybe I should have went before all this happen, before I become this disgrace to my country and my family. Before I have to go back with no choice of my own.

Jackie she think I stay because of her but that is not right. Jackie mean almost nothing to me. She was Willie Williams' girl last year and after he dump her still she come around and ask to go for a ride in his car which he call his Love Chariot. But he always say No and Get lost and one night I am so lonely I get mad and say Manny you don't have to take this shit off of Pilar that bitch you can have some fun too. So when Jackie come around at The Press Box to drink beers and shoot pool after we lose the doubleheader to Tulsa I say Willie that's no way to hurt a lady and make him say he is sorry so I don't hit him. After that she have her hands all over me. Now she stay here and sleep on Pilar's side of the bed but I want her to go because she is not Pilar. She wear a blonde wig and laugh like she is underneath angry. But she love me and go crazy with crying when I say some things like I don't want you to hang your wig on the doorknob. I can't say anything mad or she will cry and want to be dead so how can I tell her to get lost. She laugh a lot but she have a scar on both wrists from when Willie first tell her to go away. The scars look like X's cut so careful and neat, I can see her trying to make them pretty, her tongue sticking out the corner of her mouth while she do it, concentrating. I am scared she will kill herself dead so I make sex with her but I wish she would go away. She scare me with her crazy too much of love, like I scare myself.

Now I don't know what to do. Each day that pass I wait for a sign. But nothing happen. I want one minute to go home, I want that Pilar will lay on top of me and kiss me so I am lost in the dark cave of her so beautiful black hair. And I want to kiss Angelita for goodnight on her little nose and say to her like before the joke about the bed bugs biting. But another minute I want hard to be a baseball pitcher in The Bigs and hear everybody even the white people cheering my name. I want everybody to know I make the money they don't. I want a house with chandeliers and shag carpet everywhere and a swimming pool in the backyard with color lights under the water. I want all these things but I don't want Jackie with her blonde wig and eye make-up and crying. But more than this I don't want her to bleed to death because I leave her like she always threaten without saying. So I want to go and I want to stay. And that make me not want anything anymore.

That is why I don't finish the game tonight. I am pitching the ball so good they swing and grunt at my curve ball which break in the dirt and my slider low and away. It is already inning eight and still I have no hits on me. Only six more outs to a no-hitter which would make Whitey Herzog to see I am ready for The Bigs. My palm it is sweating so I turn to pick up the bag of resin and then I see on the scoreboard all the zeros and somehow it take the breath out of me it all look so perfect. I am so proud because I do it, I make all the zeros. And then I think about Pilar leaving and Jackie's scars and my dream with Angelita running on the field and my pitch hitting her dead. Why I think these things then I do not know but I think them and it make my heart to beat so hard.

When I turn back to the plate my legs they are shaking like in my first game for los Azucareros del Este when Pilar was in the stands to cheer for me and I imagine she is out there now watching me and knowing if I do good I will make The Bigs and marry with Jackie because I am scared to find her in my bathtub, the water turning red. So I look down at Gene my catcher and nod and then I throw the ball and it sail over everybody's head and up the screen, a wild pitch. Gene he signal time and run out to the mound and say Jesus Christ Manny I give you the sign for change-up not fastball what are you thinking of. I can not remember what I say but Gene he go back to behind the plate and thump his mitt and give me another sign. I nod and throw the ball and it hit the batter in the shoulder and he spin around like he want to fight but I stand there only and look at him. Then he go down to first holding his shoulder and swearing at me and Gene he say Don't worry about it kid. You'll get 'em, he say. Just take it easy.

All this time I am thinking If I throw a no-hitter I will never see my Pilar and Angelita again. Not forever. So when Gene throw the ball back to me I am not watching close and it hit the top of my glove and don't go in. I look around quick and it isn't there. Gene he jump up then and yell Second! Second! but by the time when I find the ball and turn around to throw it to Peachy, already the runner he is standing up and brushing the dirt off his uniform. I hear Coach swear loud but somehow I don't care like I should.

Settle down, Gene say then and give me a sign. I start to wind up but then I forget what pitch he ask for and I stop, a balk. The runner he walk down to third laughing. I don't look at him. Gene come out to the mound then. Calm down for Chrissakes, Gene say. If they get a hit they get a hit the main thing is win. So just rare back and hump that ball in there. Okay I say and he go back. Then he give me a sign maybe for fastball or could be slider. But I just stand there and hold the ball. He give me another sign I think for curve but I just stand there. Then Gene come out to the mound again and Coach too this time and Coach he say What's the problem Manny your arm getting sore again. I shake my head no. Then what gives, he say. What the fuck is going on. I almost can not talk the words are so far down inside of me but somehow I say Nothing but I say it in Spanish — *Nada*. I never talk on the team in Spanish because in The Bigs they want that you always talk American. But I say *Nada*. Then he look at me foreign and ask You all right. I say Fine in American and he say Good let's set 'em down, then he trot back to the dugout and Gene go behind the plate and give me one more time again the sign and this time too I do nothing. If I do nothing nothing happen because I am the pitcher, I am the one who hold the ball. I want then everything to stop, I want time to stop, I want Jackie to stop, I want being alone and sad to stop, so I hold the ball for one minute. For that one minute the world stand still, nothing change, and I can breathe.

Then the umpire step before the plate and say Throw the ball Sanchez or it is delay of the game. The batter he step out of the box and shrug his shoulders to the dugout of his team and spit. I stand there more. Then Gene say What the fuck and everybody in the stands start to yell and boo but I don't do anything.

Then out of the dugout come Coach's face looking red. All of a sudden I feel so sorry for him, so sorry for Gene and Peachy and my teammates and for Jackie and Pilar and Angelita and the umpire and the people in the stands who are booing so disappointed. I feel so bad for everybody I want to cry. Then Coach he say What the hell do you think you're doing Sanchez. I say it again—*Nada*. And he say Don't give me any of that I want to know why you aren't throwing the goddamn ball. His face is close to mine the way he get with a umpire who make a lousy call. I look down and say from somewhere My wife she leave me and my little girl is gone away. Jesus H. Christ he say then and touch his left arm which mean bring in the lefty. Then he say You're under suspension Sanchez now get your sorry ass out of this park and don't come back until your head is on straight. I don't want to see you or hear you or even *smell* you until then is that clear. I just stand there and listen to him, I can't even nod. Everything I live for is disappearing into nothing, I am becoming like a zero, and I am sad but somehow all of a sudden I am so much of nothing I am gone away and I'm there but not there too and where I am is so peaceful I want almost to cry. I want to tell Coach about this place, I want to tell everyone, but there are no words there so I only smile at him. He look away then mad and cursing but still I smile so happy.

And I am still smiling when Parisi come in to take from me my no-hitter and make me a nobody who can not go to home or stay where he is without shame. I am holding the ball and everything have stop and I am so happy and I love everybody even Coach and the fans booing and Whitey Herzog who keep me from being in The Bigs so long and Antonio who steal my wife maybe. I love everybody so much I feel like I am dead and looking down on everybody from heaven, not a man anymore but a angel with no sadness or pain or anything, just love. But then Coach take the ball away from me and give it to Parisi. He take the ball away, he take everything away, and I am standing there waiting and alone and there is no sign.

The Greatest Slump of All Time

DAVID CARKEET

"Apples" Bagwell loses it in the late innings. His shoulders slump, his curve hangs, and his fastball yawns. Into the seventh or eighth he is great, almost perfect. But then he loses it, and it always takes Grammock a few more baserunners than it should to come out from the dugout and mumble around the mound and finally signal to the bullpen. Apples comes off the field looking like a puppy about to be whipped and sighs into the dugout. He just fills that dugout with his sigh.

People talk about it. He gets tired, some say. He has a fear of losing, say others, remembering his early years in the bigs. Some believe he becomes overconfident and lets up. The profile is baffling. Late innings. A lead. A stunning performance through six or seven frames.

E.T.A. Whitaker, a bespectacled first baseman with a good mind and a social worker for a wife, finally figures it out. He takes Apples to breakfast, choosing a secluded booth at the rear of the hotel coffee shop.

"Tough game last night," E.T.A. says to Apples as he gives his menu to the waitress. "For you, I mean." Apples lost his stuff in the seventh, but Butch came in and saved the game. The team is only three games out now, with a month of the regular season left.

"Yeah," says Apples.

"Grammock shoulda left you in, Apples," says the waitress, who is buxom and toothy. "He shoulda let you work it out. You're the best."

Apples shrugs and a pitiful look, one familiar to E.T.A. of late, crosses his face.

"She likes you, you know," says E.T.A., testing his theory after the waitress has gone.

Apples looks down at the table. His lids are heavy, his cheeks pale and lifeless. "Let Jaime have her," he says without feeling. Jaime is their right fielder. He has an unquenchable lust for women and an active English vocabulary of sixty-five words.

"He has," says E.T.A. "She told him she wants you."

Apples sighs and sinks deeper into gloom.

E.T.A. knows that the way out and the way in are one and the same. "The writers are talking about you for the Cy Young Award this year, Apples."

"Great," says Apples. His face doesn't say "great." Someone watching from across the room would think he was recalling famous airline disasters.

"We're all really happy for you," says E.T.A. "The whole team." Then, twisting the knife, "We all love you, Apples. Deeply. We really do."

It works. Apples begins to sob. His face turns into a contorted mass of red flesh under his hands. The waitress, who has brought his pineapple pancakes, sees what is happening and thinks he is upset about last night's game. She crawls into the next booth and leans over him from behind and begins to knead his shoulders like a trainer, whispering comforting words into his ear.

E.T.A. watches with pity which, he begins to notice with concern, is mixed with self-pity.

"Success depresses him," E.T.A. says to shortstop Scrappy Hawthorn as they walk back to the third-base line after a warm-up run. "Give him praise and he crumbles. On the mound he sees a victory coming and he folds. He's afraid of winning."

"That don't make no sense," says Scrappy. Unlike E.T.A., who is a modern athlete in every sense and an interviewer's delight, Scrappy talks like a Coolidge-era ballplayer.

"I didn't think so at first either," says E.T.A. "But then I saw that if you think you're inferior, being good at things will only make you feel like more of a bum."

Scrappy frowns and turns to him. "Apples feels like a bum?"

E.T.A. nods. They have reached the baseline and turn to run the twelve paces again, gliding easily with synchronized strides. As they slow and turn to walk back, E.T.A. says, "Maybe deep down we all think we're bums. After all, you know yourself better than anyone else does. You know how stupid and cruel you can be. Heap success on top of that and you've got a real formula for the blues." He pats Scrappy on the fanny and they turn and run once more. E.T.A. slows to a stop and turns, but Scrappy continues running in a wide arc and jogs back to the dugout alone.

E.T.A., temporarily relieved by their talk, plays well that day. Scrappy goes oh-for-five. In the field *twice* he trips over second base as he tries to make unassisted double plays, and twice his throw sails wide of E.T.A.'s desperate reach. The second throw is much more cautious, and much worse, than the first. Then, in the ninth, he instinctively dives to his right to make an impossible game-ending catch of a line drive, his body stretched out straight as a javelin. The cheers rain down on him in the clubhouse. That night he has trouble falling asleep. He wakes before dawn and stares at the ceiling until it is time for breakfast, when he must go into society and be congratulated again.

The next day Scrappy shares his inarticulate thoughts with Bubba Phelps, the second baseman. Bubba laughs without sympathy and apparently without understanding, and then commits a judgment error in the field and later is picked off first base—a base given to him not on the merits of a hit, but because he was too slow, too torpid, too sodden with thought, to move out of the way of a high, inside pitch that grazed him on the arm. All day, and then at night, he sees that pitch again and again, only it is higher, heading for his face, and he is even slower to get out of its way.

To ease his mind, Bubba raps with Eddie Johnson, the swift center fielder. Eddie gives him wisdom and comfort. Later, when the team's flight is delayed by a mechanical problem, Eddie smashes two metal chairs in the airport lounge in a fit of impatience. He unburdens himself to his teammates in the outfield, Buford Ellenbogen and Jaime, and from Buford the word travels back into the infield to the fast-talking third baseman, Frank Joiner; Frank gives it to Narvel Adams, the catcher, and in no time at all Narvel is matching batterymate Apples sigh for sigh.

As the days wear on and the players collectively bring the team into first place, their symptoms diversify and specialize. Apples, of course, is the chief mumbler and moper. He has polished his flatness of affect beyond improvement. Between innings of work Grammock, a former pitching coach, criticizes and corrects him, telling him to bear down, goddammit, and push off the be-Jesus mound. He listens and feels each word adding measurable weight to his body. When he returns to the mound his motion is even more ponderous than before.

Frank is different. He plays well and looks normal, but his mind is full of spiders. He thinks people are talking about him. On the road he lurks just inside the door of his hotel room, listening to his teammates going down to breakfast, wondering why they haven't asked him to join them. He hears words that could be about him—words like "am" and "my"—and he aches for acceptance.

Narvel sighs a lot. This makes him light-headed and dizzy. Though only twenty-four, he concludes that his body is deteriorating. Two years, maybe three, and he will announce his retirement.

Bubba fears someone is going to break into his apartment on a dark night while he is in bed. The intruder will of course steal from him, but he will also abuse him with words. Bubba feels that the man will have every right to do this.

Eddie compares himself with others and comes out sub-human. The way Scrappy runs the bases, the way Jaime goes back on the long ball—he can't match them. He doesn't belong in the majors. Every day he is ashamed to see his name still on his locker.

Scrappy can't sleep. He awakens at 4:00 every morning as if called by God. He lies awake and stares, then lurches in bed as if having sex with the air. Then he stares some more. His afternoon naps debilitate him further. The sleep he loses at night is unrecoverable.

Buford, once featured in the hometown newspaper for the way he ate four entrees in succession at a Denny's, has lost his appetite.

E.T.A. maintains that the world has gone to hell in a cardboard suitcase. His favorite word is "point," especially when it occurs with "no" or "what's the."

Jaime, newly impotent, is exploring suicide.

Narvel calls home. His mother answers and calls with elderly enthusiasm to his father, who picks up the phone in the Rathskeller.

"Narvel! How are you, boy?"

"Fine, Dad."

"Say, you guys are lookin' good. I mean good. A steady climb into first, tough resolve in the face of challenge, a widening lead in the division. . . . I like the looks of it. I like it a lot. I like the whole pattern of the season. Another week of the same and I'd say you're uncatchable. I'd definitely say you're uncatchable. Of course I'm assuming lively run production from Eddie and a little more pizzazz in your starters, especially Apples. Nice play last night on that bad throw, by the way. You saved a run and kept the D.P. in order."

Narvel blinks heavily. His father is retired and lives for the game. This once gave Narvel pleasure.

"How are you?" asks Narvel. He knows his conversation is lifeless. He never could talk—not well, anyway.

"Us?" his father says loudly. "Fine, fine. Not bad for old folks. Your mom's back is giving her some trouble."

"I'm sorry-"

"It's nothing," says his mother. "Narvel, do you remember Mrs. Webster?"

"No."

"The Sunday School teacher?"

"No, I don't."

"He was too young, Ruth," says his father.

"She passed away," says his mother, ending the tale.

"Hunh," says Narvel. There is a long silence after this. Then he says, "Mom, Dad, do you remember an old diary I kept when I was little?"

"No," says his father.

"Of course," says his mother. "It's in the trunk in the attic." Her voice is chipper and sing-songy.

"Can you send it to me?"

"Of course."

"Gettin' sentimental, boy?" says his father suspiciously. "Seems to me you ought to be thinkin' of the future, not the past. Like tomorrow's doubleheader. Those guys will eat you for lunch if you let 'em."

"Yes, sir," he says, feeling reprimanded. His throat tightens and his voice thins out. "It's just that a bunch of us were talking about our childhoods and all, and I got wondering about mine and if it was, well, you know, what it was like and all, and I thought maybe the diary would help, because lately-"

"Of course, dear. I'll put it in the mail right away."

Narvel sighs in misery. His mother, as always, cooperates without understanding.

"The future is for the living, Narvel," his father says. "You guys have been lookin' pretty drab for a front-runner."

"Maybe it's our TV, Ralph. Ever since they built that high-rise-"

"I know a drab team when I see one," his father insists. "Do you hear me, Narvel? Talk to me."

"Yes, sir," he says, sighing again. His father understands but gives no support. Narvel suddenly sees himself as a soldier wounded in battle; his parents try to help him back to safety, but they arrive with a corpse mangled from mishandling.

Eddie plays with his daughter, Tina, and listens to his wife on the telephone. She is talking to Bubba's wife, making plans for the World Series. The playoffs start tomorrow and already she is planning for the Series. His resentment is like a cloak that warms him and darkens his life. He pulls it around himself tighter and tighter. She has come to expect satisfaction. She is never surprised when they win. She will never see his achievement for what it is—not just a well-paying job, but a glorious, precarious moment of trembling balance. An injury or a brief slump turning into a long one because he gives it too much thought—either of these could close it out and turn him into a regular guy with nothing more than a year or two of interesting history becoming less interesting as the years go by. And a bitch for a wife, because all baseball is to her is lots of money and a chance to shop in New York during the Series. She who has never touched a baseball in her life, who sits with the other wives and cheers in ignorance. She still doesn't know what a hit is. If he flies out four times in a game she will say he got four hits. She cannot know how good he is.

Neither can Tina, because she is so young. And when she is older? He imagines her future, a product of his wife's unassisted bungling because he is on the road so much: knocked up with nine kids and no man; or maybe a good Christian who prays her bruises away while her man drinks and beats up on her; or maybe a radical feminist who uses her dead father in her speeches as an example of persistent racism in the U.S. because in spite of his brains there was no room for him in baseball management after it came to an end for him in his third year because of an injury or a slump that he gave too much thought to.

A conference on the mound. It is a key game — the fourth game of the playoffs. After taking the first two from Chicago they have dropped one and fear dropping this one. Chicago would have the momentum then and would be strong for the fifth game. They are at home, up by one, in the top of the ninth. After a disputed call on a dive by Eddie for a ball hit behind second (ruled an out), Apples has hit a batsman (who stole second on the next pitch), intentionally walked a batter, and given up an infield single — a ludicrously topped ball that dribbled nowhere in particular and advanced everybody. The bases are loaded. Apples is down, but no more than usual.

Narvel shuffles out to him. Apples welcomes the rebuke implied by his approach. The infield moves to the mound. Narvel looks at their faces and sees ghosts.

"What are we gonna do?" asks Apples.

They all look down at their feet and kick at the dirt on the mound.

"I dunno, man," says Bubba. "Don't let him hit to me. I'm blue."

"And I'm fired," says sleepless Scrappy. "Make him pull it."

They all look up at the batter to see if he is right- or left-handed. They should know this already without having to look, but they don't concentrate. He is a switch hitter, and he will bat left-handed against Apples. If he pulls the ball sharply it will go to E.T.A. at first. They turn to him and he shrugs.

"Sure," he says indifferently. "I can handle it. And if I don't?" He flashes a macabre grin and his eyeglasses twinkle in the sunlight. "What does it matter? Everyone here'll be dead someday." He sweeps his eyes over the field and then up to the stands filled with hopeful supporters. His teammates follow his eyes and suddenly find themselves surrounded by sixty thousand skeletons.

"There are people dyin' every day," Narvel says thoughtfully. "People you don't even know."

"Whatever happens," says Apples—and a quiet urgency in his voice draws their close attention—"I want you guys to know I've really appreciated your support this year."

This is received glumly by all but E.T.A. He laughs loudly. "Jesus, Apples, what do you do when you're thirsty—drink ashes?" The infield begins to chuckle grimly and a dark figure approaches. Narvel sees him out of the corner of his eye and fancies it is the Grim Reaper, but it is only the home-plate ump. He tells them to stop clowning around and play ball. Meekly, guiltily, they obey.

Two things happen that decide it. First, Apples forgets there is already one out—the disputed call and subsequent hit batsman have blurred in his mind into just one hitter—so he pitches with no expectation of victory. With the bases loaded and nobody out, he thinks, Chicago is bound to take it away from them. Then after the loss tomorrow he can stay home in bed for five months.

He puts the ball right where he should.

Second, E.T.A. gets mad. As he crouches with Apples' pitch and watches the switch hitter he is reminded of a minor league coach who tried to make *him* into a switch hitter, ruining his average for a full year and slowing his rise to the major leagues. He complained about it frequently and got a bad rap as a troublemaker. When the coach got reassigned somewhere E.T.A. resumed his left-handed hitting and left the farm the next season. For the misery he caused him with his ignorance, that coach nearly destroyed his career.

In rage E.T.A. whirls and guns the ball to second even before he knows he has fielded it cleanly, and in the same motion he is on his way back to first to cover, because he knows Apples won't make it, and he takes Scrappy's low return throw out of the dirt to his right, stretching his leg as if convinced that to tear something in it is to tear that coach's heart out, and the ump's call and the cheers from the stands send him and his team to the Series.

It has been asked if it is possible for a team to win the big one without a big stick, or with a bullpen that is weak, or with rookies at the corners. A related question that has not been asked is if it is possible for a team to win the big one with an outfield on Elavil.

"Poppin' pills again?" asks Grammock as he walks through the clubhouse and sees Buford and Eddie comparing prescriptions. Eddie protests that it is legal—they're not uppers, he says, they're anti-downers. Grammock shakes his head in silence and stalks off to his office, feeling that he just doesn't understand his boys anymore. He has tried his bench, hoping that platooning his regulars would get them out of the doldrums, but as soon as his bench performs well they go logy on him too. So he sticks with his starters. If he's going to put nine zombies on the field he wants it to be his best nine.

Scrappy, who is in sit-down psychotherapy, challenges Eddie's treatment. He says that the outfielders will never truly know themselves if they rely solely on drugs.

"'Know thyself,' said Abe Lincoln," Scrappy informs him. "He knew hisself, you can bet."

"Like you?" Eddie asks mockingly.

"I'm workin' on it," Scrappy says with a tentativeness bordering on total capitulation. "It takes time."

"Yeah? How much time?"

Scrappy's eyes shift nervously. "A year, maybe. Maybe longer."

Eddie laughs loudly.

"I . . . I got a lotta issues to work through," says Scrappy.

"Issues?" says Eddie. "Issues of what—the *Sporting News?* What kind of word is that, you dirtbrain?" His words surprise everyone. Though big, black, and witty, Eddie has never been the club razzer. That was always Narvel's role, at least before he forgot how to talk.

Scrappy's face collapses and he begins to whine his arguments out. He says that drugs just cover up the sickness. Eddie says that if the sickness is bad only because of the symptoms, and if drugs take away the symptoms, then it's a harmless disease. It's as harmless, he says, as being allergic to moon dust: it makes no difference if you never go there.

Frank has been oiling his glove nervously and listening. He speaks up in a speedy, jerky way that is like his lateral movement at third base.

"Scrappy's right. He's just got the wrong kind of therapy. What is your guy—an analyst?"

"I dunno," says Scrappy.

"How often do you go?"

"Once a week."

Frank purses his lips. "Maybe not, then."

"But he wants me to come three or four times a week."

"Ah. Does he ever talk about the here-and-now?"

Scrappy looks deeply uncertain.

"You know—what's going on in your life today," Frank explains.

"Nah. He's more, I dunno, innerested in pre-school I guess."

"Yeah," Frank says knowingly. "You got the wrong persuasion, Scrappy. You should get into cognitive therapy."

"What's that?" asks E.T.A., who has joined the group.

"It's clean and simple," says Frank. "People get depressed because they have bad thoughts about themselves. Cognitive therapy helps the patient see that these thoughts are distortions of reality. Like if Jaime here thought he was a for-shit ballplayer, if I was his therapist I'd remind him of his record for doubles last year and the catch he made on Frawley's ball last week. Stuff like that." Jaime smiles, happy to be discussed this way.

"And it works?" asks Eddie, his eyebrows dancing. He looks right at Frank, into the soul of his depression.

"Well, it's *working*," says Frank.

Eddie snorts. "And what if the bad thoughts are true? Like Jaime's batting average is way down this year, and he lost us the third game of the playoffs on that pansy throw. What does a therapist do when there's evidence that the patient is a washout?" Jaime has stopped smiling.

Frank is not prepared for this argument. "Maybe he kind of puts things in perspective," he says tentatively, gesturing broadly with his hands—hands that have been called "soft" for the way they absorb ground balls.

Eddie snorts again. "If you're throwing away money on a shrink like that you better hope we win the Series. And you better help us, like by improving your bunting, for God's sake. It stinks. Did your guy tell you that?"

"I'm just trying to get better," Frank says weakly. He is not talking about his bunting.

E.T.A. has observed this dialogue closely. Eddie's anger surprises him. He remembers his own flash of hatred for his old coach in the last game of the playoffs. He looks at Apples, Narvel, and the others. Their self-hatred is suddenly as obvious to him as it would be if they were systematically mutilating their bodies with their cleats.

"Listen up, guys," he calls out with a hint of his old hopefulness. Heads turn. The faces are pale and listless, but they are interested. He speaks. His theory is simple: depression, he says, is hatred of others turned inward. It is anger unreasonable only in its direction. "We're like a little boy whose parents have yelled at him so he kicks his dog," he says, his hand darting nervously up to adjust his glasses. "Only we're the dog. We're kicking ourselves."

Buford asks him how he gets from anger to depression. They seem to him to be different emotions.

E.T.A., suddenly losing all faith in his position, says he doesn't know. Maybe it makes no sense, he admits, and maybe no one is mad at anybody he can think of, at least not right now, but all he is asking is that they give it some thought, not necessarily right now, but—

"I hate my wife," Eddie announces matter-of-factly. He looks at Scrappy, Jaime, and Frank. He has hurt them too, he sees, along with himself. His eyes moist, he says to each of them, "Hey, man . . . hey, man . . ."

"It's okay," Scrappy says softly.

"I hate *someone*," says Narvel, banging his fist into his palm. "I know I do. I can feel it." His words are followed by a long silence. It is the first time he has spoken in two days.

"When I was a kid," Bubba says suddenly, "this other kid who was older and a lot bigger than me used to wait for me and beat me up on my way to school. He had a whip, too, and sometimes he used that. He waited for me every day."

"I was an Army kid," says Frank, "and we moved around a lot, so I was switching schools all the time. It seemed like I'd never studied what the other kids had, so I was always behind. Couldn't draw or sing, either. The teachers always found me handy as a negative example, and they would talk about me all the time in front of the other kids." He pauses, then says with a dreamy smile, "I hate a whole shitload of people."

The players form a tighter circle and continue to talk. Grammock steps out of his office and opens his mouth to ask Narvel something about the New York line-up. The words don't come out. He squints at his team—all hunched up together and muttering, as isolated and freaky as those goddamned Christian athletes in Bible study.

They win the first, third, and fifth games of the Series on skill, instinct, and constructive anger. They lose the second, fourth, and sixth games in the fog of depressive relapses. The pattern has not gone unnoticed, and the sportswriters, ignorant of the pathology, pursue a mathematical whimsy and predict victory for them in game seven. The players themselves do not know what to expect, or what to hope for. For a baseball team sickened by success, winning the World Series is definitely contraindicated. They wonder if, during the game, they will sabotage victory if they see it coming. But then perhaps a win is just the thing they need. How nice, how *insuring*, to have reached the absolute top. Good material for a cognitive therapist, that. And they are getting madder every day. Old angers grow stronger—Eddie, for example, is divorcing his wife and seeking custody of Tina—and new angers erupt: Jaime has decided that he hates women, and the nervousness his discovery arouses in the clubhouse is offset by the team thrill in the knowledge that the entire outfield, in spite of their medication, is now mad as hell.

Apples and Narvel are the only ones left to make progress. They have been slow, as E.T.A. puts it, "to get in touch with their anger." But even this changes for the good in the eleventh hour, at least for Apples. During a live radio interview in the dugout just before the seventh game, the normally placid pitcher flushes with sudden annoyance at a prying question, and as he looks back at the badly dressed broadcaster who has been tailing them all season, he recalls that it was this same man who once described him as "a tall, skinny, loosey-goosey kind of pitcher," and while Apples knows that this describes his motion perfectly, he resents the implication of awkwardness and ugliness. After all, that waitress back at the hotel wanted him, didn't she? He suddenly feels that the press has never dealt with him fairly, always suggesting that because he doesn't look like a pitcher he probably isn't. He responds to the question, not even remembering what it is, with a flurry of obscenity that leaves the broadcaster speechless. The interview is carried over the radio speakers in the clubhouse, and those players still there tying their shoelaces or looking at themselves with ambivalence in the mirror hear the words in astonishment and send out a cheer for their hurler.

As for Narvel, it is obvious from the way he returns Apples' fiery warm-up throws that he's still being blue. The team sees it. E.T.A., chewing on the bitterness of his minor league experience, knows the joy of rage, and he wants Narvel to know it too, so when the game starts he directs his encouraging chatter away from Apples to the catcher, saying, "C'mon babe, c'mon Narvel babe, get mad, babe, c'mon," and Scrappy, who has been watering with tears an ancient anger toward the incompetent and belittling grandmother who reared him, yells, "Work on it, Narvel, work on it," and Frank at third interrupts a steady stream of soft curses at a grade school teacher who said his painted trees in art class looked like apple cores to shout, "Who do ya hate, Narv, who do ya hate?"

Narvel accepts the encouragement gratefully. The game seems to proceed almost without him. He drops a few balls (but nobody's hurt), he gives some bad signs (but Apples just shakes them off), and he makes a bad throw on an attempted steal (but it's backed up by swift, dry-mouthed Eddie, who charges in from center and throws the runner out as he tries to advance to third). The game remains scoreless, the only threat coming from long balls hit to the wall in fury by Eddie, Frank, and E.T.A. New York has barely touched the ball because Apples is hot, giving up just two hits, bloop singles, into the bottom of the seventh. His cheeks are flaming red, and he gets hotter as he moves through his fateful innings. He imagines he is pitching over and over to the radio broadcaster, and he rejoices in his enemy's repeated failures at bat.

In the top of the ninth, back-to-back doubles by Bubba and Jaime give them a one-run lead. Both hits are line drives to the wall on the fly — clotheslines, ropes. It happens so quickly that they are ahead before they have time to think about it. A relief pitcher enters the game for New York, and while he takes his warm-up throws each of the next three batters waits and watches, alone with his thoughts. It is the top of the ninth, after all, and the more runs they score the more likely they are to win. When play resumes, Eddie and Scrappy promptly strike out. E.T.A. fares even more poorly. Remembering his minor league coach and wishing to prove himself once and for all, he bats right-handed for the first time in eight years. He ignores Grammock's baffled shouts from the dugout, and after two swinging strikes he makes contact but is called out for several of the most ignominious reasons in the rule book. His weak undercut sends the ball straight up, spinning madly but rising no more than five feet. As it drops back down it strikes his bat as it swings around in an awkward follow-through. The ball squirts down the first-base line, where it is struck again by his bat—which has slipped out of his unaccustomed right-handed grip—and then kicked by his foot as he stumbles out of the batter's box. The ump says he is out; the opposing catcher adds, "And then some." E.T.A. takes his position in the field, gloating with a strange sense of revenge.

In the bottom of the ninth Apples retires the first batter on a pop-up to Frank that Narvel should have taken, but Frank and E.T.A. have agreed to cover for Narvel because of his deep funk. The second batter hits a ball sharply down the line at third that rolls around in the left-field corner. Buford, hungry and constipated, seems to take a day or two to come up with it, and he just barely holds him to a triple. The hometown crowd goes wild: the tying run is at third. Apples, expecting to lose now, whiffs the next batter on three pitches, and the visiting fans thunder with anticipation of the final, Series-winning out. Apples, expecting to win, walks the next batter on four pitches. He studies the runner's lead at first and remembers how the press has always criticized his pick-off move. He fires the ball to E.T.A. and the runner is safe by a wide margin. He goes into his stretch and fires again, making it a little closer. He hears Grammock yell something from the dugout but ignores it. His third throw to E.T.A. is wide and E.T.A. must come off the bag to take it. The tying run at third dances down the line, itching to get home. Grammock is joined in his yelling by some fans behind the dugout. They shout, "Get the batter, Apples! Get the last out!" Unhappy with his last throw, Apples tries again and is pleased with the improvement. Yes, this is definitely a part of the game he needs to work on. No time like the present. He tries a slightly different motion and E.T.A. blocks the ball with his chest as it bounces up out of the dirt.

Grammock jumps from the dugout and a voice from the stands yells, "Tell the moron to forget about the runner and work on the batter, Grammock." The voice is familiar to Apples—it is a friend or relative of one of the players—and he smiles toward it and toward the approaching Grammock with blank indifference. Grammock chastises him further, waving violently to the rest of the infield to stay back from the mound.

Apples sighs despondently and agrees to abandon his cause. After getting the sign from Narvel, he delivers a lackluster pitch that is outside by a foot, and Narvel surprises everyone by coming up quickly from behind the plate to try to pick the runner off at first. He too, it seems, has become caught up in Apples' obsession. But the ball doesn't go to E.T.A. at all. Instead it screams over the dugout toward the fans in the stands, and there is a shout and a pwang! as it flies into the tin crate of a beer vendor, knocking him backwards into a row of spectators. One voice rises above the others. It is Narvel's father, yelling, "What the hell are you doin', boy?" Beside him, Narvel's mother wipes spilled beer from her lap and softly weeps.

The runner at first advances to second on the throw. The runner at third comes home, tying the score, and he says something unkind and jeering to Narvel. Narvel does not hear him. His mind is numb. His body tingles with satisfaction.

The winning run at second is represented by a rookie—a pinch runner who nervously stands on one leg and grabs the ankle of the other, stretching his quadriceps. He chatters excitedly, and he reminds Bubba of the taunting teenage boy who always beat him up on his way to school. When Apples, inspired by the team's declining fortune, gets the next batter to hit a ground ball to Bubba for an easy play at first which will send the game into extra innings, Bubba guns the ball across the diamond to Frank at third in hopes of erasing the skinny bully once and for all. Though surprised, Frank takes the throw well—for he is good, his hands are soft, his cognitive therapist says so—and comes within inches of tagging the sliding runner. In the cloud of dust the call can go either way. Because Bubba's play was so stupid in the first place, the ump spreads his hands out wide and sticks his fanny up and yells, "He's there!"

The infield, agitated and without direction, draws together on the mound. E.T.A. says, "Well, the run that will beat us is at third."

"Yeah," says Frank. "We put him there too."

"You're a sport for sayin' 'we,' Frank," says Bubba. "It was my fault all the way."

"I put him on base to begin with," says Apples.

"And I got him to second," says Narvel.

E.T.A grins. "A team effort. That's what we'll say to the press afterward. Better yet, we'll let Apples tell them." They all chortle, producing a cacophonous death rattle that reaches the fans in the first few rows and chills their hearts. "It's funny," continues E.T.A., "you'd think depressed people wouldn't want to be around other depressed people, but we seem to get along all right. I think it's even been good for team spirit."

"You didn't start this on purpose, did you, E.T.A.?" asks Bubba. "Jis' to bring us together? You wouldn't do that, would you, man?"

"He couldn't have," says Apples. "He didn't start it. *I* did."

"But he put it into words," says Bubba. "He made it contagious."

"Nobody started it," Frank says firmly. "It just happened. We were all ripe. Maybe everybody's ripe."

Scrappy nods slowly. "Ain't it a bitch the way it takes hold of you? And it's never over, is it? Even when you think you're getting' better."

"It's never over until it's over," says Narvel.

As the infield pauses to ponder this, the ump steps out and rudely orders them to break it up. As he turns his back he receives a blistering chorus of illegal epithets. Their anger is like a pitching machine gone wild, spraying the ball park with vengeful sallies. The ump flinches but keeps walking to the plate. He should eject them all, but he lets it pass. His judgment has been dulled by nine innings of Narvel's sighing listlessness at his feet.

In mutual consolation for their season in hell together, and to warm one another for the long, cold off-season ahead of them, the infield forms a hugging circle and squeezes hard. With a moaning cheer they break the circle and return to their positions. Apples bends down and picks up the rosin bag. He wants to give this one some thought, and the rule book says that with a man on base a pitcher may take as long as he likes.

Meanwhile, at third, Frank and the rookie pinch runner chat, as opposing players will do, even under the most tense of circumstances. The rookie, grown cocky with his progress to third base and his instant national importance, asks Frank why his club is so weird. Apples' delay behind the mound gives Frank ample opportunity to speak about the suffering of his team. He describes the symptoms and possible origins of clinical depression, stressing his team's particular nemesis: the psychic perils of success. Frank understands the problem well and speaks about it intelligently. The upshot of their discussion is that when Apples finally goes into his stretch and looks at the rookie at third and sighs so heavily that he balks, thus automatically scoring the runner (who must trot home and touch the plate to end the game—a formality, but a necessary formality), the rookie freezes in uncertainty at third base.

Basepaths

JERRY KLINKOWITZ

The foul lines are crooked, the outfield too shallow, and the infield's in crying need of repair. But it's a diamond nevertheless, with the same ninety feet along its basepaths that Kenny has seen big leaguers run all summer.

As bullpen coach for the Kansas City Royals, his view has been somewhat oblique, not really close to the action until a guy rounds second and makes the turn to third. If it's one of his, Kenny cheers. If it's an enemy runner, he listens for the bullpen phone to ring or the pitching coach holler "left" or "right" from the dugout.

Here in Massachusetts he's finishing up a quick visit to Salem State College, taking a last look at the school's diamond from above as he sits ten rows up with the painfully young athletic director.

"It sure would be nice to have you with us," the kid is saying. "Ken Boyenga of the Cincinnati Reds."

"I'm with Kansas City now," Kenny tries to remind him, but all he hears is blather about those Reds teams, the last of which he'd rather forget. Didn't he spend nearly all his career with the Redlegs, the AD's now asking; wasn't he their rookie of the year?

"No, no," Kenny demurs. "I was a slow starter, a late bloomer, like they say. And I came up with the Cubs, not the Reds."

"Really?" The young man brightens, then tries to excuse himself. "I guess that was before my time."

There's a silence the athletic director fills with some chatter about how Ken would like coaching here. "In a year we might have some staff for you," he's told. "A full-time groundskeeper in addition to the guys from physical plant, and maybe even a pitching coach."

"Oh, really?" Kenny asks, trying to sound interested.

"Most of those guys you caught in Cincy are novice coaches now," the kid is saying, "just starting in JuCo or even prep. I know you were pretty good friends with Don Kruse and Jeff Copeland, and Copeland even put in for the job you're looking at now."

"No lie?" Kenny wants to say, but stops short. Knowing Kruse and Copeland doesn't make for a good set of references. But this potential employer of his seems to know all about his days with the Reds, even if his first three years in Chicago are a dark mystery. For his day and a half on campus all those wild stories never came up—but now, an hour before he leaves for the airport, he's getting a this-is-your-life treatment from someone who must have been a teenager at the time.

"Ken Boyenga," the AD's saying again. "Only catcher who could handle the mound that staff writers said was the craziest in baseball. You could handle our student athletes here, no doubt!"

"No doubt," Ken repeats, looking for a way to say goodbye and ask where's his ride.

"Do you mind if I call you Kenny?" he's asked.

"Nope."

"Was that the only nickname you had in pro ball?"

"Yep."

"Wasn't there some problem when Kruse, or was it Copeland, tried to change his name? I mean his real name?"

This is just the conversation Kenny doesn't want to have, so he ignores the question and asks if they shouldn't be thinking about his flight. It's an indirect one, routed through Chicago rather than directly to Minneapolis, where the Royals are starting a weekend series, thanks to the airline he'd rather use being on strike. He really can't be late or risk getting bumped. But the kid is still full of questions. Isn't there time for just one? OK.

"Have you considered managing in the minors? I shouldn't really mention this, but as one old Redlegs fan to another, the others on our short list have done that."

Kenny's not a Reds fan and never has been, he wants to clarify, but decides to give an honest answer. "Haven't before," he says, thinking how his baseball career has come to this or nothing, as he's been told KC has someone else in mind for bullpen coach next year, an ex-Royal just released by the Yankees. "But to be honest with you, it's going to be that or this."

"I really do hope it's this," Kenny hears the kid saying, and is touched by his sincerity. Well, maybe he hopes so too, and takes a last look at this college diamond that despite all the work it needs still sparkles enough in the bright sunlight to make his eyes shed tears.

Back at the AD's office he retrieves his bag and is introduced to the school's driver who'll run him in to Logan. But today must be nostalgia day in old Salem, for the guy wastes most of an hour bringing Kenny into Boston the long way, past the river and through the academic area, where student traffic from three big universities slows them to a crawl. "There it is," the driver says excitedly and points to another field not unlike Salem State's. "What's that?" Kenny asks, forgetting why they've come this way, and is told that over there's the original diamond from old Braves Field. "Spahn, Sain, and pray for rain!" the driver waxes, and Kenny notes that the day is crystal clear.

Great flying weather, but he gets to the desk just ten minutes before flight time and learns he's too late, his seat's been taken. Worried she'll be cursed, the agent assures him he's already been booked on a later flight with almost the same routing. "Almost?" he asks skeptically, and is told he's still set for a nonstop to Chicago that connects to Minneapolis–St. Paul. "Just one stop," he's assured.

"For Christ's sake, where?" he asks, wondering what's between Chicago and the Twin Cities.

"Mason City. That's in Iowa."

"I know," he says, recognizing the name. "We have a farm team there," then immediately regrets the reference, fearing another interview about baseball.

"That *is* a good place for young salespeople to start," she agrees. "Maybe someday they'll be selling out of Boston or Minneapolis like you!" She beams brightly, handing him his ticket and some coupons.

"What's all this?" he asks.

"Your flight doesn't leave 'til eight," she announces, and before he can complain adds that these are coupons for a dinner and complimentary drink at the airport VIP room.

"One crapping drink?" he blurts out and at once apologizes, but she's already smiling something more than her company-school smile and handing him a fistful of extra coupons.

"You didn't get them from me, did you," she advises with a wink, and Kenny says of course he didn't, he made them.

Feeling better than he should, he grabs a cabin tag for his bag and heads off toward where she's said he'll find the VIP club. But first a phone call to the Hyatt's desk in MSP, message for Marshall Adesman, Kansas City's traveling secretary, saying he'll be late but ready to rejoin the team as promised. He's happy not to have missed a single game, easy as it seems they get along without him. What a way to end what should have been a dream career, he thinks: half a year on the Royals' bench, a boring winter back home in Cincinnati, and this spring and summer working as a bullpen coach, psyching out and warming up Kansas City's relievers. Now, as August ends, he's down to just two options: college coaching and minor league managing.

The one thing he won't do is coach in the minors. He's thought it over and there's nothing in Triple-A Tacoma or Double-A Chattanooga, let alone Single-A Sonoma, Mason City, or Charleston (not to mention the rookie clubs in Elmira and Bradenton) that could make him be anything less than captain of his destiny. Well, tonight he'll get his first look at one of the places he could be if Salem State doesn't pan out, at least as much as one can see from the airport.

In the swanky club he orders a surf 'n' turf, forks over a drink coupon, and counts the rest: over a dozen. Geez Louise, he mutters, and for the second time today thinks of Don Kruse and Jeff Copeland, for either of whom these would not have been enough. Well, maybe for Kruse, who swore he preferred to keep himself clean—for worse mayhem later. Damn that kid for bringing all this up. He heard about it when Kansas City picked him up and still must fend off requests for stories when the charter flights run late from the coast. Is it why they're not asking him back as bullpen coach? No, that makes no sense, since the minor league managing job they've teased him with is just as responsible, if not more.

Oh, what the hell, he muses, getting dizzy from the quandary. Fingering the coupons he knows he won't use, he nevertheless starts humming a line Jeff Copeland used to boom out on the charters from San Diego, Frisco, and LA after they'd been up for hours with many more yet to go: "It's all right, 'cause it's midnight, an' I got two more bottles of wine." Somebody must know the song, Kenny realizes with a start, for from behind him a voice is calling, "Cheers, fella!"

By the time they're in the air it's twilight, but Kenny doesn't mind. Always a nice view in the evening, the old city's population packed so tight that street lights cluster like a field of diamonds. The takeoff has sent them out across the bay; but now, as the jumbo jet swings back toward land, the urban map passes beneath as if it's moving and he's standing still. Dotting that map are reference points more focused than anything the natural landscape can offer: the gold-domed statehouse, the huge bridge over to Cambridge, and—nestled along the Back Bay and named for the marsh-lands drained for its construction so long ago—Fenway.

Although the plane is several miles away and already five thousand feet high, Fenway Park stands out as the brightest of Boston's lights. Such white luminescence compared to the city's amber, whiter still for being banked off the green he can discern even from here. Several minutes later the amber's turned to blue, a blue that's fuzzing away in the haze, but the striking glare of the Red Sox' stadium can still be distinguished. To Ken's amazement it remains a distinct point, so much brighter and whiter than everything else that half an hour later he can see it poking through the gloom. I'm five miles up, he thinks in amazement, and probably two hundred, maybe two hundred and fifty miles away: I don't believe this! Now he keeps his eye on it, compulsively, craning around in his seat even as the lights of Buffalo and Toronto come into view ahead. If he didn't know it was Boston back there, he could never guess it, or even imagine that the one fine point sparkling in its dim smudge on the trailing horizon was Fenway Park.

Then, just as the last hint of it fades away, something else catches Ken's attention. The pilot has said they're passing over Toronto, and it is a rather nice looking carpet of light stretching right up to the sudden darkness of the lake. But up ahead he sees some dimmer clusters, probably London or Kitchener-Waterloo, and beyond them another sparkling

island: Detroit. And at the island's near edge he sees a point of light so
much brighter than all the rest. He makes a bet that it's Tiger Stadium,
Briggs Stadium as they called it in his youth and where, on a trip with
his father, he saw the visiting Red Sox and Ted Williams beat the Tigers
with a home run. For the next half-hour he keeps his eye trained on it,
until they're over Windsor. He can see the international bridge, and follows the trailing lights of its off-ramp to the ballpark itself.

Thirty-two thousand feet, the captain says. That's over six miles high,
Kenny calculates, and marvels that, directly over the stadium as they are,
he can distinguish infield brown from outfield green. Can't see the bases,
couldn't bet he'd see the players, though he tries. But from the shape of
things, even so far away, he can visualize the basepaths. Maybe someone's
rounding them right now, sweeping past second and aiming, for a
moment, at one of those little cages down the lines they use as bullpen
benches. God, how he hates sitting out there, and here's where the team
is coming after their weekend with the Twins. But how he loves this old
park.

He hates to take his eyes away from it, but steals a moment to open
the USA Today that's been sitting on his lap unread the whole flight.
Toronto at Detroit, starting time 7:30. Nine o'clock now, could be fourth
or fifth inning. At takeoff the Red Sox must have been just getting under
way; right, New York at Boston, 7:30 start. It amuses him to think that for
twelve or thirteen games a year he's almost face to face with the guys down
there, playing before the same crowds. He knows half the Detroit players
and even some of the regular fans, aficionados with season tickets in the
first row over the near-in bullpens. He looks down and Tiger Stadium's
still there, glowing green within and white without. See ya Tuesday, he
says with a nod, then figures he's been staring out the window long
enough and turns back to his paper. But there's the pitching line for Minnesota at Chicago, and even as he's figuring where the Twins will be in
their rotation for his game tomorrow it dawns on him that he just might
see his third ballpark tonight.

What time? Seven o'clock start, and it's 9:15 now with well over an
hour to go. No way. But Carlton Fisk calls the slowest game in baseball;
the Sox are never out of there before ten. Who's pitching for the Twins
again? Kenny notes the knuckleballer, thinks piteously of the catcher, and
decides if the plane loops into O'Hare from the south and approaches the

city before 10:30 there's a chance. Of course there is: he's gained an hour because of central time.

Looking back, Tiger Stadium's a harder dot to focus on than Fenway, given that the greater part of metro Detroit stretches past it to the west. But it's there, Kenny is sure. Then he wonders if he could have picked up Municipal Stadium across the lake in Cleveland; check the paper—no way, the Indians are out in Seattle. Maybe the Browns were having a workout tonight, it's their exhibition season. But who cares if it's football? And probably not, anyway, as he recalls looking south from Toronto where the lights would have been; if the ballpark were alight, right there on the southern shore, he would have seen it, an easier shot than he has at Chicago now.

And Chicago's there, he can see it, a string of lights running perpendicular to his course: the western shore of Lake Michigan. He traces the lights south and there, a little inland, is a spot so much brighter than the rest he has no doubts that it's Comiskey.

Please, he prays, as his ears pop and he feels the plane slow a bit and tilt forward: come in from the south. They're heading right for the Loop, and at the north of it he can see the John Hancock sticking up above the rest like black tinkertoys. Again, all the other lights are blue or amber, but Comiskey sparkles in pure whiteness. It strikes him that these are the three oldest ballparks he's seen tonight, lit like freight yards with hundreds of incandescents boxed atop metal towers. He's wondered how the new parks can be just as bright with half the power, and now knows why: all that excess wattage at Fenway, Briggs, and Comiskey is going straight up and out. He thinks of the bullpens at Chicago, stuck out there beneath that tiny bleacher section beyond the center field fence, and remembers looking up to count the floodlights on each pole. An even hundred, ten across and ten down. How many poles? He'll count those when they end the season here in five—what is it—five and a half weeks.

Suddenly the plane makes a steep bank to the left, sending Ken's glance straight down into the blackness of Lake Michigan, and he realizes he's in luck, the pilot's going to cruise along the lakefront before turning inland a couple miles south. Make it three miles and he'll see the park. Another bank to the right and the shoreline passes beneath. Cars on the Outer Drive, there's a college campus—IIT, a tough one. Geez Louise, they're coming right down Wentworth Avenue at about five thousand feet.

Less than a mile up, and he can see a person, at least a figure, at a mile, if he knows where to look. Holy cripes, Ken's thinking, breathing fast and as excited as a child on a first flight ever. Things are rushing past and he no sooner sees the Dan Ryan and its heavy traffic than the ancient stands loom up and his vision pours into the outfield. White on the grass. Who's behind the plate? Unless he's been lifted, and he wouldn't be unless hurt, it's Carlton Fisk, a thousand miles from the park that made him famous but one that Kenny was looking at just a couple hours ago.

At O'Hare Kenny sees he's got less than twenty minutes to make his connection, but he darts inside a terminal bar where he sees a TV set aglow. A commercial's showing, but the channel light reads 32, not 9, so it's the Sox. The game's back on with a scoreboard shot they're holding too long, something about it being knotted in the tenth. "Who's catching?" Kenny asks the bartender. "Catching?" the guy asks in return. "Who the hell do you think?" and that's answer enough for Ken.

"What's the deal, fella?" he's being asked by the salesman he pushes past, hurrying from the bar, and Kenny has to ask himself what is—after all, he was standing fifteen feet from Carlton Fisk three weeks ago in Kansas City, and can introduce himself right here in Chicago on October first, second, or third. He could tell Fisk about the answer to a trivia question: Which ex-Cub did the White Sox trade to make room for free agent Carlton Fisk? For the year and a half they've worked in the same ballparks Kenny's never had the nerve to do that, but maybe he should, especially now that he can say he's seen him from an airplane as well.

From an airplane? I've been in this game too long, he thinks, as he lets the Mississippi Valley Airlines agent check his bag that's too big for carry-on in these different dimensions of commuter flying. Too long. It's what he's been thinking about all day, his day and a half the Royals let him have off between series so he could look into this college job. Professor Boyenga? What comes next, President of Yale? It really wasn't worth the effort. Nor does he find it worth the effort to look from the window of this small, noisy plane as it climbs westward from O'Hare and angles slightly to the north for Minneapolis. Can't look into the Humpty Dome, he tells himself; and besides, it's dark, the Twins are here and so is he. "There," he corrects himself, and leans back to have a last look at Chicago. But at this low altitude the city's out of sight.

He slips into a shallow sleep, then wakes with a start as the stewardess eases his seat upright. Minneapolis already? No, Mason City, and he realizes he'd forgotten the stop. This is what he's supposed to be looking at—one-in-five chance, really one-in-three he could be here next year if he tells Salem State to take a walk. He tries to focus out the window but sees nothing. Because there is nothing, he soon realizes, and waits for the lightless countryside to pass. Then some lights come into view, yard lights from farms, corners where sections meet, a small town way off to the right, and to the far left some lights that must be the interstate he presumes they'll follow to the Twin Cities. Then the edge of what might be considered suburban sprawl; they even have that here. Then a river he guesses will lead to town. And suddenly something so bright it actually hurts his eyes.

A ballpark. Jesus, four-for-four, Kenny thinks, realizing they're about to pass over the minor league field where the Mason City Royals, if that's what they're called up here, play. My God, it must be near eleven, midnight Boston time. Then he remembers how late his own games in the minors could go, ineffective hitting rarely able to break out in a lead and sloppy fielding letting those leads slip away. Or it could be the second game of a doubleheader; bet they have to make up lots of wash outs and cold outs from April and early May, the poor suckers.

His interest aroused, Ken pushes his face against the window to look down. They're much lower, yet not as fast as over Comiskey, and he has time to see not only that white's in the field, visitors batting, but that the bleachers are stone cold empty while what he can see of the grandstand looks pretty sparse. Maybe their start was four or five hours ago too, who knows. Anyway, in a moment the ballpark's gone, there are some open fields, a factory (Closed? No lights, so at least no night shift), some tract houses, and right away a runway. Nothing more to see, not even a view of downtown. Ten minutes on the ground and they take off, banking right before they join the interstate and follow it at twelve thousand feet to the airport south of Minneapolis–St. Paul.

Kenny cabs it to the Hyatt, gives the bellman a five to take his bag upstairs, and heads right for the bar. No players here, he knows; players can't drink in the place they're staying—bad image. Not even encouraged for the coaching staff, and their manager has a favorite place across town where Billy Martin once had a famous fight and baseball folks can still cadge a drink. But Marshall Adesman's here, and he wants to be sure the traveling secretary knows he's back in time, before midnight, to merit meal money.

That's on Adesman's mind too, as his eyes leave Kenny's face and dart to his watch, missing because he's left it in his room, and to the bar's clock, which is such a mess of colored lights he can't read it. But the cagey secretary tries a guess nevertheless.

"12:01," he says as a greeting. "No fifty-five bucks."

"12:01 bar time, 11:46 real time," Kenny answers. "Cough up." Realizing he's been tricked with his own shamming, Marshall pulls an oversized wallet from his jacket pocket and counts out two twenties and three fives. "So I'm tipping fives all night, huh?" Kenny objects, and Adesman tells him to stow it, he'll pay for drinks and cover the tip as well. Kenny feigns surprise and the traveling secretary demurs, making an elaborate wave-off motion while muttering, "Unless you've got your buddies Kruse and Copeland along."

"Hell," Kenny laughs, "they're my coaching staff at Salem State, where we're all professors of intercollegiate athletics," and Marshall cracks up at the line, never guessing how true it could have been.

Nor will Kenny tell him, for at just this moment he's decided he'll forget about college and start talking seriously about managing in the minors, even if it's in that godforsaken park they just dive-bombed in Mason City. Mason City, he realizes, is in the same chain with Royals Stadium, which he hasn't seen since Tuesday night, and Fenway, Tiger Stadium, and Comiskey, where he tells Adesman he's seen games tonight. Salem State sure ain't, he reminds himself. Let Copeland and Kruse have it.

"So you really saw old Briggs Stadium from the plane?" Marshall accepts the stories about Fenway and Comiskey, taking off and landing, but tries to argue that you can't see anything that small from that altitude. "Small?" Kenny protests, remembering how big the park looked when he was fifteen. "Maybe you thought you saw it," the traveling secretary allows, but this makes Kenny even madder.

They switch topics to Mason City, and Adesman asks if Kenny saw a pitcher there named Freddie Guagliardo.

"Huh?" Kenny asks, and is told the kid will be joining them September first in Detroit.

"Small world," the two friends agree.

Infield

PHILIP F. DEAVER

I have a flash of Skidmore, playing first base, whose father played first base before him. He's stretching to take a throw from me at shortstop, and the throw goes over his head, mainly because it's thrown too high but also because he stretched out real fancy before he knew where the ball was going, then couldn't get up to reach it, because it was high and not in need of one of his goddamned fancy first-baseman's stretches.

I can still remember perfectly how it feels to snag a grounder. I remember the jerk in the shoulder from an overhand baseball throw, hard, from deep short and on the run, the rhythm of it, the whip of the arm crossing the body in the follow-through. These were great feelings. But there was pain in it too, for me anyway. Later I learned there's pain in almost all good feelings.

"What kind of throw was that?" Skidmore's making a scene, yelling at me to get the heat off himself.

The runner rounds first, tears for second. Skidmore's standing next to the bag, his arms out. "Seriously, what kind of throw was that?"

The right fielder sees that Skidmore won't be chasing the ball, gets it himself, and manages to stop the runner from scoring. Skidmore comes to the middle of the field, still looking at me. He's fourteen. This is Pony

League, and in those days we played in Levi's and T-shirts colored to differentiate the teams.

"I need to know what kind of throw you think you're making out here," he says.

I'm staring at him, standing at the far edge of the grass between second and third.

"Let's have it. I'm serious. What kind of throw was that?"

He's brilliant, and can be very funny. His movements are gawky with a rough adolescence. For some reason I even liked him back then, but he had a terrible mean streak that used to rise up out of him like a second personality—evil, angry, driven.

In adult life, I've accused him of this in letters. I forget when, but it's been just a couple of years ago he wrote me that none of that in the old days was meanness at all. He said it was all irony and I just failed to catch it.

But it was Cliff Webb and Junior Guthrie who got me thinking about baseball, plus the fact that today was opening day for the Cubs up at Wrigley. Like Skidmore, Cliff was an old baseball pal of mine when we were all growing up in this town, and he and I ran into each other in a bar the night before, after all these years.

On this particular morning I had decided to make a tour of our rental properties, to catalogue the repairs that were needed. My wife had been nagging me to get this done for two months—it was tax time. And, of course, on the day I finally got to it, because of Cliff, I had a headache, so I'd gone to the IGA to get some Extra Strength Anacin, even though it was too late (in order to avoid a hangover, you have to have the presence of mind to take aspirin and drink much water precisely at the time you have no presence of mind—one of the little Zen perplexities we learn to live with).

Incredibly, on the way back to my car on my aspirin run I encountered Junior Guthrie, another old baseball crony, now with a big beer belly, meandering around out in the IGA parking lot wearing a yellow American Legion bowling shirt and a Chicago Cubs ball cap.

"Hey, pal, can you jump me?" he was saying. Something about the eyes, I could still spot the old Junior, still down in there somewhere.

"Wha'd'ya say. I'm parked right over here." He raised his arm and pointed so I could see how convenient his car was to mine.

I had the headache and really didn't want to.

"Sure," I said. "You have cables?"

"Pal, you got a car like mine, you carry jumper cables." He was already heading back to his car, gesturing to me. "It's just right over here, no problem."

The gravelly asphalt lot was depressing, especially in my condition. I drove around to his rusted-out tan-and-brown Cordoba, the vinyl roof fried off by the sun. By then Junior had the hood up. I popped mine, then let him hook us up while I chased aspirin with coffee from home. I switched on the radio to see if I could catch some news. I think I stayed in the car for fear Junior would recognize me and I'd get blasted with another round of nostalgia, this while the effects of the first round were still with me. Suddenly I noticed that there was a little raisin of a woman sitting behind the wheel of his car, staring at me. She had small, brown, nervous eyes like a squirrel. He'd shout directions at her.

"Okay, crank her." "Okay, shut her off." "Okay, give her a try." "Okay, stop pumpin' her, lay off it."

He was shouting through the crack that appears between the motor and the hood when the hood's open. She huddled behind the wheel following directions.

Watching Junior was difficult for me. I remembered clearly an eleven-year-old second baseman with big white teeth and light brown floppy hair. I remembered his almost pony-like run and unending hubbah-hubbah chatter. The optimism of a child. This is what it had come to?

Finally he looked toward me and said, "Okay, don't rev her. Let her be. Needs to store it up a minute." He enjoyed my obedience.

Then, too quickly, he said, "Okay, now rev her!" And then he said to the woman, "PUMP that son-of-a-bitch, Mama—that's it. Okay, hit it!"

He had the distributor completely loosened and no air filter over the carb. When she'd hit the starter to turn it over, he'd go halfway into the dying thing's gaping mouth and wrench back and forth on the distributor like it was a whale's wisdom tooth and he was the dentist. His feet were clear off the ground. He had a stub of a cigar all chewed and sweated on, which he would light between rounds.

"Ain't gettin' no good contact," he said to me, "—yur battery's one of them sidewinders, never can get no good contact. I'll find somebody else, she'll fire right up."

Translated, this meant his car troubles were my fault.

"Get this goddamned thing goin', I'll take it to the junkyard, head back to Kentucky, get me another one. Got this one down there, cost me one-fifty. Put sixty thousand miles on her. Guy I play softball with—out at Cabot—he's from Kentucky, told me about it. Lot of stolen cars down there, he says. Stop pumpin' her so much, Mama, like I goddamned tol' ya."

"I wasn't pumpin' her!" the woman crackled back at him.

"What?" He hurried around to her window. "Wha'd'ya say?" She sank down in her seat like he was going to belt her. "You was pumpin' her, honey. I know that much."

Her face was real wrinkled, resembled the cracked vinyl of the Cordoba's dashboard. She was dirty, desperate looking, bent down in that old seat like she was ashamed. For all I know I might have gone to school with her, too, but she was beyond recognition now.

"Okay, crank her up," he says to her, back in front of the car, and she tries, the motor making a terrible grinding noise. Never jump somebody when you've got a headache. I was not optimistic that his car would ever start again.

"Goddamned starter's the problem. Get this thing started, I'll head over to the parts shop—there's a parts shop around here somewhere—head over there and get me another starter. And some starter fluid. If she's gonna start, she'll start with starter fluid. NOW, Mama. HIT IT!! That's it, PUMP the son of a bitch. Hold it, you're floodin' her. Damn. Flooded."

He comes around to my window, bends down so our noses, or rather my nose and the end of his cigar, are eight inches apart. "That there's my girl friend," he says so she can't hear. "She loves me—hard to figure, I know. You'd think my brother could buy me a car. I gave him a kidney and he ain't rejected it yet. Doc says most of 'em are rejected by now, but not mine. Never paid me nothin', some brother."

I got out of my running car and went up with him beside the front end. I watched him climb in and out of his motor.

"You did what?" I said. "You gave your brother a kidney?"

"Damn straight," he says. He pulls up his dirty bowling shirt and there's a scar. It starts just above the tip of his pelvis on the right, and heads northeast most of the way to the opposite shoulder. Half of an X, right up his body, pink and angry looking like my hernia scar, only two feet longer and heading across tender territory, the white and light-blue flabby sticking-out giant human frog abdomen. "Yeah, worked all his life and he never knew he had a bad heart, eighteen hours a day without givin' it a thought."

I was trying to remember Junior Guthrie's brother. Couldn't.

"Then they tell him his heart's givin' out and he gets all these bypasses, and then his kidney gives out 'cause his heart gave out, and he gets a kidney from me, two hundred bucks a week on drugs to keep him from rejecting it—you know that new stuff they got now? Well, my brother's fadin' fast after all this help he's gettin' from doctors, but they all own big houses and my kidney's cooking along independently like nothin' ever happened, shit."

Again he dives down into the motor, his feet kicking in the air. Over his shoulder, he yells above the grinding of the car, "Doc says if he dies they'll get it back for me."

His whole body is pivoting on his beer belly, which is pressed down over the fender into the area where the containers for windshield-wiper fluid and coolant used to be.

"Hit it, honey, that's it," he says to the woman, and wrenches the distributor for all it's worth. And, incredibly, the car starts. "Yup, my brother's in the garbage business and trucks is always breakin' down. We got a couple of 'em on their ass in the garage all the time, all spread out all over everywhere getting rebuilt. Don't tell me about distributors, I tell 'em, it's just the timing's off and the chain has to come around, and you gotta hit it just right. Good work, Mama," he says.

I climb back in my car. He unhooks the cables and thanks me, latches down my hood with appreciated reverence for my car, and comes around to my window again.

"This is a fine automobile." Big hand on the roof above my head, he's bending down, squinting at me, smiling. He turns his head and spits a piece of his cigar. "I know you, right?"

"I don't know. I don't think so," I said. "You a Cub fan?"

"What?"

"I see your cap—you gonna watch the Cubs this afternoon? First day of the season."

"Nah. This here's my brother's hat. And be that as it may, the Cubs suck." He laughed, looked over at K-Mart, then back to me. "You're Carl Landen, am I right? Took me a while, because of the beard. Makes you look like a salesman. I'm Junior Guthrie, remember?"

"Junior," I said. I went for a look of surprise, but who knows if it worked. "Good to see you."

"Hey, honey, this here's Carl Landen, guy I played ball with. His dad was that doctor that died, remember I told ya? Long time ago?" Smiling, he looked back at me. Then there was a little blank spot where neither of us could think of anything to say.

"Well," I said finally, "you take care."

"You knew it, didn't you?" He was asking hopefully, as if trying in a friendly way to find out if he'd not changed so much after all.

As I backed out, I saw he had a ball glove in the back window of the car.

"I wasn't sure, Junior. You know how that goes. You take care."

The rest of the morning I toured the rentals, head hurting and kind of cranky except I was by myself so maybe also a little lonesome—I think I was lonesome for my boy. I wanted to talk baseball with him. He was at school, age eleven, sitting at a desk, bored and hungry.

I mooched three fingers worth of whiskey from the cleaning ladies at one of our places around noon. Under the sink I found a glass left by the last tenants and washed it with some cleaning ladies' Spic and Span. They must have thought they had a pretty cool boss, to tip one with them out there on the job.

I planned this to be the house I hit around noon, because it was partially furnished, a few things from the previous tenants (the U-Haul must have been full) and the rest from inventory. It had a TV and the cable hadn't been turned off yet so I could pick up WGN. There was a cot in the house, and a lamp—shiny black and shaped like the head of a horse, red lamp shade. I was in business.

The headache hadn't given out with the first hit of aspirin, and I'd taken more around ten-thirty, but still no give. So about noon, after I belted down the cleaning ladies' whiskey and they were gone, I stretched out on the cot, the TV droning with a soap opera. I think I still had the headache, but I couldn't feel it.

Lying out on that cot in our rental, I started thinking about my dad and baseball and Skidmore and all those kids I knew like Junior and Cliff who grew up, and all the things I learned. Now my own son was learning the same stuff.

From the upstairs window, the back bedroom, at my childhood home across town (my mom still lives there), I remember looking down into the yard one night. There wasn't a moon; the light from the stars lit the yard only a little. Near the doghouse, on a long chain, was my springer spaniel, Tad. He was lying down, but his head was up, on guard. He was looking deep into the black shade of the lilacs. His chain would clink in the dark. He was guarding his very best pal, my father, who was stretched out on the picnic table nearby, watching the stars.

From my lighted room, through the window screen and down into the dark, I could barely see him. He didn't move. I was listening to the Cardinal game on the radio—Harry Caray, Jack Buck, Joe Garagiola. Vinegar Bend Mizell was on the mound, high kicking lefty. Infield of Stan Musial, Don Blasingame, Alvin Dark, Eddie Kasko. Outfield, Wally Moon in left, maybe Curt Flood in center but for some reason I never can exactly remember, Joe Cunningham for sure in right. Behind the plate, Hal Smith. They were playing the Pirates, 1957. This was when I was eleven.

"Who's winning?" Dad asked me. He could see me clearly.

"Cards. Cunningham stole home again."

"Great." His voice was barely audible.

His father had died that winter. He'd missed a last chance to see him alive in the previous fall. Dad had gone out on a quick trip to hunt pheasants and had neglected swinging through the old Nebraska hometown to see his folks. He was having a hard time with it.

"What're you doing?"

"Looking at the stars. You start to see the dimensions after a while. Come here."

I went out and sat next to him on the table. He pointed out a dim formation overhead that, if you looked away from it just a bit, you could see was really a kite-shaped cluster of seven stars.

"Pleiades," he said. "Look real close and you can tell some of them are farther away than others. You can catch the depth of it. Go get the binoculars."

I got them but we didn't use them long. We just sat there talking. I knew what was on his mind.

"What was it Grandpa said, in the hospital?" I asked him.

He sighed. "He said, 'Jesus, Mary, and Joseph.' Then he took a real deep breath, and he died."

He was quiet a minute or so. "He was a good guy," he said. "The bishop, out in Lincoln, he says they're going to name Grandpa a Knight of St. Benedict. It's a pretty big deal. The Pope has to do it."

"You think Grandpa's looking down on us right now?"

He was staring into the sky, breathing quietly. It wasn't a question to answer, really, but just to think about. In those days the rural Illinois night sparkled deep and black.

Finally my dad muttered, "I don't know."

That summer I saw my first professional baseball game, in the old Busch Stadium on Grand Avenue in St. Louis. My father, his good friend and partner Bob Swift, and I stayed in a nearby hotel called the Fairgrounds, and drove across town to the zoo that Sunday morning.

On the way, we went to mass in the St. Louis Cathedral, unfinished in a hundred years of work, scaffolding high in the vaulted ceiling where the man who made the mosaics labored day after day, the altar candles far below. As we drove around the city, I sat in the back seat, and up front Dad and Bob talked about patients, or investments, or other things that were too convoluted for me to pay attention to. So I sat quietly, staring out the window, absorbing the warm, sunny streets of St. Louis.

We ate lunch near the stadium, in a bar, sitting toward the back. Right now I can summon the smell of beer and primitive air conditioning, see the reflection of the front windows and the gleam of traffic off the dark linoleum, taste the ham sandwich eaten too fast, the anticipation of the ball park in less than an hour.

But when we came through the gates of old Sportsman's Park, when we came up the walkway to find our seats, we popped into a strange, fin- ished, green world like I'd never seen before. Every angle was planned, every hue was coordinated—baseball was urbane and civilized, not like the pasture-type game, dry and weedy and rough, that we played at home. The afternoon air was heating up. People who behaved randomly and at odds outside acted in concert at the ball park, standing together and cheering and laughing when Cards manager Freddie Hutchinson kicked the dirt or someone stumbled rounding first. The crowd had a rousing, a great, comforting, somehow knowing, collective voice.

Bob Swift had interned at Barnes Hospital in St. Louis, and knew all there was to know about the Cardinals and their ball park. Hand on my shoulder, he pointed out, against the back screen, Harry Caray, in slicked-back hair and black-and-white checked pants, conducting the dugout show for radio, interviewing Larry Jackson, last night's winning pitcher. The big batting cage loomed over the plate, and the venerable old catcher Walker Cooper, wad of tobacco in his jowl, stood at the side of it cracking line drives. At home, I pictured the ballplayers as kids. At the ball park, I was startled by the dark shadow beard on the face of Blasingame, "the Blazer" as he was called. He was littler than I thought. Moon's eyebrows were astonishing, Kasko wore glasses, Cunningham was bald. Those were men out there.

The first time I saw Musial at the plate, his unusual stance (often described on the radio) absorbed my attention. Perhaps I had pictured Babe Ruth or a drawing I had of Casey at the Bat, or the action photo I had of Ted Williams hitting the long ball with a vicious Y-chromosome rip. In reality, Musial's stance seemed soft, relaxed, almost like dance. The front foot was pointed forward, toward the pitcher, the rear foot back toward the catcher. The front knee bent inward, graceful, the bat was held too high and way too far back. The head was out over the plate and tilted a little. For me, at eleven, the batter's stance told a lot—it was the posture one assumed for battle, the very definition of ready. Musial's stance communicated artistry, individuality, himself. By then he was getting to be a grand old man of baseball, his late thirties. During the game, when he blasted a home run, the crack of the bat communicated immediately that the park would never hold it. The enormous swelling roar of the crowd conveyed respect. The ball bounced on the roof of the right field stands, at the base of the light tower. The scoreboard Budweiser eagle flapped its wings and a little red Cardinal made of neon darted around the stadium. The stroke itself had been a level, easy, sweeping movement, not a wild-ass swing like you'd get from Kaline, Clemente,

Frank Robinson. Not the tight, big-armed body turn of Yogi Berra. Somewhere along the base path Musial broke the cadence of a sprint and settled into the relaxed stride of the home-run hitter in his parade lap, the
crowd standing, pleased, respectful, happy.

"Wow, wow, wow, he tagged that one!" Bob Swift shouted as he took
his seat again.

I noticed baseball was different without the interpretation of Harry
Caray on the radio. You had to really watch. The game was happening at
some distance away. On that day, we were far down the left-field line,
almost to the outfield wall, nearly a block away from home plate. The
crack of the bat arrived a moment after the swing, the ball already lofting
high across the background of the white-, blue-, red-shirted crowd in the
upper deck across the way. Or on grounders the third baseman might
already have reacted to his right, the ball skipping into this glove, as the
sound of the hit finally made it to us.

Vernon Law was on the mound for the Pirates that day. A tall straight
man, kind of thin. Even sitting as far from the plate as we were, you could
still hear the pop of his fastball in the catcher's glove.

On a ball to left I remember watching Wally Moon peg the ball to second. The handsome young Texan, rookie of the year three years before,
who replaced the retired and venerable Enos Slaughter, reached back
and, in a thrilling overhand motion like the hammer of a pistol, laid the
ball on the flat plane of green air. All I could compare the geometry and
motion to was pool, the green carpet of perfectly groomed grass like a pool
table, flat, the smooth flight of the ball as though it were coasting not
across the hot afternoon air but green felt, flat marble. Low and fast—the
ball skipped like a bullet on the infield dirt, the Blazer taking it on the
short hop right at the bag. Big league, I thought to myself.

My dad got up from the seat next to me in the third inning, asking if
Bob or I wanted something, saying he'd be right back. Bob Swift stayed
with me, one empty seat away. He'd lean over and fill me in on things—
like the enormous black man selling beer, sweating in the Sunday heat,
his voice full and shouting, for fifteen years an institution at Sportsman's
Park.

I couldn't get enough. I stared through the binoculars at the players
and the crowd. My dad's absence bothered me a little, but not terribly—
sometimes I'd say something to him, forgetting he was gone. I stared until

the heavy steel on my nose and against my eyes began to hurt, but I kept staring. The binoculars were powerful, and because I'd used them on the planets I could focus them as sharply as they could be focused. The creamy white, scarlet, blue, and yellow of those old Cardinal uniforms was dazzling against the green of the grass under brilliant sun.

As long as I live I'll remember one strange thing that happened at that game. Using the binoculars, I followed a foul ball up and back into the crowd. The fans scrambled and laughed and spilled their Coke, and one old lady laughed at her friends, and the guy who got the ball turned and waved at Harry in the radio booth, knowing Harry would observe on the radio, "Nice catch by a fan down along the first base line!"

But suddenly, as I panned the crowd, something caught me, and I panned back to find it. There in my vision, though it took me a moment to realize it, was my own dad. Far away from me, he was standing in the shade of the concourse, leaning against a steel pillar, a beer in hand, watching the game alone from shadows.

I remember my father very well in those times, at my ballgames. He stood out by the railroad maple down beyond third base—the very field where my own son plays now. The Illinois Central had put out a plaque, inlaid in a sort of gravestone, commemorating the planting of the tree on Arbor Day 1905, and my father would invariably be sitting on this stone during the games, if he could be there at all. A few times he had the old 8-mm Brownie with him and would level it at me. I remember how I felt then, but I've recently seen the films again and the impression is inescapable. I was a lot littler than I thought I was.

As I've said, I was playing short in those days. Later, in college, I played third. They don't now, and really never did, expect a shortstop to be a hitter. I console my own son with this to no avail. There was only one thing a shortstop need be able to do, and that was cover the ground. His area in the big leagues is seventy feet of real estate from behind second base to twenty feet on the second-base side of third, and in addition he must be able to drop into shallow left for pop-ups and range into foul territory behind third, about where the IC maple was at our old Pony League diamond, to rein in foul balls the third baseman has no angle on. The shortstop makes this play somewhat facing the infield, somewhat set to throw. When the shortstop fields grounders to his right, he must glove the ball backhanded; then he must be able to plant his back foot and throw overhand to first, putting a vertical spin on the ball or else the throw will sail. When he fields to his left, behind second, he must turn back into himself, tricky footwork, then throw sidearm, quick and snappy like a second baseman, or with a long whipping action if he is throwing from farther out. In turning the double play, he must choose which side of the bag to work as he pivots, according to how the runner coming into second decides to try to take him out, and also according to how the ball arrives from the second baseman or the first baseman, whoever initiates the play.

In those Pony League days, just as in the days of American Legion, Skidmore played first because his father played first, and his father, Leonard Skidmore, was our coach. My father was a local doctor, and he played shortstop as a boy. He and Leonard Skidmore were good friends. Now my boy plays shortstop. So there you are. The infield has continuity through the ages.

Another memory: I'm standing across the street from the Catholic church, on the vast lawn of the Douglas County courthouse. Father O'Daniel is pacing his front sidewalk, reading his breviary. I sit against the old silver maple under which an earlier generation of kids in the neighborhood had fashioned a makeshift home plate. Unlike the IC maple, this tree was tall and old and many times broken by lightning meant for the steeple it sheltered. It was a workhorse, a government tree. Its limbs were white with the shit of starlings and pigeons. A bored ballplayer years before had chiseled "Honus Wagner was here" into the trunk. Later someone in a generation with less time and less art had lightly and artlessly knifed "Honus Wagner sucks"—the wood and bark of the old thing took it all in and displayed it.

"How's sixth grade?" Father O'Daniel shouts over to me after a while. "It's going okay?"

"Yes, Father."

He's the one I confess self-abuse to every Saturday afternoon. No telling what all those other people are confessing to him, who stand silently with me in the confession line along the back wall of the church. There was a show on *Ford Theatre* one night of a priest who had had a murder confessed to him, then couldn't help the police because of the confidentiality code of the confessional.

Father O'Daniel had been in a car accident several months before, hurrying back to town to do a wedding after playing golf too long, and for what seemed like an endless number of spring Sundays he said mass on crutches, the altar boys, mostly eighth graders, helping him to the pulpit where he stormed after the parishioners to get them to contribute more, more for the new Catholic school he dreamed of.

I served mass on weekdays that summer. I walked to his house on those early mornings, and together we'd walk across to the church, not saying much, and in the sacristy dress for the celebration. He muttered to himself in Latin, kissed the stole before putting it on. The wood floor creaked. I rinsed and filled the cruets with water and wine. Then he rang a little bell, and we walked onto the altar, me first. Two little ladies and a farmer, the morning's congregation, rose to their feet. And the tone-deaf lady who provided the music let it rip from the balcony.

Now, on the front sidewalk, he paced too quickly, trying to heal the leg and say his office at the same time. Two birds, one stone. Like Jackie Gleason, a little traveling music. Sometimes he turned and went down the narrow white sidewalk between the church and the rectory. He'd been the local parish priest for thirty years.

"Want me to pop you a few?" he said just when I was afraid he wasn't in the mood.

"Yes, Father. If you have time."

He came across Van Allen Street, book in hand. "Did you bring the 33?"

"Yes, Father. The 30's cracked anyway." Father O'Daniel liked my Larry Doby 30 inch, but he liked my Duke Snider 33 even more.

He put his breviary on the courthouse pedestal, above a bronze frieze of a scene from the Civil War, Columbia leading the wounded Union soldiers to safety. He was raised in Ireland and didn't play baseball as a boy. But he was a talented golfer and therefore could hit rain-making fly balls. I remember how the ball became a tiny speck against the blue sky, and the thrilling speed it would gather in its fall, and the occasional tricks of the warm and humid wind. Major league infield pop-ups.

Father O'Daniel raved and raved at how I could range under those flies and haul them in. The courthouse lawn was dotted with trees, several smaller ones, of course the Honus Wagner silver maple, and one very tall cottonwood. I learned to catch a fly ball even when it nicked a few leaves, or thocked off a solid limb and went a strange direction. I would chase it, dive for it. The ground was soft loam, sweet-smelling. The satisfaction of catching the ball before it hit the ground has stayed with me my whole life. Sometimes my boy will let one drop right in front of him. He does it to drive me crazy, but still I don't see how he can stand it.

Actually, though I never told Father O'Daniel, the 33 was too big for me. I bought it at Western Auto one afternoon, for him to use.

"How's your mom?"

"Great," I said.

"How's your dad?" he asked me. He was my dad and mom's friend. He probably knew them better than I did. I often wonder.

"I don't know how he is," I said. "I don't see him much."

The pain I had in my arm in my baseball years was a dull ache, inside and just above the elbow. It wasn't the slack disconnected feeling when the rotator cuff goes. That's the shoulder, the beginning-of-the-end pain the veteran ballplayer dreads. This arm pain I had came, I'm sure, from the action of throwing a hardball, which God did not design an arm, and particularly an elbow, to do. It especially hurt on those cold blue evenings of spring when the team was out there getting ready for the season but the season hadn't come begun yet because it was too cold to play baseball. Many nights I couldn't sleep because of my arm, and I worried that it was the beginning-of-the-end pain and kept it a secret so no one would know. Baseball was everything to me then.

I was playing with other pains, too. Pony League was the first level of youth baseball in which steel spikes were worn, and at shortstop you'd get spiked covering second on double plays. I had been stitched in one knee for what seemed like the better part of that particular summer. I'd chased a fly ball down the third-base line, chased it beyond foul territory out onto the access road—there was no fence then—I could not let this ball fall to the ground—and ran full speed head-on into two girls who were riding by on their bikes. We all went down in a heap, and the ball landed among us. Thus, it was an inane but somehow heroic wound, and after putting the stitches in, my dad went on with work and summer, apparently forgetting they were there. Every move I made that summer, it seemed, tore the stitches.

In those days, too, we had the usual strawberries on our butts and legs from sliding on the hard sandy base paths. The worst place to slide in back-country (that is, not professional) baseball was home, because invariably the dirt had eroded from around the plate, which had dried out and gotten brittle and extracted its pound of flesh as you sliced over it in your desperate desire to score. Invariably the dirt of the back-country baseball infield was either gritty and sandy or like cracked concrete, bad bad bad for sliding.

Another common wound was a swollen mouth, from bad bounces. If the infielder was getting swollen ears instead, he got benched. He wasn't watching the ball. I tell my son, watch the ball.

In one of those baseball summers, I came to understand my father was an alcoholic, and so, back then, there was also an oppressive pain of the spirit that seemed to invade everything. The films he took of me playing ball tended to hop a little sometimes, and the focus was often dubious. Many young men, I know now, will recall the same experience — miserable and humiliating. Your father would stand beneath the IC maple down by third, and he would embarrass you with distracting, weak, complaining taunts, some of which would bring laughter from the other parents in the crowd. The time came when I dreaded him showing up.

In my sophomore year in high school, after six years of handling all this the best I could, the culminating thing of my childhood happened. He had come to one of my games, as usual not falling-down drunk but well on his way — flushed and belligerent and loud. That night I got home before he did after the game. I waited for him in the garage. I sat around, on the lawnmower, on a pile of drying logs, in a swing in the backyard, eventually on the back bumper of Mom's car. Waiting. I didn't know what I was going to say, but I'd decided I wasn't going to take any more of this shit from him.

Finally, just at dusk, his car headlights swept up the driveway. Instinctively, I retreated. I jumped for a crossbeam and swung up into the dark upper reaches of the garage where we stored scrap lumber and extra shingles.

He pulled in right under me. I noticed, watching him from above as he climbed out of the car, how alone and tired he seemed. He pulled a box from the back seat and hid it carefully under logs at the back of the garage. Then he straightened himself, straightened his shirt, and shuffled in his leather soles out into the evening light and across the gravel to the house.

It was a cache of Old Fitzgerald that he'd hidden. I got my .22 from the basement and I set the box on the hood of his car and, with ten loud shots at very close range, I reduced it to sweet-smelling glassy rubble and put a couple of rounds through the windshield for good measure.

On the stairs in the house later that night, he caught me going down, him coming up. He'd slipped out there for a nightcap and made the discovery. "Watch yourself, Junior," he said to me. He had a hold of my shirt. "I'm not perfect. I never said I was." He didn't seem like my father as he said this. I looked right in his eyes and got a terrible feeling. He was giving me a warning from the underworld, one bad boy to another.

Memory: The sun is going down. Irv, an older man, holds an old 34-inch Nelly Fox thick-handled bat, the handle wrapped with friction tape. Irv is wearing bib overalls, black workboots he scuttles through the dust in. I'm sitting on the bleachers, ball glove next to me. Home from college, 1966. Irv shouts at his boy, who is out in left waiting for the ball. "Keep it low," he says. "Just 'cause the guy hits you a high one doesn't mean you throw a damned pop-fly back in." He spits. He gestures low. "Think of it," he says. "Shortest distance between two things."

Now he lifts the bat to his shoulder. It has gotten four shades of darkness darker since the lowness lecture began. He smacks a hard line drive, left center. The boy comes across, takes it on the bounce, and fires it to the plate—you hear him grunt. He's six or seven years younger than me, maybe a freshman in high school. The ball hisses as it flies, skips once and slams against the green boards of the backstop behind the plate.

"Hell of a throw, son." Irv smiles, the bat down again at his side, staring out toward the outfield. "That was a great throw."

I applaud. I want into the action. Like all people in this town, when Irv looks at me it's with the searching-through-time look—can he find a face in my face that's a face he knows?

"Wanna shag a few?" he says.

"I'll take the cut-off," I tell him, and his son backs up to the fence as I trot out to shortstop. Left fielders need to hit the cut-off man.

Now, after a number of years away, I'm standing on the Pony League field I played on, about eighty yards from the Little League field where I learned. A thousand evenings like this come to mind. I remember this diamond when it had no grass, was solid dirt, and the wind would always kick it up into your eyes. And I remember, with a lot of pain, the railroad maple where Dad would stand to watch my ballgames, and the commemorative stone beneath its now embracing shade.

From there he'd point the old Brownie movie camera at me. In our home movies, blanching out with age, the leaves of this old tree when it was years younger wave in the foreground. "Gives it depth," the photographer would tell us from the dark on projection night.

There had been old white outhouses on the far end of the park, and I remember sitting in there on a one-holer looking at the splayed obstetrical graffiti and not knowing what I was looking at or if the drawing was for some reason upside down. The word *fuck* was frequently carved with pocketknives in the pine of the outhouses. Successive paint-jobs had miserably failed to cover over generations and tides of *fuck* going back who knew how far. I looked around from my position to see if the outhouses were still out there. They weren't.

"You're Landen's boy," Irv says to me, points at me with the bat. He found my face. "Aren't ya?"

"Yes."

"We were real sorry," he says. He cracks a line drive to his son, down the left-field line.

I move over to the line and out, until I'm between third and Irv's son and have both hands in the air for the cut-off. The boy sends the ball way over my head, all the way to the plate. Before it gets there, his dad is yelling. "What are you *doing?* Everybody's running! You can't throw people out from there! Hit the shortstop! Hit him! His dad brought you into this world!"

That kid, Irv's son, later married a girl named Missy Stowe.

In college, 1966, two years after my father was killed in a car wreck, Skidmore and I had a major falling-out. It was simple why. At a party which I did not attend, he'd quietly passed along to those who were attending that my father had had, in earlier days, an affair with some woman in town. I never knew the source of this rumor, but always suspected Skidmore's dad was somehow at the root of it.

The next morning I was in bed when my mom yelled up that I had a phone call.

"Hi, it's me." It was a girl named Kitty whom I'd sometimes dated.

"Last night," she said, "your pal Skidmore said something I think you ought to know about. He said your dad had an affair a few years ago, with the lady Mrs. Stowe, at the hospital."

I sat there. Something like that had never occurred to me. In fact, it took me a laughable ten seconds to imagine what Kitty meant by the word "affair." Then my initial reaction was that this was another vicious thing Skidmore dreamed up to say, being mean in a lot of ways. But then I realized something about him—that his meanness was rarely in outright lies, more often in the brutal administering of the truth.

"He said there might even have been a child," Kitty said.

I knew Mrs. Stowe's youngest daughter, who was then about nine. By subtraction, we came to the summer of 1957. I recalled seeing him through the binoculars, standing alone in the shadows, my first trip to the ball park.

I could tell you a great story about Leonard Skidmore, my old coach. He was a first baseman way back when, but when the war came, World War II, and he was drafted, he went to Europe and you might think in the middle of war he forgot baseball. It happened that he was in the Battle of the Bulge, and so was Warren Spahn. In the evenings Leonard would scout out a catcher's mitt and let Spahnie throw him a few. Spahn was already well known, famous even. His return from his duty fighting the war was anxiously awaited by Johnny Sain and the Boston Braves. To hear him tell it, Leonard had to get a slab of ham from the mess officer to put inside the mitt, to take out a little of the big league sting. Anyway, there they were, my friend Skidmore's dad and Warren Spahn, playing catch at the Battle of the Bulge.

Cliff Webb, who provided me with my Opening Day hangover, was three years older than me, and it turned out that he had mostly played catcher later on. He had always seemed easy-going, but now, in middle age, he had very oily skin and nervous, worried eyes. He'd sat down next to me at the bar (I'd been there a while), recognized me past the beard in just a few seconds, and, even though we hadn't seen each other in twenty years, a minute didn't pass before he embarked on a long joke about tits and the Pope.

I had heard that he had a reputation for being tough on wives — in fact, had been in jail for beating up one of them. Which was a lot like his father, who'd been in jail for something right during the time Cliff and I'd been playing ball together. I assumed the scars on his face were where his women raked him as they were going down for the count.

"I remember your dad," he said to me. "Yelling at you to hit behind the runner. Hell, at the time I didn't even know what he meant. He'd yell, 'Okay, touch any base, touch any base!'" Cliff was laughing. "There we were, twelve or whatever. Your dad, he must have known a lot about baseball."

"The game got inside him early. Like us." I told Cliff that one night, after going to a game between the Cardinals and the Giants, how Dad and I had wandered into the coffee shop at the hotel (it was where the Giants were staying) and Dad ended up sitting at the counter talking baseball with Harvey Kuenn. "Remember Harvey?"

"Managed the Brewers in '82, right? Against St. Louis in fact, and the Cardinals won."

"Yikes, Cliffy! That's good!" Cliff knew his baseball. "Back then though, Harvey was playing third for the Giants. '62. Chase Park Plaza in St. Louis. By that time they were even letting Willie McCovey swim in the hotel pool."

Cliff looked toward the mirror behind the bar. "Well, he was something, your dad. I'll bet everyone on our team remembers how he yelled for you."

"*At* me, more like it." I laughed but a couple of memories hit me that weren't so funny.

"Whatever happened to that asshole Skidmore?"

I always wonder how people weather time in other people's minds.

"Lives in Nebraska, I think. Somewhere out there. He's an attorney."

"Oh boy, that's about what I'd expect. He go to Vietnam, do you know?"

"Nope."

"You?"

"Nope."

I could see stuff well up in Cliff. He needed to talk about Vietnam, so we did, getting plowed on beer which he was buying for us by the pitcher. I was turned on my stool and had a good view of the whole bar. In fact, I was deep in eye games with a woman sitting at a corner table way off behind Cliff. She was my age, maybe younger, but hard—maybe older, who could tell in the dark?

He was talking about Vietnam, but now he sold for State Farm and a lot of that kind of language invaded his speech and bored me. After he told me about the war, he briefly skirted his marriages, then hit upon the topic of an old fishing rod he loved. Once in a while I'd glance over his right shoulder at the woman in the corner. She seemed shy in a way, looking down. But then she'd be looking my way the next time I looked hers. A couple of times we held the gaze a moment before one or the other of us looked away. He was repeating himself—I'd missed something in the conversation. He seemed to reach for my arm to regain my attention: "Hey, you ever play softball?"

"No."

"Pretty good shape. Ought to."

"Nope. Wish I did. Maybe sometime."

The woman in the corner, her hair was dark brown, held back with a ribbon and flower.

"Wish I did," I said.

Vietnam found its way back into the conversation. Cliff had been a marine, and had a very rough time. Fifteen years had passed, and it still wasn't settled inside of him. He said he'd like to go back. He said it was where he knew himself best. I was thinking it was where he *left* himself.

The woman in the corner half smiled at me once. She seemed to be alone, although in a little town like this it was in bad taste for a woman to show up at a bar alone.

Cliff was talking about Hill 881, and how he'd watched from a hilltop as NVA tanks ran over a number of little villages on the way to the siege of Khe San. Once the woman seemed almost to toast me with her beer—she raised it, nodded my way. Suddenly Cliff lost the sort of flat drone and raised his voice. "Hey. Now look. You gonna listen to me or you gonna play games with her?" I looked at him. I was disoriented, because I'd just been deep in a little game with her. He was looking right at me, his eyes watering. There was a question on the floor. He swiveled on his bar stool, looked at her, then back at me. "Really. Forget it. I'm supposed to meet some people anyway." He polished off the last of his beer and was getting up to leave.

"Sorry, Cliff, I really am."

"Well, damn. It's real irritating."

"Yeah."

He'd gotten my apology but he was angry and seemed to want more. "I *hate* talkin' to somebody, their eyes climbing the wall."

"I don't blame you."

"I mean, you gonna talk to me, or you gonna watch her," he said, his face red in its many creases.

"Well, since you ask, Cliff," I said, putting my hand on his shoulder, "—I'm gonna do both." I poured us more beer from the pitcher. "I'm not perfect either."

The woman in the bar, she wasn't Missy Stowe, who is probably my half sister. The town isn't *that* small.

I know the people in this town too well. I really ought to move away. When I go to my boy's ballgames, I frankly can't stand to watch the game from the bleachers, among old classmates who now work at the post office and the plant, among Dad's old patients who will take the time to tell me about an ailment or ask me something I don't know the answer to about how things have turned out since he died. And I don't know what his last words were—car wrecks can kill you without last words. I don't know if he's up there looking down. I don't know what to say to people, so I dodge them the way Dad did. I take the video camera and find that great shade down beyond third base under the IC maple, where the angle on the infield is good for picture-taking and a fellow can have a drink if he needs one.

Baseball

RAY GONZALEZ

The home run ball rose over right field and disappeared before it started its downward arc. The right fielder backed to the warning path, but there was no ball to catch. He stood dazed as the roar of the crowd turned to confusion. Thousands of fans were on their feet for the home run. But, where was it? The hitter, a national hero who led the league in home runs, slowed to a hesitant jog as he rounded first base. The first and second basemen stood at their positions, one of them removing his cap from his head as he searched the night sky for the ball. The hitter nodded to the closest umpire, as if asking permission to keep running the bases, though he kept going. Managers, coaches, and players from both benches came out of the dugout. Unable to lower their heads from searching for the ball, some of the players stumbled over each other in front of the dugouts. The manager of the team at bat waved to his batter to keep running. The opposing manager ran toward one of the umpires. There was no ball, just the memory of the loud whack as the player's bat met the ball and sent it rocketing toward the right field bleachers. The ball's rapid trajectory was the last thing anyone recalled before it vanished. Thousands of witnesses amplified their stunned silence with a magnetic restlessness. With two men on base, the home run would give the visiting team a 3–2 lead in the first game of the World Series. It was the bottom half of the sixth inning. Where was the ball? As the hitter, his mouth agape, rounded third and headed home, the right fielder ran as fast as he could toward the second base umpire. With his confused manager joining him, both men screamed at the umpire to do something. The right fielder claimed the ball had not been hit hard enough for a home run. He screamed that he was in position to catch it when it vanished. His manager yelled that the three runs should not count because there was no ball hit out of the park. The opposing manager was welcoming his hero at home plate. He was not going to argue with anybody, even though he had no idea what had happened to the ball. In his book, it was a home run and the ball's speed and height made that obvious to the entire stadium before it disappeared. The beleaguered umpire at second base walked toward the umpire at first. He was surrounded by angry players and one red-faced manager. The first base umpire was coming to his defense when, suddenly, the ball appeared in the night sky. It fell where the right fielder was previously standing and settled in the warning path. Thousands of spectators saw it and both teams saw it. They pointed, screamed, and waved, but it was too late. The bases had been run, the three men had scored, and it would be ruled an inside-the-park home run. The last thing reported in the sports pages of every major newspaper was the right fielder running from the umpire he had been attacking, to the ball in the right field corner. He picked it out of the dirt and stared at it. What was not reported was his surprise at how old and yellow the baseball was. The stitches were coming off, and the ball was slightly warped. Some balls looked like that after a good hit, but this one was different. He threw it to the cut-off man at second, who also noticed how old the ball was. He picked it out of his glove and handed it to the umpire who was recovering from being attacked. When the umpire realized he had not seen this brand of baseball since his dirt lot days in the fifties, he tucked it into his coat pocket. The home plate umpire threw out another ball. When the papers carried the story, the second base umpire was surprised no sports writer asked him about the ball. Maybe it was because the home team won by a score of 5–3, three more runs coming on base hits. After the game, the umpire took his coat off in the umpire's dressing room and searched the pockets, but couldn't find the antique ball.

Pray for Rain

KIP KOTZEN

I can still remember exactly what was for dinner that night, even though I didn't eat a thing. Grilled asparagus, a beet risotto, and an entire Alaskan king salmon stuffed with fresh herbs and baked in salt. Gus had handwritten the menu on the inside cover of gold-foil matchbooks and sent them out as invitations. The dessert was Rum Baba, and all that morning on the phone, Gus couldn't stop saying those two words, interjecting them randomly into every single sentence. "Hey Rum Baba it's Gus Rum Baba. There's Rum Baba some stuff I need. Can Rum Baba you pick up Rum Baba some things for me."

"What's with all the Rum Babas. What are you talking about?" I asked.

"Rum Baba, Rum Baba, Rum Baba. It's all I can think about. It's the dessert."

I took out my matchbook, and there it was, etched carefully at the bottom of the menu, right above the date, Rum Baba. I'd thought it was kind of crazy that Gus had mailed me an invitation because he had been telling me daily about this dinner for a month.

"What exactly is Rum Baba?" I regretted my question almost as I said it. If he got rolling, Gus's explanation could take an hour. He was only truly passionate about three things: food, baseball, and Maggie, and of the three, food was the only one he'd discuss. He'd start talking about shitake mushrooms and his eyes would get a faraway look.

Instead of rambling though, he was very succinct. All he said was, "You'll see tonight."

He was wrong. All that I ever saw of the Rum Baba that night was a big bowl of batter and a half empty bottle of rum that Gus was sucking down like soda pop. I've seen Rum Baba offered on dessert menus twice since that evening, but I haven't ordered it, and I never will. The true nature of Rum Baba has become one of life's little mysteries that I hold on to dearly.

Maggie was coming into New York from Los Angeles just for this dinner party. Then Gus and Maggie were flying to San Francisco the next night and then driving to Mendocino for their wedding. The ceremony would be just family: Gus's mom, his sister Ruthie, and Maggie's mom. Gus's father was dead, and Maggie was an only child, and her dad, well nobody was really sure where he was.

That's the way Gus wanted it—have a dinner party in New York with his closest friends, then fly back to California for the wedding. I really don't think Gus wanted any of his friends to be at the wedding. I think what he really wanted was Maggie all to himself. He'd have been perfectly happy with a judge and an anonymous witness, then a honeymoon on a deserted island. Other than the dinner, the only thing that Gus planned to do in New York was to go to Yankee Stadium to see the Red Sox. I told Gus that it seemed like an inordinate amount of flying for Maggie, back and forth from California to New York in two days.

"First of all," Gus had told me, "I'm making a very special meal. And secondly, Clemens is pitching."

Gus's dad had played in the majors. He spent most of the nineteen forty-eight season with the Boston Braves. He didn't play much, but the Braves won the pennant and in the last week of the season he caught back-to-back shutouts from Warren Spahn and Johnny Sain and hit a homer in each game. When the season ended, he volunteered for the Service, and the next spring, when he should have been battling for the starting catcher's job, he went to fight in Korea and took a .50mm slug in his hip. He bounced around the minors for ten years as a coach before he met Gus's mom. Gus's mom's father had made a mint selling those curly french fries that you get at amusement parks and state fairs. The ones they spell K-u-r-l-e-y F-r-y-e-s with the Old English–style letters, and Gus's dad left baseball to become a french fry salesman.

I learned some of Gus's family history from some old newspapers that he had neatly bundled in a cardboard box under his bed and I had found in college snooping around for his stash of marijuana, and also from two long letters from his mother that Gus had started to burn one night when he was drunk and he passed out in mid-singe, almost torching the apartment we shared in college in the process.

The rest I learned from his little sister, though that was before I really knew Gus at all. Gus and I met on Martha's Vineyard the summer before our senior year in high school. A girl named Amanda Curtis introduced us, really by accident. It was the last day of the summer, nineteen eighty-two, and we were at a party in Oak Bluffs, just at the top of Circuit Ave. Amanda and I were in the bathroom on the second floor and we were both pretty drunk. The tile in the shower was alternating squares of pink and green, and it was making me dizzy. I had just taken her bra off when she asked me where I was from and I told her, "Manchester, New Hampshire."

"I thought so," she slurred, "because Gus Exel is from Manchester and I've been dying to meet him. He's downstairs right now. Will you introduce me?" Then she passed out cold.

I put her shirt back on, kept her bra as a souvenir, very gently stretched her out on the bathroom rug, and went downstairs to look for Gus. I had been desperately angling for a ride home, some way to avoid the Peter Pan Line bus-ride-from-hell that made something like seventy-three stops before you'd even get to Boston, and I realized that Amanda was actually an angel sent to deliver me. I found him sitting by himself, puffing on a fat joint. Our conversation was memorable only for its brevity.

"Are you Gus Exel?"

"Yeah."

"Are you from Manchester?"

"Yeah."

"Got a ride home?"

"Yeah."

"Can I come?"

"I guess so. But I'm leaving tomorrow morning on the seven o'clock boat from Vineyard Haven. Don't miss the ferry, because we won't wait for you." Then he took a nice drawn out toke on his joint, held it for what seemed like much too long for his own good, and got up and went back into the party.

Gus's mom was waiting for us in Falmouth when we got off the ferry. She had brought along Gus's little sister Ruthie and they were in the parking lot, leaning up against a new green station wagon.

"It's avocado," Ruthie blurted out to me as I bent down to say hello. As she spoke, a small piece of her spit flew up and across and landed right underneath my left eye. "That's the color of our station wagon. Avocado. Mom let me pick it out myself." Almost as an afterthought she added, "Did I spit on you? I've been doing that a lot lately. I do it when I say contractions. The ones with s's. Not don't or can't or words like that."

I looked over at Gus. He had his hands wedged in his pockets and was balancing on one leg like a stork. He seemed different; nervous, edgy, like he really just wanted to get this ride home over with and if he hadn't been so stoned the night before he wouldn't have ever said I could come along.

When we started to get near the New Hampshire border, Gus and his mom started to argue. The only thing was that they were doing it so obliquely that I had no idea what they were talking about. It had something to do with going somewhere and I started to get the feeling that I was the reason that Gus didn't want to go there. I guess Gus's mom won the argument because when we got to Nashua we pulled off the highway and Gus said he had to go and visit his dad in the hospital.

We drove for ten miles or so, through what seemed like the worst part of Nashua, past dilapidated factories and through empty train yards. Finally, standing alone, surrounded by a giant chain-link fence with rolls of barbed wire on top was a huge yellow-brick hospital. The guard at the gate waved us through immediately.

Mrs. Exel parked in the visitors' lot. Gus told me I could stay in the car if I wanted to and I was going to until I found out that his mom was going to stay in the car too, so I got out of the car and went inside the hospital with Gus and Ruthie. I wasn't sure if Gus was too polite or was just too nervous to tell me he didn't want me to come in with him.

Mr. Exel was in the psychiatric ward on the sixth floor. When we got to his room Gus knocked on the door. There was no answer and so we went right in. Mr. Exel didn't even acknowledge us. The room was bare, not even a dresser, just a hospital cot and a big oil panting of an old sailboat on one wall that looked like it was done with a paint-by-numbers kit. Gus's dad was squatting by the side of his bed, rocking back and forth like he was still balanced behind home plate at Braves Field. We stepped into the room and as we got closer, we could hear him murmuring something to himself, barely audibly. "Spahn and Sain and pray for rain. Spahn and Sain and pray for rain," he said, over and over. Ruthie went over and gave him a hug, but he didn't seem to even notice her. Gus just stood there, his arms clenched tightly across his chest, and stared down at the floor.

After a few minutes, which seemed like hours, I went over to Ruthie, who was perching near her dad, telling him about learning ballet in summer camp. "I think it's time to go," I told her, and she turned and left with me. Gus stayed in the room for a moment, let us get down the hall a bit, then followed us to the elevator, shuffling his feet all the way.

And that was the defining moment of our friendship. I had seen his father and it was as though I had peered into the depths of Gus's soul for a brief moment in time when he had entered there himself and had forgotten to close the door behind him. The polished veneer of cool that he had worn at the party on Martha's Vineyard had now been officially shattered.

When we got back to the parking lot, Gus wandered away, and Ruthie, who had grabbed on to my thumb in the elevator on the way down and hadn't let go, told me all about their father, or at least all that she knew. I'm always amazed and often overjoyed by the candor, straightforwardness, and uncensored nature of kids under the age of seven. Turning seven seems to signal an increased awareness and a higher level of understanding, and with it, unfortunately, comes caution and reticence. What goes, usually forever it seems, is honesty.

Ruthie was still six. I walked with her around the grounds of the General R. G. Slocum Memorial Veteran's Administration Hospital in Nashua, New Hampshire, and she clenched my thumb like it was the only handle of understanding left to her in the world. She said that he was just like everybody else's daddy until she was four and he went into one of those batting cages with the pitching machines at the Vermont State Fair.

"He set it super fast, like Roger Clemens, and Daddy wouldn't get out. Then he went into a fug." I had heard of people snapping, of fugues, of people being put away, but until that moment, walking across the neatly mowed grass behind the V.A. hospital with Ruthie Exel, it never seemed real. Now it was more real than I wanted it to be.

No one spoke much on the rest of the trip. Ruthie and I were in the back, and she fell asleep, her canary yellow Pro-Keds wedged tightly between the seat and my back. When the Exels dropped me off at my house, my mom came out to invite them in, but I knew from the look on Gus's face that it was a bad idea. "No, Mom. Everyone's tired. I think the Exels just want to go home."

After that, it seemed like Gus and I had to become best friends. It was that or never speak again. Gus's dad died the next year, right after we got to college. We never talked about that day at the hospital but it spawned our secret mantra, to be used only on the very rare special occasion of unbridled joy or tortured despair. Gus said it first. It was our first year at Brown. He had just met Maggie for the first time and he came back to our apartment breathless. When he caught his breath he crouched down and started chanting, "Spahn and Sain and pray for rain. Spahn and Sain and pray for rain." He knew I remembered and I'll never forget the way he looked at me, like nothing this important had ever happened to him before. "I just met the woman I'm going to marry," he finally said. He looked dizzy. He repeated the mantra and then looked at me solemnly. "Go ahead, say it," he told me, "it's okay." And I did, again and again, letting it drip off my tongue. It was like a Vedic chant, and I swear that Gus could repeat it for hours on end.

It made sense that it was a baseball phrase that meant so much to Gus. Baseball was his religion, and his father was the martyred saint, but Gus was more the reluctant missionary than the evangelical minister. Gus kept a scorecard for every game he watched, even on television, his left hand curled around the scorecard like a kid hiding the answers to an algebra quiz. He wouldn't even let me look at them. He kept them in neat stacks by home team by season. I think the combination of his father's aborted career and being a lifetime Red Sox fan was more than one person should be allowed to bear. When the ball rolled through Bill Buckner's legs and Ray Knight raced home from second base in game six of the '86 World Series he really almost keeled over. Gus and I were in a bar in Providence. I had dragged him away from the TV in his room. "When the Sox win tonight," I told him, "you should be able to share some joy." The bar was packed and it turned out that ninety-eight percent of the people in the bar were Mets fans. It was impossible to hear the television over the din of the drunken crowd, but Gus had brought his headphone radio. Not the puny modern kind, but the kind with the big padded ear-muffs and an antenna like the Eiffel Tower. He looked as if he was ready to signal an airplane that the runway was all clear as he stood at the bar, as close to the TV as possible, oblivious to everyone around him.

The game ended with Bill Buckner standing alone near first, arms akimbo, staring blankly out into space, the "Mookie Ball" lying in state near the right field line twenty million miles behind him. Gus, standing at the bar, had the same lost look as Buckner. The Mets were leaping joy-ously around home plate and the Mets fans at the bar were going wild, high five-ing each other and shaking up long-neck Buds, spraying every-body in sight. Gus clutched the worn wooden rail of the bar as if it was a Louisville Slugger. I grabbed Gus's arm and led him outside and took him home. He went straight to bed, his earmuff radio still humming. "There's still one more game, there's still game seven," I kept telling him, but we both knew it was over, that the Curse of the Bambino had struck once again, and that the Sox would never win the World Series again.

That night I couldn't fall asleep, and around two in the morning I knocked softly on Gus's door. The light next to his bed was on but Gus's eyes were closed. I went to turn off the light and Gus spoke.

"No. That's okay. You can leave it on." His voice was smooth and even. "Hey. Do you remember that clipper ship?" Gus asked me.

I didn't know what he was talking about.

"The painting of the clipper ship in my dad's room at the hospital. Do you remember it?"

I did remember it now and I mumbled a yes.

"You know, I painted that myself." He lay there for a moment, his eyes still closed. "I guess you can turn the light off now."

The guests for the dinner party had just started to arrive and Gus was in full swing racing around the kitchen when the phone rang. Gus answered it, but didn't say a word, just listened intently and then put the phone back into its cradle slowly and carefully, like it was injured and had to be nestled gently for it to survive.

"That was Maggie. She's not coming. She never got on the plane.

She's still in Los Angeles." Gus sounded out each syllable, breaking up the words into small staccato noises like a stuttering child.

"What? You're kidd-" I stopped myself abruptly when I saw that he wasn't. "What is she going to do? What did she say to you?"

"I don't know. She said something about spending some time in Palm Springs. She spent the day driving through the desert and now she's at her mom's condo. She said she couldn't do it. She decided that it wasn't right."

"'Wasn't right?' What the hell is that supposed to mean?" As I said this I looked right into Gus's eyes. What scared me wasn't that he looked devastated but was that he looked so completely resigned.

"She's not coming. She's not coming," Gus mumbled and as I looked once again into his eyes, I could see the reflection of his father, rocking slowly back and forth on his heels. "Here," he said, handing me his favorite marine blue ceramic bowl, overflowing now with shiny grilled asparagus, "these are done." He was crying now. Tears plopped down right into the bowl, each drop pausing for a fraction of a second on the glistening surface of the asparagus, then disappearing forever amongst the slender green stalks. "You know what? She was happy when I was with her."

"What the fuck are you going to do now?" I blurted. It was the wrong question, or the right question asked too soon, but it just popped out.

"Well, I guess I'll go to Mendocino anyway. I can't get the money back on the cottage." He paused for a moment and looked right through me. He seemed strangely calm, like all this had happened before over and over in his head a million times. "I'll sit on the porch and stare at the ocean and I'll pray for rain."

Gus came back to New York last summer. He stayed in Mendocino for almost two years, and during the entire time he was gone I only spoke to him twice. He called me a week after he left and told me he didn't think he'd be coming back anytime soon and asked me if I could give Ruthie, who was going to be a freshman at Columbia, the extra set of keys to his apartment. He sounded very distant. The next time he called me was the week he moved back to New York. He had gotten married in Mendocino. His wife was twenty-one years old, her name was April, she wanted to be an actress, and she had lived her whole life in Mendocino, California.

Ruthie was the one who told me all of this. At first I thought she was kidding me, but she wasn't.

When Gus came back, he opened a coffee bar on Spring Street, just around the corner from my office. I went in the day it opened to congratulate him and he gave me a gold embossed card with the words "Free Coffee" on one side. Without thinking I started to say that it reminded me of his invitations to his dinner party for Maggie. I caught myself before I really said anything at all, but it wasn't quite in time. I know Gus knew what I was about to say. He looked at me and shook his head. "This is just for free coffee."

"Free coffee. All I want. How long is it good for, a week, two weeks?" I was a bit incredulous. "How many of these things are there? It's probably some promotion that just ended yesterday."

"It's good until the Red Sox win the World Series," Gus told me, deadpan as ever. "Or forever. Whichever comes first. And there are two cards." He looked at me very seriously and we both knew who the other card was for and it wasn't April. April was in the corner of the room, sitting at a table. She seemed different than Maggie in every single way, except for her mouth. She had Maggie's mouth and I knew that was what had drawn Gus to her. She was reading sides of a script, almost audibly, her full moist lips sounding out each syllable. Gus looked at April, then looked at me, then back at April again. Then he spoke very solemnly, "I don't think people fall out of love. I think they just try to fall in love again."

Maggie still calls me about once a month, sometimes in the middle of the night. She always uses the exact same line. "I didn't wake you, did I?" She takes her time getting around to talking about Gus, but she always does. "Seen Gus lately?" she'll ask and I always answer the same way, that I see him almost every day, that I just can't resist unlimited free coffee, but that we don't talk much. "What's he like now?" she asks me again and again and I always tell her the same thing: "I don't really know."

Maggie called me again last night. I think that she was a little bit drunk. I had never asked her about the party that Gus had thrown for her. We'd always shadow-boxed around it, a few feints, a lot of backpedaling. But last night she brought it up.

"I don't know what you thought I did that night but I never told Gus that I was coming to New York or that we were getting married," she said to me. "I mean he asked me to marry him and he invited me to New York. He even sent me a first class plane ticket and a ticket to a baseball game and a gold matchbook with a menu in it but I never said I was coming to New York. I never said I was coming. I hadn't even talked to him in almost a month. He had made me stop calling him. He said it was just too difficult to talk to me if we weren't going to be together. Then he just sent a ticket and told me he didn't want me to call. He just wanted me to come or not to come." She paused to catch her breath and I could hear that gentle gulping sound that follows when words spill out too fast. "The weird thing is how close I came to going. I even packed a bag and drove myself to the airport. I think I must have circled around that loop at LAX about thirty times. It just seemed like each time I was going to veer off to long-term parking, there was always a car in my way, and then I finally just went home."

I've never told Gus this, and I never will, but I wanted the Mets to beat the Red Sox. I'm still not exactly sure why. Maybe I just liked the Mets more, thought that Keith and Doc and Daryl were a hell of a lot cooler than Calvin Schiraldi and Wade Boggs, but maybe it was because Gus wanted the Sox to win so badly. Maybe we can only want so much happiness for our friends. Maybe what we really want most is for our friends to need us more than we need them. For them to fail and then we'll pick them up and dust them off.

I don't know if Gus and Maggie made a mistake, if they really were meant to be together. I think that Gus loved Maggie because she would never commit to him and Maggie would never commit to Gus because he really did love her, but I'm not sure. I'll never understand what Gus and Maggie had together, and that's okay, because I can't. We can't understand why other people love each other, or why they don't. It's impossible. Friendship is chemistry, full of equations that can be written on a chalkboard, two molecules of hydrogen plus one molecule of oxygen equals water. Love is different. Love is alchemy, two people trying to change something common into something precious, and in the end, only they can know if they've turned lead into gold.

The Barbarians

PATRICIA HIGHSMITH

Stanley Hubbell painted on Sundays, the only day he had to paint. Saturdays he helped his father in the hardware store in Brooklyn. Weekdays he worked as a researcher for a publishing house specializing in trade journals. Stanley did not take his painting very seriously: it was a kind of occupational therapy for his nerves recommended by his doctor. After six months, he was painting fairly well.

One Sunday in early June, Stanley was completing a portrait of himself in a white shirt with a green background. It was larger than his first self-portrait, and it was much better. He had caught the troubled frown of his left eyebrow. The eyes were finished—light brown, a little sad, intense, hopeful. Hopeful of what? Stanley didn't know. But the eyes on the canvas were so much his own eyes they made him smile with pleasure when he looked at them. There remained the highlight to put down the long, somewhat crooked nose, and then to darken the background.

He had been working perhaps twenty minutes, hardly long enough to moisten his brushes or limber up the colours on his palette, when he heard them stomping through the narrow alley at the side of his building. He hesitated, while half his mind still imagined the unpainted highlight down the nose and the other half listened to find out how many there were going to be this afternoon.

Do it now, he told himself, and quickly bent toward the canvas, his left hand clutching the canvas frame, his right hand braced against his left forearm. The point of his brush touched the bridge of his nose.

"Let's *have* it, Franky!"

"*Yee-hoooo!*"

"Ah, g'wan! *What dyuh think I wanna do? Fight the whole god-damn . . .*"

"Ah-ha-*haaaaaaah!*"

"Put it *here,* Franky!"

Thud!

They always warmed up for fifteen minutes or so with a hard ball and catchers' mitts.

Stanley's brush stopped after half an inch. He paused, hoping for a lull, knowing there wouldn't be any. The braying voices went on, twenty feet below his window, bantering, directing one another, explaining, exhorting.

"*Get the goddamn bush outa the way! Pull it up!*" a voice yelled. Stanley flinched as if it had been said to him.

Two Sundays ago they had had quite an exchange about the bushes. One of the men had tumbled over them in reaching for the ball, and Stanley, seeing it, had shouted down: "Would you please not go against the hedge?" It burst out of him involuntarily—he was sorry he had not made the remark a lot stronger—and they had all joined in yelling back at him: "What d'yuh think this is, your lot?" and "Who're you, the gardener?—Hedges! Hah!"

Stanley edged closer to the window, close enough to see the bottom of the brick wall that bounded the far side of the lot. There were still five little bushes standing in front of the wall, forlorn and scraggly, but still standing, still growing—at this minute. Stanley had put them there. He had found them growing, or rather struggling for survival, in cindery corners of the lot and by the ash-cans at the end of the alley. None of the bushes was more than two feet tall, but they were unmistakably hedge bushes. He had transplanted them for two reasons; to hide the ugly wall somewhat and to put the plants in a spot where they could get some sunshine. It had been a tiny gesture toward beautifying something that was, essentially, unbeautifiable, but he had made the effort and it had given him satisfaction. And the men seemed to know he had planted them, perhaps because he had shouted down to watch out for them, and also because the superintendent, who was never around and barely took care of the garbage cans, would never have done anything like set out hedge bushes by a brick wall.

Moving nearer the window, Stanley could see the men. There were five of them today, deployed around the narrow rectangular lot, throwing the ball to one another in no particular order, which meant that four were at all times yelling for the ball to be thrown to them.

"Here y'are Joey, *here!*"

Thud!

They were all men of thirty or more, and two had the beginnings of paunches. One of the paunchy men was redheaded and he had the loudest, most unpleasant voice, though it was the dark-haired man in blue jeans who yelled the most, really never stopped yelling, even when he caught and threw the ball, and by the same token none of his companions seemed to pay any attention to what he said. The redheaded man's name was Franky, Stanley had learned, and the dark-haired man was Bob. Two of the others had cleated shoes, and pranced and yelled between catches, lifting their knees high and pumping their arms.

"*Wanna see me break a window?*" yelled Franky, winding up. He slammed the ball at one of the cleat-shod men, who let out a wail as he caught it as if it had killed him.

Why was he watching it, Stanley asked himself. He looked at his clock. Only twenty past two. They would play until five, at least. Stanley was aware of a nervous trembling inside him, and he looked at his hands. They seemed absolutely steady. He walked to his canvas. The portrait looked like paint and canvas now, nothing more. The voices might have been in the same room with him. He went to one window and closed it. It was really too hot to close both windows.

Then, from somewhere above him, Stanley heard a window go up, and as if it were a signal for battle, he stiffened: the window-opener was on his side. Stanley stood a little back from the window and looked down at the lot.

"Hey!" the voice from upstairs cried. "Don't you know you're not supposed to play ball there? People're trying to sleep!"

"*Go ahead'n sleep!*" yelled the blue jeans, spitting on the ground between his spread knees.

An obscenity from the redhead, and then, "Let's go, Joey, let's *have* it!"

"Hey!—I'm going to get the law on you if you don't clear out!" from the upstairs window.

The old man was really angry—it was Mr. Collins, the night-watchman—but the threat of the law was empty and everybody knew it. Stanley had spoken to a policeman a month ago, told him about the Sunday ballplayers, but the policeman had only smiled at him—a smile of indulgence for the ballplayers—and had mumbled something about nobody's being able to do anything about people who wanted to play ball on Sundays. Why couldn't you, Stanley wondered. What about the NO BALLPLAYING written on the side of his own building and signed by the Police Department? What about the right of law-abiding citizens to spend a quiet Sunday at home if they cared to? What about the anti-noise campaign in New York? But he hadn't asked the policeman these questions, because he had seen that the policeman was the same kind of man the ballplayers were, only in uniform.

They were still yelling, Mr. Collins and the quintet below. Stanley put his palms on the brick ledge of the windowsill and leaned out to add the support of his visible presence to Mr. Collins.

"*We ain't breakin' any law! Go to hell!*"

"I mean what I say!" shouted Mr. Collins. "I'm a working man!"

"*Go back to bed, grampa!*"

Then the redheaded man picked up a stone or a large cinder and made as if to throw it at Mr. Collins, whose voice shut off in the middle of a sentence. "*Shut up or we'll bust yuh windows!*" the redheaded man bellowed, then managed to catch the ball that was coming his way.

Another window went up, and Stanley was suddenly inspired to yell: "Isn't there another place to play ball around here? Can't you give us a break one Sunday?"

"Ah, the hell with 'em!" said one of the men.

The batted ball made a sick sound and spun up behind the batter, stopping in mid-air hardly four feet in front of Stanley's nose, before it started its descent. They were playing two-base baseball now with a stick bat and a soft ball.

The blonde woman who lived on the floor above Stanley and to the left was having a sympathetic discussion with Mr. Collins: "Wouldn't you think that grown men—"

Mr. Collins, loudly: "Ah, they're worse than children! Hoodlums, that's what they are! Ought to get the police after them!"

"And the language they use! I've told my husband about 'em but he works Sundays and he just can't *realize!*"

"So her husband ain't home, huh?" said the redheaded man, and the others guffawed.

Stanley looked down on the bent, freckled back of the redheaded man who had removed his shirt now and whose hands were braced on his knees. It was a revolting sight—the white back mottled with brown freckles, rounded with fatty muscle and faintly shiny with sweat. I wish I had a BB gun, Stanley thought as he had often thought before. I'd shoot them, not enough to hurt them, just enough to annoy them. Annoy them the hell out of here!

A roar from five throats shocked him, shattered his thoughts and left him shaking.

He went into the bathroom and wet his face at the basin. Then he came back and closed his other window. The closed windows made very little difference in the sound. He bent toward his easel again, touching the brushtip to the partly drawn highlight on the nose. The tip of his brush had dried and stiffened. He moistened it in the turpentine cup.

"*Franky!*"

"*Run, boy, run!*"

Stanley put the brush down. He had made a wide white mark on the nose. He wiped at it with a rag, trembling.

Now there was an uproar from below, as if all five were fighting. Stanley looked out. Frank and the other pot-bellied man were wrestling for the ball by the hedges. With a wild, almost feminine laugh, the redhead toppled onto the hedges, yelping as the bushes scratched him.

Stanley flung the window up. "Would you please watch out for the hedge?" he shouted.

"*Ah, f'Chris' sake!*" yelled the redhead, getting up from one knee, at the same time yanking up a bush from the ground and hurling it in Stanley's direction.

The others laughed.

"You're not allowed to destroy public property!" Stanley retorted with a quick, bitter smile, as if he had them. His heart was racing.

"What d'yuh mean we're not allowed?" asked the blue jeans, crashing a foot into another bush.

"*Cut that out!*" Stanley yelled.

"Oh, pipe down!"

"I'm gettin' thirsty! Who's goin' for drinks?"

Now the redhead man swung a foot and kicked another bush up into the air.

"Pick that hedge up again! Put it back!" Stanley shouted, clenching his fists.

"Pick up yer ass!"

Stanley crossed his room and yanked the door open, ran down the steps and out. Suddenly, he was standing in the middle of the lot in the bright sunshine. "You'd better put that hedge back!" Stanley yelled. "One of you'd better put all those bushes back!"

"Look who's here!"

"Oh, dry up! Come on, Joey!"

The ball hit Stanley on the shoulder, but he barely felt it, barely wondered if it had been directed at him. He was no match for any of the men physically, certainly not for all of them together, but this fact barely brushed the surface of his mind, either. He was mad enough to have attacked any or all of them, and it was only their scattered number that kept him from moving. He didn't know where to begin.

"Isn't any of you going to put those back?" he demanded.

"No!"

"Outa the way, Mac! You're gonna get hurt!"

While reaching for the ball near Stanley, the blue jeans put out an arm and shoved him. Stanley's neck made a snapping sound and he just managed to recover his balance without pitching on his face. No one was paying the least attention to him now. They were like a scattered, mobile army, confident of their ground. Stanley walked quickly toward the alley, oblivious of the laughter that followed.

The next thing he knew, he was in the cool, darkish hall of his building. His eye fell on the flat stone that was used now and then to prop the front door open. He picked it up and began to climb the stairs with it. He thought of hurling it out his window, down into the midst of them. The barbarians!

He rested the stone on his windowsill, still holding it between his hands. The man in blue jeans was walking along by the brick wall, kicking at the remaining bushes. They had stopped playing for some reason.

"Got the stuff, fellows! Come 'n get it!" One of the pot-bellied men had arrived with his fists full of soft drink bottles.

Heads tipped back as they drank. There were animal murmurs and grunts of satisfaction. Stanley leaned farther out.

The redheaded man was sitting right below his window on a board propped up on a couple of rocks to make a bench. He couldn't miss if he dropped it, Stanley thought, and almost at the same time, he held the stone a few inches out from his sill and dropped it. Ducking back, Stanley heard a deep-pitched, lethal-sounding crack, then a startled curse.

"Who did that?"

"Hey, Franky! *Franky!* Are you okay?"

Stanley heard a groan.

"We gotta get a doctor! Gimme a hand, somebody!"

"That bastard upstairs!" It came clearly.

Stanley jumped as something crashed through his other window, hit the shade and slid to the floor—a stone the size of a large egg.

Now he could hear their voices moving up the alley. Stanley expected them to come up the stairs for him. He clenched his fists and listened for feet on the stairs.

But nothing happened. Suddenly there was silence.

"Thank—God," Stanley heard the blonde woman say, wearily.

The telephone would ring, he thought. That would be next. The police.

Stanley sat down in a chair, sat rigidly for several minutes. The rock had weighed eight or ten pounds, he thought. The very least that could have happened was that the man had suffered a concussion. But Stanley imagined the skull fractured, the brain partly crushed. Perhaps he had lived only a few moments after the impact.

He got up and went to his canvas. Boldly, he mixed a colour for the entire nose, painted over the messy highlight, then attacked the background, making it a darker green. By the time he had finished the background, the nose was dry enough for him to put the highlight in, which he did quickly and surely. There was no sound anywhere except that of his rather accelerated breathing. He painted as if he had only five minutes more to paint, five minutes more to live before they came for him.

But by six o'clock, nobody had came. The telephone had not rung, and the picture was done. It was good, better than he had dared hope it would be. Stanley felt exhausted. He remembered that there was no coffee in the house. No milk, either. He'd have to have a little coffee. He'd have to go out.

Fear was sneaking up on him again. Were they waiting for him downstairs in front of the house? Or were they still at the hospital, watching their friend die? What if he were dead?

You wouldn't kill a man for playing ball below your window on Sunday—even though you might like to.

He tried to pull himself together, went into the bathroom and took a quick, cool shower, because he had been perspiring quite a bit. He put on a clean blue shirt and combed his hair. Then he pushed his wallet and keys into his pocket and went out. He saw no sign of the ballplayers on the sidewalk, or of anyone who seemed to be interested in him. He bought milk and coffee at the delicatessen around the corner, and on the way back he ran into the blonde woman of about forty who lived on the floor above him.

"Wasn't that awful this afternoon!" she said to Stanley. "I saw you down there arguing with them. Good for you! You certainly scared them off." She shook her head despairingly. "But I suppose they'll be back next Sunday."

"Do they play Saturdays?" Stanley asked suddenly, and entirely out of nervousness, since he didn't care whether they played Saturdays or not.

"No," she said dubiously. "Well, they once did, but mostly it's Sundays. I swear to God I'm going to make Al stay home one Sunday so he can hear 'em. You must have it a little worse than me, being lower down." She shook her head again. She looked thin and tired, and there was a complicated meshwork of wrinkles under her lower lids. "Well, you've got my thanks for breakin' 'em up a little earlier today."

"Thank you," Stanley said, really saying it almost involuntarily to thank her for not mentioning, for not having seen what he had done.

They climbed the stairs together.

"Trust this super not to be around whenever somebody needs him," she said, loud enough to carry into the superintendent's second-floor apartment, which they were then passing. "And to think we all give him big tips on Christmas!"

"It's pretty bad," Stanley said with a smile as he unlocked his door. "Well, let's hope next week's a little better."

"You said it. I hope it's pouring rain," she said, and went on up the stairs.

Stanley was in the habit of breakfasting at a small café between his house and the subway, and on Monday morning one of the ballplayers — the one who usually wore blue jeans — was in the café. He was having coffee and doughnuts when Stanley walked in, and he gave Stanley such an unpleasant look, continued for several minutes to give him such an unpleasant look, that a few other people in the cafe noticed it and began to watch them. Stanley stammeringly ordered coffee. The redheaded man wasn't dead, he decided. He was probably hovering between life and death. If Franky were dead, or if he were perfectly all right now, the dark-haired man's expression would have been different. Stanley finished his coffee and passed the man on the way to pay his check. He expected the man to try to trip him, or at least to say something to him as he passed him, but he didn't.

That evening, when Stanley came home from work at a little after six, he saw two of the ballplayers — the dark-haired man again and one of the paunchy men who looked like a wrestler in his ordinary clothes — standing across the street. They stared at him as he went into his building. Upstairs in his apartment, Stanley pondered the possible significance of their standing across the street from where he lived. Had their friend just died, or was he nearer death? Had they just come from the funeral, perhaps? Both of them had been wearing dark suits, suits that might have been their best. Stanley listened for feet on the stairs. There was only the plodding tread of the old woman who lived with her dog on the top floor. She aired her dog at about this time every evening.

All at once Stanley noticed that his windows were shattered. Now he saw three or four stones and fragments of glass on the carpet. There was a stone on his bed, too. The window that had been broken Sunday had almost no glass in it now, and of the upper halves of the windows, which were panelled, only two or three panels remained, he saw when he raised the shades.

He set about methodically picking up the stones and the larger pieces of glass and putting them into a paper bag. Then he got his broom and swept. He was wondering when he would have the time to put the glass back—no use asking the super to do it—and he thought probably not before next weekend, unless he ordered the pieces during his lunch hour tomorrow. He got his yardstick and measured the larger panes, which were of slightly different sizes because it was an old house, and then the panels, and recorded the numbers on a paper which he put into his wallet. He'd have to buy putty, too.

He stiffened, hearing a faint click at his doorlock. "Who's there?" he called.

Silence.

He had an impulse to yank the door open, then realized he was afraid to. He listened for a few moments. There was no other sound, so he decided to forget the click. Maybe he had only imagined it.

When he came home the next evening he couldn't get his door open. The key went in, but it wouldn't turn, not a fraction of an inch. Had they put something in it to jam it? Had that been the click he had heard last night? On the other hand, the lock had given him some trouble about six months ago, he remembered. For several days it had been difficult to open, and then it had got all right again. Or had that been the lock on his father's store door? He couldn't quite remember.

He leaned against the stair rail, staring at the key in the lock and wondering what to do.

The blonde woman was coming up the stairs.

Stanley smiled and said. "Good evening."

"Hello, there. What happened? Forget your key?"

"No, I—The lock's a little stiff," he said.

"Oh. Always something wrong in this house, ain't there?" she said, moving on down the hall. "Did you ever see anything like it?"

"No," he agreed, smiling. But he looked after her anxiously. Usually, she stopped and chatted a little longer. Had she heard something about his dropping the rock? And she hadn't mentioned his broken windows, though she was home all day and had probably heard the noise.

Stanley turned and attacked the lock, turning the key with all his strength. The lock suddenly yielded. The door was open.

It took him until after midnight to get the panes in. And all the time he worked, he was conscious of the fact that the windows might be broken again when he got home tomorrow.

The following evening the same two men, the paunchy one and the dark-haired one who was in blue jeans and a shirt now, were standing across the street, and to Stanley's horror they crossed the street so as to meet him in front of his door. The paunchy one reached out and took a handful of Stanley's jacket and shirtfront.

"Listen, Mac," he said in Stanley's face, "you can go to jail for what you did Sunday. You know that, doncha?"

"I don't know what you're talking about!" Stanley said quickly.

"Oh, you *don't?*"

"No!" Stanley yelled.

The man let him go with a shove. Stanley straightened his jacket, and went on into his house. The lock was again difficult, but he flung himself against it with the energy of desperation. It yielded slowly, and when Stanley removed his key, a rubbery string came with it: they had stuffed his lock with chewing gum. Stanley wiped his key, with disgust, on the floor. He did not begin to shake until he had closed the door of his apartment. Then even as he shook, he thought: I've beaten them. They weren't coming after him. Broken windows, chewing gum? So what? They hadn't sought out the police. He had lied, of course, in saying he didn't know what they were talking about, but that had been the right reply, after all. He wouldn't have lied to a policeman, naturally, but they hadn't brought the police in yet.

Stanley began to feel better. Moreover, his windows were intact, he saw. He decided that the redheaded man was probably going through a prolonged crisis. There was something subdued about the men's behaviour, he thought. Or were they planning some worse attack? He wished he knew if the redheaded man were in a hospital or walking around. It was just possible, too, that the man had died, Stanley thought. Maybe the men weren't quite sure that it was he who had dropped the rock—Mr. Collins lived above Stanley and might have dropped it, for instance—and perhaps an investigation by the police was yet to come.

On Thursday evening, he passed Mr. Collins on the stairs as he was coming home. Mr. Collins was on his way to work. It struck Stanley that Mr. Collins' "Good evening" was cool. He wondered if Mr. Collins had heard about the rock and considered him a murderer, or at least some kind of psychopath, to have dropped a ten-pound rack on somebody's head?

Saturday came, and Stanley worked all day in his father's hardware store, went to a movie, and came home at about eleven. Two of the small panes in the upper part of one window were broken. Stanley thought them not important enough to fix until the weather grew cooler. He wouldn't have noticed it, if he hadn't deliberately checked the state of the windows.

He slept late Sunday morning, for he had been extremely tired the night before. It was nearly one o'clock when he set up his easel to paint. He had in mind to paint the aperture between two buildings, which contained a tree, that he could see straight out his window above the lot. He thought this Sunday might be a good Sunday to paint, because the ballplayers probably wouldn't come. Stanley pictured them dampened this Sunday, at least to the extent that they would find another vacant lot to play in.

He had not quite finished his sketch of the scene in charcoal on his canvas, when he heard them. For a moment, he thought he was imagining it, that he was having an auditory hallucination. But no. He heard them ever more clearly in the alley—their particular sullen bravado coming through the murmuring, a collective murmur as recognizable to Stanley as a single familiar voice. Stanley waited, a little way back from the window.

"Okay, boys, let's *go-o-o!*"

"*Yeeeeee-hoooooo!*" Sheer defiance, a challenge to any who might contest their right to play there.

Stanley went closer to the window, looking, wide-eyed for the red-headed man. And there he was! A patch of bandage on the top of his head, but otherwise as brutishly energetic as ever. As Stanley watched, he hurled a catcher's mitt at a companion who was then bending over, hitting him in the buttocks.

Raucous, hooting laughter.

Then from above: "F'gosh sakes, why don't you guys grow up? Why don't you beat it? We've had enough of you around here!" It was the blonde woman, and Stanley knew that Mr. Collins would not be far behind.

"*Ah, save yer throat!*"

"C'mon down 'n get in the game, sister!"

There was a new defiance in their voices today. They were louder. They were determined to win. They had won. They were back.

Stanley sat down on his bed, dazed, frustrated, and suddenly tired. He was glad the redheaded fellow wasn't dead. He really was glad. And yet with his relief something fighting and bitter rose up in him, something borne on a wave of unshed tears.

"Let's have it, Joey, let's *have* it!"

Thud!

"Hey, Franky! Franky, look! Ah-ha-*haaaaaa!*"

Stanley put his hands over his ears, lifted his feet onto the bed, and shut his eyes. He lay in a Z position, his legs drawn up, and tried to be perfectly calm and quiet. No use fighting, he thought. No use fighting, no use crying.

Then he thought of something and sat up abruptly. He wished he had put the hedge bushes back. Now it was too late, he supposed, because they had been lying out on the ground for a week. But how he wished he had! Just that gesture of defiance, just that bit of beauty launched again in their faces.

Sunny Billy Day

RON CARLSON

The very first time it happened with Sunny Billy Day was in Bradenton, Florida, spring training, a thick cloudy day on the Gulf, and I was there in the old wooden bleachers, having been released only the week before after going o for 4 in Winter Park against the Red Sox, and our manager, Ketchum, saw that my troubles were not over at all. So, not wanting to go back to Texas so soon and face my family, the disappointment and my father's expectation that I'd go to work in his Allstate office, and not wanting to leave Polly alone in Florida in March, a woman who tended toward ball players, I was hanging out, feeling bad, and I was there when it happened.

My own career had been derailed by what they called "stage fright." I was scared. Not in the field—I won a Golden Glove two years in college and in my rookie year with the Pirates. I love the field, but I had a little trouble at the plate. I could hit in the cage, in fact there were times when batting practice stopped so all the guys playing pepper could come over and bet how many I was going to put in the seats. It wasn't the skill. In a game I'd walk from the on-deck circle to the batter's box and I could feel my heart go through my throat. All those people focusing on one person in the park: me. I could feel my heart drumming in my face. I was tighter

From *Plan B for the Middle Class* by Ron Carlson. Copyright © 1992 by Ron Carlson. Used by permission of W. W. Norton & Company, Inc.

than a ten-cent watch—all strikeouts and pop-ups. I went .102 for the season—the lowest official average of any starting-lineup player in the history of baseball.

Ketchum sent me to see the team psychiatrist, but that turned out to
be no good, too. I saw him twice. His name was Krick and he was a small
man who was losing hair, but his little office and plaid couch felt to me
like the batter's box. What I'm saying is: Krick was no help—I was afraid
of him, too.

Sometimes just watching others go to bat can start my heart jangling
like a rock in a box, and that was how I felt that cloudy day in Bradenton
as Sunny Billy Day went to the plate. We (once you play for a team, you
say "we" ever after) were playing the White Sox, who were down from
Sarasota, and it was a weird day, windy and dark, with those great loads of
low clouds and the warm Gulf air rolling through. I mean it was a day that
didn't feel like baseball.

Billy came up in the first inning, and the Chicago pitcher, a rookie
named Gleason, had him 0 and 2, when the thing happened for the first
time. Polly had ahold of my arm and was being extra sweet when Billy
came up, to let me know that she didn't care for him at all and was with
me now, but—everybody knows—when a woman acts that way it makes
you nervous. The kid Gleason was a sharpshooter, a sidearm fastballer
who could have struck me out with two pitches, and he had shaved Billy
with two laser beams that cut the inside corner.

Gleason's third pitch was the smoking clone of the first two and Sunny
Billy Day, my old friend, my former roommate, lifted his elbows off the
table just like he had done twice before and took the third strike.

It *was* a strike. We all knew this. We'd seen the two previous pitches
and everybody who was paying attention knew that Gleason had nailed
Billy to the barn door. There was no question. Eldon Finney was behind
the plate, a major league veteran, who was known as Yank because of the
way he yanked a fistful of air to indicate a strike. His gesture was unmis-
takable, and on that dark day last March, I did not mistake it. But as soon
as the ump straightened up, Sunny Billy, my old teammate, and the most
promising rookie the Pirates had seen for thirty years, tapped his cleats
one more time and stayed in the box.

"What's the big jerk doing?" Polly asked me. You hate to hear a girl use a phrase like that, "big jerk," when she could have said something like "rotten bastard," but when you're in the stands, instead of running wind sprints in the outfield, you take what you can get.

On the mound in Bradenton, Gleason was confused. Then I saw Billy shrug at the ump in a move I'd seen a hundred times as roommates when he was accused of anything or asked to pay his share of the check at the Castaway. A dust devil skated around the home dugout and out to first, carrying an ugly litter of old sno-cone papers and cigarette butts in its brown vortex, but when the wind died down and play resumed, there was Sunny Billy Day standing in the box. I checked the scoreboard and watched the count shift to 1 and 2.

Eldon "the Yank" Finney had changed his call.

So that was the beginning, and as I said, only a few people saw it and knew this season was going to be a little different. Billy and I weren't speaking—I mean, Polly was with me now, and so I couldn't ask him what was up—but I ran into Ketchum at the Castaway that night and he came over to our table. Polly had wanted to go back there for dinner—for old times' sake; it was in the Castaway where we'd met one year ago. She was having dinner with Billy that night, the Bushel o' Shrimp, and they asked me to join them. Billy had a lot of girls and he was always good about introducing them around. Come on, a guy like Billy had nothing to worry about from other guys, especially me. He could light up a whole room, no kidding, and by the end of an hour there'd be ten people sitting at his table and every chair in the room would be turned his way. He was a guy, and anybody will back me up on this, who had the magic.

Billy loved the Castaway. "This is exotic," he'd say. "Right? Is this a South Sea island or what?" And he meant it. You had to love him. Some dim dive pins an old fishing net on the wall and he'd be in paradise.

Anyway, Polly had ordered the Bushel o' Shrimp again and we were having a couple of Mutineers, the daiquiri deal that comes in a skull, when Ketchum came over and asked me—as he does every time we meet—"How you feeling, kid?" which means have I still got the crippling heebie-jeebies. He has told me all winter that if I want another shot, just say so. Well, who doesn't want another shot? In baseball—no matter what you hear—there are no ex-players, just guys waiting for the right moment for a comeback.

I told Ketchum that if anything changed, he'd be the first to know. Then I asked him what he thought of today's game and he said, "The White Sox are young."

"Yeah," I said. "Especially that pitcher."

"I wouldn't make too much out of that mix-up at the plate today. You know Billy. He's a kind that can change the weather." Ketchum was referring to the gray preseason game a year before. Billy came up in a light rain when a slice of sunlight opened on the field like a beacon, just long enough for everyone to see my roommate golf a low fastball into the right-field seats for a round trip. It was the at-bat that clinched his place on the roster, and that gave him his nickname.

"Billy Day is a guy who gets the breaks." Ketchum reached into the wicker bushel and sampled one of Polly's shrimp. "And you know what they say about guys who get a lot of breaks." Here he gave Polly a quick look. "They keep getting them." He stood up and started to walk off. "Call me if you want to hit a few. We don't head north until April Fools' Day."

"I don't like that guy," Polly said when he'd left. "I never liked him." She pushed her load of shrimp away. "Let's go." I was going to defend the coach there, a guy who was fair with his men and kept the signals (steal, take, hit-and-run) simple, but the evening had gone a little flat for me too. There we were out to celebrate, but as always the room was full of Billy Day. He was everywhere. He was in the car on the way back to the hotel; he was in the elevator; he was in the room; and—if you want to know it— he was in the bed too. I knew that he was in Polly's dreams and there he was in my head, turning back to the umpire, changing a strike to a ball.

The papers got ahold of what was going on during the last week of March. It was a home game against the Yankees and it was the kind of day that if there were no baseball, you'd invent it to go with the weather. The old Bradenton stands were packed and the whole place smelled of popcorn and coconut oil. Polly was wearing a yellow sundress covered with black polka dots, the kind of dress you wear in a crowded ballpark if you might want one of the players to pick you out while he played first. By this time I was writing a friendly little column for the *Pittsburgh Dispatch* twice a week on "Lifestyles at Spring Training," but I had not done much with Billy. He was getting plenty of legitimate ink, and besides—as I said—we weren't really talking. I liked the writing, even though this was a weird time all around. I kind of *had* to do it, just so I felt useful. I wasn't ready to go home.

It was a good game, two-two in the ninth. Then Billy made a mistake. With one down, he had walked and stolen second. That's a wonderful feeling being on second with one out. There's all that room and you can lead the extra two yards and generally you feel pretty free and cocky out there. I could see Billy was enjoying this feeling, leaving cleat marks in the clay, when they threw him out. The pitcher flipped the ball backhand to the shortstop, and they tagged Billy. Ralph "the Hammer" Fox was umping out there, and he jumped onto one knee in his famous out gesture and wheeled his arm around and he brought the hammer down: OUT! After the tag, Billy stood up and went over and planted both feet on the base.

"What?" Polly took my arm.

Ralph Fox went over and I could see Billy smiling while he spoke. He patted Ralph's shoulder. Then Fox turned and gave the arms-out gesture for safe—twice—and hollered, "Play ball." It was strange, the kind of thing that makes you sure you're going to get an explanation later.

But the ballpark changed in a way I was to see twenty times during the season: a low quiet descended, not a silence, but an eerie even sound like two thousand people talking to themselves. And the field, too, was stunned, the players standing straight up, their gloves hanging down like their open mouths during the next pitch, which like everything else was now half-speed, a high hanging curve which Red Sorrows blasted over the scoreboard to win the game.

Well, it was no way to win a ballgame, but that wasn't exactly what the papers would say. Ralph Fox, of course, wasn't speaking to the press (none of the umpires would), and smiling Sunny Billy Day only said one thing that went out on the wire from coast to coast: "Hey guys, come on. You saw that Mickey Mouse move. I was safe." Most writers looked the other way, noting the magnitude of Red Sorrows's homer, a "towering blast," and going on to speculate whether the hit signaled Sorrows's return from a two-year slump. So, the writers avoided it, and in a way I understand. Now I have become a kind of sportswriter and I know it is not always easy to say what you mean. Sometimes if the truth is hard, typing it can hurt again.

There were so many moments that summer when some poor ump would stand in the glare of Billy's smile and toe the dirt, adjust his cap, and change the call. Most of the scenes were blips, glitches: a last swing called a foul ticker; a close play called Billy's way; but some were big, bad, and ugly—so blatant that they had the fans looking at their shoes. Billy had poor judgment. In fact, as I think about it, he had no judgment at all. He was a guy with the gift who had spent his whole life going forward from one thing to the next. People liked him and things came his way. When you first met Billy, it clicked: who is this guy? Why do I want to talk to him? Ketchum assigned us to room together and in a season of hotel rooms, I found out that it had always been that way for him. He had come out of college with a major in American Studies, and he could not name a single president. "My teachers liked me," he said. "Everybody likes me."

He had that right. But he had no judgment. I'd seen him with women. They'd come along, one, two, three, and he'd take them as they came. He didn't have to choose. If he'd had any judgment, he never would have let any woman sit between him and Polly.

Oh, that season I saw him ground to short and get thrown out at first. He'd trot past, look back, and head for the dugout, taking it, but you got the impression it was simply easier to keep on going than stop to change the call. And those times he took it, lying there a foot from third dead out and then trotting off the field, or taking the third strike and then turning for the dugout, you could feel the waves of gratitude from the stands. Those times I know you could feel it, because there weren't many times when Billy Day took it, and as the season wore on, and the Pirates rose to first place, they became increasingly rare.

Sunny Billy Day made the All-Stars, of course. He played a fair first base and he was the guy you couldn't get out. But he was put on the five-day disabled list, "to rest a hamstring," the release said. But I think it was Ketchum being cagey. He wasn't going to gain anything by having a kid who was developing a reputation for spoiling ball games go in and ruin a nice July night in Fenway for fans of both leagues.

By August, it was all out: Billy Day could have his way. You never saw so much written about the state of umping. Billy was being walked most of the time now. Every once in a while some pitcher would throw to him, just to test the water. They were thinking Ketchum was going to pull the plug, tell Billy to face the music, to swallow it if he went down swinging, but it never happened. The best anybody got out of it was a flyout, Billy never contested a flyout. And Ketchum, who had thirty-four good years in the majors and the good reputation to go with them, didn't care. A good reputation is one thing; not having been in the Series is another. He would be seventy by Christmas and he wanted to win it all once, even if it meant letting Billy have his way. Ketchum, it was written, had lost his judgment too.

I was writing my head off, learning how to do it and liking it a little more. It's something that requires a certain amount of care and it is done alone at a typewriter, not in the batting box in front of forty thousand citizens. And I found I was a hell of a typist; I liked typing. But I wasn't typing about my old roommate—at all. I missed him though, don't think I didn't miss him. I had plenty to say about the rest of the squad, how winning became them, made them into men after so many seasons of having to have their excuses ready before they took the field. Old Red Sorrows was hitting .390 and hadn't said the word "retirement" or the phrase "next season" in months. There was a lot to write about without dealing with Billy Day's behavior.

But, as September came along, I was getting a lot of pressure for interviews. I had been his roommate, hadn't I? What was he like? What happened to my career? Would I be back? Wasn't I dating Billy Day's girl? I soft-pedaled all this, saying "on the other hand" fifty times a week, and that's no good for athletes or writers. On the topic of Polly I said that we were friends. What a word. The papers went away and came out with what they'd wanted to say anyway: that Billy Day's old roommate had stolen his girl and now he wouldn't write about him. They used an old file photograph of Billy and Polly in the Castaway and one of Billy and me leaning against the backstop in Pittsburgh, last year, the one year I played in the major leagues. Our caps are cocked back, and we are smiling.

During all this, Polly stopped coming to the games with me. She'd had enough of the Pirates for a while, she said, and she took a job as a travel agent and got real busy. We were having, according to the papers, "a relationship," and that term is fine with me, because I don't know what else to say. I was happy to have such a pretty girl to associate with, but I knew that her real ambition was to be with Billy Day.

The Pirates won their division by twenty-eight games, a record, and then they took the National League pennant by whipping the Cardinals four straight. With Billy talking the umps into anything he wanted, and the rest of the team back from the dead and flying in formation, the Pirates were a juggernaut.

It took the Indians seven games to quiet the Twins, and the Series was set. Pirate October, they called it.

The Cleveland Press was ready for Billy. They'd given him more column inches than the Indians total in those last weeks, cataloguing his "blatant disregard for the rules and the dignity of fair play." Some of those guys could write. Billy had pulled one stunt in the playoffs that really drew fire. In game four, with the Pirates ahead five-zip, he bunted foul on a third strike and smiled his way out of it.

As one writer put it, "We don't put up with that kind of thing in Cleveland. We don't like it and we don't need it. When we see disease, we inoculate." As I said, these guys, some of them, could write. Their form of inoculation was an approved cadre of foreign umpires. They brought in ten guys for the Series. They were from Iceland, Zambia, England, Ireland, Hungary, Japan (three), Venezuela, and Tonga. When they met the press, they struck me as the most serious group of men I'd ever seen assembled. It looked good: they knew the rules and they were grim. And the Tongan, who would be behind the plate for game one, looked fully capable of handling anything that could come up with one hand.

Polly didn't go out to Cleveland with me. She had booked a cruise, a month, through the Panama Canal and on to the islands far across the Pacific Ocean, and she was going along as liaison. She smiled when she left and kissed me sweetly, which is just what you don't want your girl to do. She kissed me like I was a writer.

So I went out alone and stayed in the old Hotel Barnard, where a lot of the writers stay. It was lonely out there in Ohio, and I thought about it. It was the end of a full season in which I had not played ball, and here I was in a hotel full of writers, which I had become, instead of over at the Hilton with my club.

I was closing down the bar the night before the Series opener when Billy Day walked in. I couldn't believe my eyes.

"I thought I'd find you here," he said.

"Billy," I said, waving the barman to bring down a couple of lagers.

"I'm a writer now. This is where the writers stay. You're out after curfew."

He gestured back at the empty room. "Who's gonna write me up, you?" He smiled his terrific smile and I realized as much as I had avoided him for eight months, I missed him. I missed that smile.

"No," I said. "I don't think so." Our beers came and I asked him, "What's up?"

"It's been a rough season."

"Not from what I read. The Pirates won the pennant."

"Jesus," he said. "What is that, sarcasm? You gonna start talking like a writer too?"

"Billy, you've pulled some stunts."

He slid his beer from one hand to the other on the varnished bar of the Hotel Barnard. And then started to nod. "Yeah," he said. "I guess I did. You know, I didn't see it at first. It just kind of grew."

"And now you know."

"Yeah, now I know all about it. I know what I can do."

"So what brings you out on a night to the Hotel Barnard?" I pointed at his full glass of beer. "It's not the beer."

"You," he said, and he turned to me again and smiled. "You always knew what to do. I don't mean on the field. There was no rookie better. But I mean, what should I do? This is the Series."

"Yeah, it's the Series. If I were you, I'd play ball."

"You know what I mean. Ketchum wants me to use it all. He doesn't care if they tear down the stadium."

"And you?"

"I don't know. All my life, I played to win. It seems wrong not to do something that can help your team. But the people don't like it."

I looked at the clouds crossing the face of Sunny Billy Day, and I knew I was seeing something no man had ever seen there before: second thoughts.

"These new umps may not let you get away with anything."

"Kid," he said to me, touching my shoulder with his fist, his smile as wide and bright as the sun through a pop-up, "I've been missing you. But I thought you knew me better than that. I've lived my life knowing one thing: everybody lets me get away with everything. The only thing I ever lost, I lost to you. Polly. And I didn't even think about it until she was gone. How is she?"

"I'd get her back for you if I could," I said, lifting my glass in a toast to my old friend Billy Day. "Polly," I told him, "is headed for Tahiti."

Billy was right about the umps. They looked good, in fact, when they took the field and stood with their arms behind their backs along the first-base line, they looked like the Supreme Court. The people of Cleveland were ready for something too, because I noted in the article I wrote for the *Dispatch* that the squadron of umpires received a louder ovation when they took the field than the home team did. Everybody knew that without an iron heel from the umps, the Indians might as well take the winter off.

Okay, so it was baseball for several innings. Ohio in October smells sweet and old, and for a while I think we were all transported through the beautiful fall day, the stadium bathing in the yellow light and then pitching steeply into the sepia shadow of the upper decks. See: I was learning to write like the other guys.

Sunny Billy Day hadn't been a factor, really, walking twice and grounding a base hit into left. It was just baseball, the score two to one Cleveland in the top of the eighth. Now, I want to explain what happened carefully. There were seventy-four thousand people there and in the days since the Series I've heard almost that many versions. The thirty major papers disagreed in detail and the videotapes haven't got it all because of the angle and sequence. So let me go slow here. After all, it would be the last play of Sunny Billy Day.

I wasn't in the press box. The truth is that the season had been a little hard on me in terms of making friends with my fellow reporters. I'd had a hundred suppers in half-lit lounges and I don't think it came as a surprise that I didn't really care for the way they talked—not just about baseball, for which they had a curious but abiding disdain. And I'm not one of these guys who think you have to have played a sport—or really done anything—to be able to write about it well. Look at me—I was good in the field, but I can't write half as good as any of the guys I travel with. But sportswriters, when they are together at the end of the day, a group of them having drinks waiting for their Reuben sandwiches to arrive, are a fairly superior and hard-bitten bunch. You don't want to wander into one of these hotel lounges any summer evening if you want to hear anything about the joy of the sport. These guys don't celebrate baseball, and really, like me, they don't analyze it very well. But they have *feelings* about it; I never met a man who didn't. That's why it's called the major leagues.

Anyway, I don't want to get going on writers and all that stuff. And don't get me wrong. Some of them—hell, most of them—are nice guys and quick about the check or asking how's it going, but it was October and it was all getting to me. I could see myself in two years, flipping my ash into somebody's coffee cup offering a weary expert's opinion. So I wanted to sit where someone might actually cheer or spill a little beer when they stood up on a third strike or a home run. Journalists are professionals, anyone will tell you this, and they don't spill their beer. I ended up ten rows behind third in a seat I paid for myself, and it turned out to be a lucky break given what was going to happen.

With one out in the top of the eighth, Billy Day doubled to right. It was a low fastball and he sliced it into the corner.

On the first pitch to Red Sorrows, Coach Ketchum had Billy steal. He's one run down with one out in the eighth, a runner in scoring position, and a fair hitter at the plate, and Ketchum flashes the steal sign— it's crazy. It means one thing: he's trading on Billy's magic all the way. When I saw Ketchum pinch his nose and then go to the bill of his cap, which has been the Pirate's steal sign for four years, I thought: Ketchum's going to use Billy any way he can. The pitch is a high strike which Sorrows fouls straight back against the screen, so now everybody knows. Billy walks back to second. I have trouble believing what I see next. Again Ketchum goes to his nose and his cap: steal. The Cleveland hurler, the old veteran Blade Medina, stretches and whirls to throw to second with Billy caught halfway down and throws the ball into center field. He must have been excited. Billy pulls into third standing.

Okay, I thought, Ketchum, you got what you wanted, now *stop screwing around*. In fact, I must have whispered that or said it aloud, because the guy next to me says to my face, "What'd I do?" These new fans. They don't want to fight you anymore, they want to know how they've offended you. Too much college for this country. I told him I was speaking to someone else, and he let it go, until I felt a tap on my shoulder and he'd bought me a beer. What did I tell you? But I didn't mind. A minute later I would need it.

Sorrow goes down swinging. Two outs.

It was then I got a funny feeling, on top of all the other funny feelings I'd been having in the strangest summer of my life, and it was a feeling about Ketchum, and I came to know as I sipped my beer and watched my old coach walk over to Billy on the bag at third that he was going to try to steal home. Coach Ketchum was the king of the fair shake, a guy known from Candlestick to Fenway as a square shooter, and as he patted Billy on the rump and walked back to the coach's box, I saw his grin. I was ten rows up and the bill of his cap was down, but I saw it clearly—the grin of a deranged miser about to make another two bucks.

Billy had never stolen home in his career.

Blade Medina was a tall guy and as he launched into his windup, kicking his long leg toward third, Billy took off. Billy Day was stealing home; you could feel every mouth in the stadium open. Blade Medina certainly opened his. Then he simply cocked and threw to the catcher, who tagged Billy out before he could decide to slide.

Ketchum was on them before the big Tongan umpire could put his thumb away. For a big guy he had a funny out call, flicking his thumb as if shooting a marble. I have to hand it to Billy. He was headed for the dugout. But Ketchum got him by the shirt and dragged back out to the plate and made him speak to the umpire. You knew it was going to happen again—and in the World Series—because all the Indians just stood where they were on the field. And sure enough after a moment of Ketchum pushing Billy from the back, as if he was some big puppet in a baseball suit, and Billy speaking softly to the umpire, the large official stepped out in front of the plate and swept his hand out flat in the air as if calming the waters: "Safe!" he said. He said it quietly in his deep voice. Well, it was quiet in Cleveland, do you see? I sat there like everyone else looking at the bottom of my plastic glass of beer and wishing it wasn't so. Seventy-four thousand people sitting in a circle feeling sour in their hearts, not to mention all the sad multitudes watching the televised broadcast.

Then my old coach Ketchum made it worse by hauling Billy over to touch the plate; Billy hadn't even stepped on home base yet. Just typing this makes me feel the ugliness all over again.

But then the real stuff started to happen, and, as I said, there were no good reports of this next part because of everybody looking at their shoes, programs, or their knuckles the way people in a restaurant read the menu real hard when a couple is arguing at the next table. But I saw it, and it redeemed Sunny Billy Day forever to me, and it gave me something that has allowed me, made me really, get out my cleats again and become a baseball player. I'm not so bad a writer that I would call it courage, but it was definitely some big kick in the ass.

What happened was, halfway back to the dugout, *Billy turned around*. His head was down in what I called *shame* in my report to the *Pittsburgh Dispatch*, and he turned around and went back to home plate. Ketchum was back at third, smug as a jewel thief, and he caught the action too late to do anything about it. Billy took the ump by the sleeve and I saw Billy take off his cap and shake his head and point at the plate. We all knew what he was saying, everybody. The ballpark was back, everyone standing now, watching, and we all saw the big Tongan nod and smile that big smile at Ketchum, and then raise his fist and flick his thumb.

Oh god, the cheer. The cheer went up my spine like a chiropractor. There was joy in Ohio and it went out in waves around the world. I wrote that too. Not joy at the out; joy at order restored. It was the greatest noise I've ever heard. I hope Billy recognized the sound.

Because what happened next, as the Cleveland Indians ran off the field like kids, and Ketchum's mouth dropped open like the old man he would become in two minutes, surprised everyone, even me.

When the Pirates took the field (and they ran out joyfully too—it was baseball again), there was something wrong. The Pirates pitcher threw his eight warm-up pitches and one of the Cleveland players stepped into the box. That is when the Irishman umping first came skittering onto the field wheeling his arms, stopping play before it had begun, and seventy-four thousand people looked over to where I'd been staring for five minutes: first base. There was no one at first base. Sunny Billy Day had not taken the field.

I wish to this day I'd been closer to the field because I would have hopped the rail and run through the dugout to the clubhouse and found what the batboy said he found: Billy's uniform hung in his locker, still swinging on the hanger. I asked him later if he got a glimpse of a woman in a yellow dress, but he couldn't recall.

And now, this spring, I'm out again. I'd almost forgotten during my long season in the stands how much fun it was to play baseball. I still have a little trouble at the plate and I ride my heartbeat like a cowboy on a bad bull, but I want to play, and if I remember that and hum to myself a little while I'm in the box, it helps. The new manager is a good guy and if I can keep above .200, he'll start me.

Oh, the Indians won the series, but it went six games and wasn't as one-sided as you might think after such an event. Ketchum stayed in the dugout the whole time, under heavy sedation, though I never mentioned that in my stories. And I never mentioned the postcards I got later from the far island of Pago Pago. I still get them. Sometimes I'll carry one in my pocket when I go to the plate. It's a blue-and-green place mainly, and looks like a great place for a lucky guy and a woman who looks good in summer clothing.

Sunny Billy Day was a guy with a gift. You could see it a mile away. Things came his way. Me, I'm going to have to make my own breaks, but, hey, it's spring again and it feels like life is opening up. I'm a lot less nervous at the plate these days, and I have learned to type.

After the Game

ANDRE DUBUS

I wasn't in the clubhouse when Joaquin Quintana went crazy. At least I wasn't there for the start of it, because I pitched that night and went nine innings and won, and the color man interviewed me after the game. He is Duke Simpson, and last year he was our first baseman. He came down from the broadcasting booth, and while the guys were going into the clubhouse, and cops and ushers were standing like soldiers in a V from first to third, facing the crowd leaving the park, I stood in front of the dugout with my jacket on, and Duke and I looked at the camera, and he said: "I'm here with Billy Wells."

This was August and we were still in it, four games back, one and a half out of second. It was the time of year when everybody is tired and a lot are hurt and playing anyway. I wanted a shower and a beer, and to go to my apartment for one more beer and then sleep. I sleep very well after I've pitched a good game, not so well after a bad one, and I sleep very badly the night before I pitch, and the day of the game I force myself to eat. It's one of the things that makes the game exciting, but a lot of times, especially in late season, I long for the time when I'll have a job I can predict, can wake up on the ranch knowing what I'm going to do and that I'm not going to fail. I know most jobs are like that, and the people who have them don't look like they've had a rush of adrenaline since the time somebody ran a stop sign and just missed colliding broadside with them, but there's always a trade-off and, on some days in late season, their lives seem worth it. Duke and I talked about pitching, and our catcher Jesse Wade and what a good game he called behind the plate, so later that night I thought it was strange, that Joaquin was going crazy while Duke and I were talking about Jesse, because during the winter the club had traded Manuel Fernandez, a good relief pitcher, to the Yankees for Jesse. Manuel had been Joaquin's roommate, and they always sat together on the plane and the bus, and ate together. Neither one could speak much English. From shortstop, Joaquin used to call to Manuel out on the mound: *Baja y rapido.*

We ended the interview shaking hands and patting each other on the back, then I went between the cops and ushers but there were some fans waiting for autographs at one end of the dugout, so I went over there and signed three baseballs and a dozen scorecards and said thank you twenty or thirty times, and shook it seemed more hands than there were people, then went into the dugout and down the tunnel to the clubhouse. I knew something was wrong, but I wasn't alert to it, wanting a beer, and I was thinking maybe I'd put my arm in ice for a while, so I saw as if out of the corner of my eye, though I was looking right at it, that nobody was at the food table. There was pizza. Then I heard them and looked that way, down between two rows of lockers. They were bunched down there, the ones on the outside standing on benches or on tiptoes on the floor, stretching and looking, and the ones on the inside talking, not to each other but to whoever was in the middle, and I could hear the manager Bobby Drew, and Terry Morgan the trainer. The guys' voices were low, so I couldn't make out the words, and urgent, so I wondered who had been fighting and why now, with things going well for us, and we hadn't had trouble on the club since Duke retired; he was a good ballplayer, but often a pain in the ass. I went to the back of the crowd but couldn't see, so took off my spikes and stepped behind Bruce Green on a bench. Bruce is the only black on the club, and plays right field. I held his waist for balance as I brought my other foot from the floor. I stay in good running shape all year round, and I am overly careful about accidents, like falling off a bench onto my pitching elbow.

I kept my hands on Bruce's waist and looked over his shoulder and there was Joaquin Quintana, our shortstop, standing in front of his locker, naked except for his sweat socks and jockstrap and his gold Catholic medal, breathing through his mouth like he was in the middle of a sentence he didn't finish. He was as black as Bruce, so people who didn't know him took him for a black man, but Manuel told us he was from the Dominican Republic and did not think of himself as a black, and was pissed off when people did; though it seemed to me he was a black from down there, as Bruce was a black from Newark. His left arm was at his side, and his right forearm was out in front of him like he was reaching for something, or to shake hands, and in that hand he held his spikes. It was the right shoe.

Bruce looked at me over his shoulder.

"They can't move him," he said. Bruce was wearing his uniform pants and no shirt. I came to Boston in 1955, as a minor-league player to be named later in a trade with Detroit, when I was in that organization, and I have played all my seven years of major-league ball with the Red Sox; I grew up in San Antonio, so Bruce is the only black I've ever really known. People were talking to Joaquin. Or the people in front were trying to, and others farther back called to him to have some pizza, a beer, a shower, telling him it was all right, everything was all right, telling him settle down, be cool, take it easy, the girls are waiting at the parking lot. Nobody was wet or wrapped in a towel. Some still wore the uniform and some, like Bruce, wore parts of it, and a few had taken off as much as Joaquin. Most of the lockers were open. So was Joaquin's, and he stood staring at Bobby Drew and Terry Morgan, both of them talking, and Bobby doing most of it, being the manager. He was talking softly and telling Joaquin to give him the shoe and come in his office and lie down on the couch in there. He kept talking about the shoe, as if it was a weapon, though Joaquin held it with his hand under it, and not gripped for swinging, but like he was holding it out to give to someone. But I knew why Bobby wanted him to put it down. I felt the same: if he would just drop that shoe, things would get better. Looking at the scuffed toe and the soft dusty leather and the laces untied and pulled wider across the tongue folded up and over, and the spikes, silver down at their edges, resting on his palm, I wanted to talk that shoe out of his hand too, and I started talking with the others below me, and on the bench across the aisle from me and Bruce, and the benches on the other side of the group around Joaquin.

That is when I saw what he was staring at, when I told him to come on and put down that shoe and let's go get some dinner, it was on me, and all the drinks too, for turning that double-play in the seventh; and Bruce said And the bunt, and Jesse said Perfect fucking bunt, and I saw that Joaquin was not staring at Bobby or Terry, but at nothing at all, as if he saw something we couldn't, but it was as clear to him as a picture hanging in the air right in front of his face.

I lowered myself off the bench and worked my way through the guys, most of them growing quiet while some still tried to break Joaquin out of it. A few were saying their favorite curse, to themselves, shaking their heads or looking at the floor. Everyone I touched was standing tense and solid, but they were easy to part from each other, like pushing aside branches that smelled of sweat. I stepped between Bobby and Terry. They were still dressed, Bobby in his uniform and cap, Terry in his red slacks and white tee shirt.

"Quintana," I said. "Joaquin: it's me, old buddy. It's Billy."

I stared into his eyes but they were not looking back at me; they were looking at something, and they chilled the backs of my knees. I had to stop my hands from going up and feeling the air between us, grabbing for it, pushing it away.

There is something about being naked. Duke Simpson and Tommy Lutring got in a fight last year, in front of Duke's locker, when they had just got out of the shower, and it was not like seeing a fight on the field when the guys are dressed and rolling in the dirt. It seemed worse. Once in a hotel in Chicago a girl and I started fighting in bed and quick enough we were out of bed and putting on our underpants; the madder we got the more clothes we put on, and when she ended the fight by walking out, I was wearing everything but my socks and shoes. I wished Joaquin was dressed.

"Joaquin," I said. "Joaquin, I'm going to take the shoe."

Some of the guys told him to give Billy the shoe. I put my hand on it and he didn't move; then I tried to lift it, and his arm swung a few degrees, but that was all. His bicep was swollen and showing veins.

"Come on, Joaquin. Let it go now. That's a boy."

I put my other hand on it and jerked, and his arm swung and his body swayed and my hands slipped off the shoe. He was staring. I looked at Bobby and Terry, then at the guys on both sides; my eyes met Bruce's, so I said to him: "He doesn't even know I'm here."

"Poor bastard," Bobby said.

Somebody said we ought to carry him to Bobby's couch, and Terry said we couldn't because he was stiff as iron, and lightly, with his fingertips, he jabbed Joaquin's thighs and belly and arms and shoulders, and put his palms on Joaquin's cheeks. Terry said we had to wait for Doc Segura, and Bobby told old Will Hammersley, the clubhouse man, to go tell the press he was sorry but they couldn't come in tonight.

Then we stood waiting. I smelled Joaquin's sweat and listened to his breathing, and looked up and down his good body, and at the medal hanging from his neck, and past his eyes, into his locker: the shaving kit and underwear and socks on the top shelf, with his wallet and gold-banded wristwatch and box of cigars. A couple of his silk shirts hung in the locker, one aqua and one maroon, and a sport coat that was pale yellow, near the color of cream; under it some black pants were folded over the hanger. I wondered what it was like being him all the time. I don't know where the Dominican Republic is. I know it's in the Caribbean, but not where. Over the voices around me, Tommy Lutring said: "Why the *fuck* did we trade Manuel?" Then he said: "Sorry, Jesse."

"I wish he was here," Jesse said.

The guys near Jesse patted him on the shoulders and back. Lutring is the second baseman and he loves working with Joaquin. They are something to see, and I like watching them take infield practice. In a game it happens very fast, and you feel the excitement in the moments it takes Joaquin and Tommy to turn a double-play, and before you can absorb it, the pitcher's ready to throw again. In practice you get to anticipate, and watch them poised for the ground-ball, then they're moving, one to the bag, one to the ball, and they always know where the other guy is and where his glove is too, because whoever's taking the throw knows it's coming at his chest, leading him across the bag. It's like the movies I used to watch in San Antonio, with one of those dances that start with a chorus of pretty girls, then they move back for the man and woman: he is in a tuxedo and she wears a long white dress that rises from her legs when she whirls. The lights go down on the chorus, and one light moves with the man and woman dancing together and apart but always together. Light sparkles on her dress, and their shadows dance on the polished floor. I was a kid sitting in the dark, and I wanted to dance like that, and felt if I could just step into the music like into a river, the drums and horns would take me, and I would know how to move.

That is why Tommy said what he did. And Jesse said he wished Manuel was here too, which he probably did but not really, not at the price of him being back with the Yankees where he was the back-up catcher, while here he is the regular and also has our short left field wall to pull for. Because we couldn't do anything and we started to feel like Spanish was the answer, or the problem, and if just somebody could speak it to Joaquin he'd be all right and he'd put down that shoe and use his eyes again, and take off his jockstrap and socks, and head for the showers, so if only Manuel was with us or one of us had learned Spanish in school.

But the truth is the president or dictator of the Dominican Republic couldn't have talked Joaquin into the showers. Doc Segura gave him three shots before his muscles went limp and he dropped the shoe and collapsed like pants you step out of. We caught him before he hit the floor. The two guys with the ambulance got there after the first shot, and stood on either side of him, behind him so they were out of Doc's way; around the end, before the last shot, they held Joaquin's arms, and when he fell Bobby and I grabbed him too. His eyes were closed. We put him on the stretcher and they covered him up and carried him out and we haven't seen him since, though we get reports on how he's doing in the hospital. He sleeps and they feed him. That was three weeks ago.

Doc Segura had to wait thirty minutes between shots, so the smokers had their cigarettes and cigars going, and guys were passing beers and pizza up from the back, where I had stood with Bruce. He was still on the bench, drinking a beer, with smoke rising past him to the ceiling. I didn't feel right, drinking a beer in front of Joaquin, and I don't think Bobby did either. Terry is an alcoholic who doesn't drink anymore and goes to meetings, so he didn't count. Finally when someone held a can toward Bobby he didn't shake his head, but got it to his mouth fast while he watched Doc getting the second needle ready, so I reached for one too. Doc swabbed the vein inside Joaquin's left elbow. This time I looked at Joaquin's eyes instead of the needle: he didn't feel it. All my sweat was long since dried, and I had my jacket off except the right sleeve on my arm.

I know Manuel couldn't have helped Joaquin. The guys keep saying it was because he was lonesome. But I think they say that because Joaquin was black and spoke Spanish. And maybe for the same reason an alcoholic who doesn't drink anymore may blame other people's troubles on booze: he's got scary memories of blackouts and sick hangovers and d.t.'s, and he always knows he's just a barstool away from it. I lost a wife in my first year in professional ball, when I was eighteen years old and as dumb about women as I am now. Her name was Leslie. She left me for a married dentist, a guy with kids, in Lafayette, Louisiana, where I was playing my rookie year in the Evangeline League, an old class C league that isn't there anymore. She is back in San Antonio, married to the manager of a department store; she has four kids, and I hardly ever see her, but when I do there are no hard feelings. Leslie said she felt like she was chasing the team bus all season long, down there in Louisiana. I have had girlfriends since, but not the kind you marry.

By the time Joaquin fell I'd had a few beers and some pizza gone cold, and I was very tired. It was after one in the morning and I did not feel like I had pitched a game, and won it too. I felt like I had been working all day on the beef-cattle ranch my daddy is building up for us with the money I send him every payday. That's where I'm going when my arm gives out. He has built a house on it, and I'll live there with him and my mom. In the showers people were quiet. They talked, but you know what I mean. I dressed then told Hammersley I wanted to go into the park for a minute. He said Sure, Billy, and opened the door.

I went up the tunnel to the dugout and stepped onto the grass. It was already damp. I had never seen the park empty at night, and with no lights, and all those empty seats and shadows under the roof over the grandstand, and under the sky the dark seats out in the bleachers in right and centerfield. Boston lit the sky over the screen in left and beyond the bleachers, but it was a dull light, and above the playing field there was no light at all, so I could see stars. For a long time, until I figured everybody was dressed and gone or leaving and Hammersley was waiting to lock up, I stood on the grass by the batting circle and looked up at the stars, thinking of drums and cymbals and horns, and a man and woman dancing.

Caught

CRIS MAZZA

B *reathless, still shirtless, familiar taste of blood still in his mouth, 7 A.M.,*
parked beside the chain link fence he usually never even glances at. He
always thought his days leaning against a chain fence, waiting to take some
swings, were over. But now he moves directly, without a flicker, a bare-
chested man on a city sidewalk beside early rush traffic, unsurprised at him-
self, also not surprised at his lack of surprise. He opens his trunk, heads for
his catcher's mitt. Swings around, standing in the gutter, his back to the
car, mitt clutched to his chest. Some cars pass, faces turn toward him, then
they're gone so quickly. He sits on the curb to replace his shoes with cleats,
metal spikes, veterans of real games that counted.

I barely know Mario but followed him into a dark, blank-faced club—how
long ago, only eight hours? Was blinded on the inside by colored neon,
deafened by stereo thump, suffocated by pressing hot bodies. But was I
stunned?

A hardball is jammed in the deepest corner of his trunk, tucked inside a fielder's mitt. He needs them both, digs them out, holds the almost-black fielder's mitt between his knees while he rubs the ball into the catcher's mitt. Heavy, smooth strokes — he grinds the ball into the dark stain in the padded pocket, both a necessity and a ritual before a game.

Mario was immediately sucked into the very center of the heartbeat — the knot of bodies on the dance floor. I never saw him again. The room breathed for me, pulled and pushed my diaphragm and ribs, prodded my heart with a heavy fist. And the lights throbbed. From every corner of the ceiling, from the walls, embedded into the floor: lights. A glob of color hanging from the center of the ceiling, mostly red like new blood, but also blue, teasing glimmers of green. Spurting color. The strands of neon were strings for puppet dancers. A room made out of rhythm.

Gravel crunches underfoot as he turns in his tracks and moves alongside the fence toward the gate. He isn't afraid. Not of this. Neither losing a game nor a hissing crowd nor hard words nor freak injury terrified him on a baseball field. If his heart is straining now, and if he's sweating too heavily and he can't seem to swallow, it is not because he's squeezing under the chain lock, crawling onto the dirty, ill-kept field. No bases, no plate, just hollows in the dirt, but he heads for his place in front of the backstop.

Not possible that I was ever afraid on a ballfield. Even squatting behind the man with the bat, never once thought: he could kill me by mistake. I was 20 years old and life was slow motion, plenty of time, like catching a pop foul: head back, eyes up, watching the speck of a ball arcing gracefully over, peaking, curving back toward earth, toward me, lifting my legs without effort, matching the flight of the ball with my circling, twirling dance. They said I had instinct. Understood the pattern of the game. Never stopped to think about what it was I was supposed to understand so innately. Kids, just fooling around, my roomie Rick wearing his jockstrap like a gas mask, jumping out of the bushes to scare tourists. And our fast-back contests — like a simple game of catch, but throw it back as fast as possible, catch him before he's ready, try to hit him with the ball, honing our 20-year-old reflexes. Then eel-tag or underwater lobster fights, illicitly using the pool after midnight ("Stay outta the pool, boys, it'll sap your strength"), so we had to glide around without splashing, without breaking the smooth surface of the water. He was a journeyman infielder but my place was always in front of the backstop.

I wouldn't let anything I couldn't see get behind me—I kept the wall at my back. I held a wet beer bottle. I may have sipped from it, but never with my eyes shut. People dancing, lights flashing, ice plinking, conversation pushing under a steady bass and cymbal upbeat. Just people dancing and talking, a kiss here, slapped face there, dark booths with black-outlined human forms, two heads together. That's all. Hard to breathe at my own rate without hiccuping—a hard jerk from my stomach which bounced my head—so I didn't fight the rhythm any more, breathed when everyone else did. We sucked the air out of the room together, blew it back in. The walls moved in and out. I didn't search long for women. Just slender men, like grass blowing with the swirling wind on the dance floor, or sleek seals you'd like to swim with, cutting still water while holding on, feeling the muscles which propel them.

From the bathroom came a queen with a round ass in a mini-skirt, a tight flat sweater, smooth hairless arms and legs which looked yellow in the neon. A thin boy in jeans took the queen's hands out on the dance floor. The music was elastic, pushing forward and holding back. Finally each beat was both a relief and a headache. And the boy smiled, turned his partner around, still holding only the yellow hands. They were still for a moment, a second, a long flexible fraction of time, and the downbeat hit as the round ass in its purple skirt pressed into the front of the boy's tight crotch. Their hips made one rhythm. Heavy, grinding, rolling strokes, jeans and skirt, ass and crotch. I couldn't catch a breath, I must've been dead, for a while at least.

The music changed and someone shrieked, a long full-moon howl. Everyone cheered. The mini-skirt was goosed, turned and slapped the boy with yellow palm and jeweled fingers. He never lost his grin. They grinned together and left, together, holding hands. He opened the door and the skirt stepped outside. My beer bottle, still full, still wet and cold, was pressed to my face. I'm not sure for how long. I never noticed any numbness—of either hand, my cheeks nor forehead. Not like holding that icepack to my mouth, flat on my back, game over, my own syrupy blood draining down my throat, watching my teammates shower, moving like demons in and out of the steam. Their hair darkened and stuck to their skin, making patterns on their legs and asses as the water streamed down. The radio was on, harsh bounce of rock, but they never danced—would slip on the slick shower floor. They talked about the rhythm of the pitcher who'd broken their bats that day, his mesmerizing pump and throw. The steam was made of their sweat and breath, thick and sweet, turning to water on the metal lockers, and on me. I wiped their wetness from my own skin. Their hair dripped and the steam was white and the yellow water gurgled down the drain.

The field is cool, feels ready for rain or just damp air left over from a foggy dawn. His jaw aches. Another guy runs laps, circling this field and another—around the back of one backstop, across first base, into right center, over the line and he touches left center on the far field, tags the worn-out hole marking third base, around the backstop and heads for first again—wearing gray shorts and a pale gold shirt, damp in front, down the middle, not a big guy, footsteps marked by a grunt from his chest, then he takes in air on the upbeat, perfect rhythm.

The catcher waits as the other guy comes across from the opposite diamond, across this outfield, toward this backstop. The runner's hair is damp-dark, he doesn't look up, doesn't break stride, comes around the backstop where the catcher halts him with his arm in his path, catches him with a mitt in his gut, then grabs the runner's arm with his throwing hand. "We're gonna play catch."

"Hey, no, I'm—"

The catcher is pressing the mitt into the guy's chest. He squirms like a bug being pinched between thumb and forefinger.

"Leave me alone." He tries to punch a knee into the catcher's balls.

The catcher shakes him. Can't do much else—he's only actually holding one of the guy's arms, but still mashing the mitt against the guy's chest with his own glove-hand. Shaking upsets the runner's effort, has to lower his knee to stand on two feet. But he swings a fist. So the catcher moves close against him. His arm flails, the catcher saying in his ear, "I bite, kid. Now let's play." The runner stops struggling. "Throwing and catching is all we're going to do. Just throw and catch, throw and catch, keep it going."

The runner puts his hands over the mitt, holds it against his chest by himself. So the catcher removes his hand, both his hands, begins to back away. The runner stares. His mouth is sucked hard against his teeth. He hurries to push his hand into the glove as the catcher shoots the ball toward him, backs him up to second base where he stays when shouted at to stop. That's where he'll take the throw-down from the catcher. He's around twenty years old. He bites the middle finger of the mitt and stares at the catcher over the top.

I didn't dance.

For a long time no one approached, no one asked. The tunes seemed to end faster and faster, and with the beginning of each, the renewed possibility of being asked, being taken, being led, being dragged to the dance floor. I mouthed my neat "no," practiced my placid shrug, watched the partners change, redistribute. They traded mid-dance, everyone danced with everyone else.

He had gray sideburns and matching gray wavy hair combed straight back, a gold chain at his throat, and he appeared at my side, from nowhere, touched my arm with ten fingers, raised his slim gray eyebrows and said, "Dance?"

Did my body relax a moment, seem to be swayed by him? No! His fingers tightened, tugging slightly, and he smiled. Perfect teeth, beautiful caps, not unlike my own phony set. Did he get his for the same reason? Did he deserve it? I wrenched my arm away. Turned my back. Dizzy. Out of breath. My jaw ached.

The music became faster, erratic, unpredictable, unsteady, unsatisfied, and the lights did the same for the sake of any deaf dancers, or those going deaf. But I was aware of something steady, calm, clear, cool, confident: Pat's eyes, watching me through the people. I kept glancing back, catching him looking, but his eyes never flitted away. Steady and strong. And I glanced back more often, and looked longer, and leaned against the wall. And when I thought to smile, and the thought was still only a shadow on my lips, he split the crowd to join me. He wore number twenty-one on a baseball sweatshirt.

He was a professional, hard-throwing catcher and the inexperienced 20-year-old across the diamond from him hides behind the fielder's mitt. The catcher is throwing hard enough to bruise the bone.

My nickname, bone-bruiser, as a promising minor league catcher. The game was a rhythm in me. Catch and throw or swing and connect. I was more than good. Tobacco in my cheek, running, hitting, sliding, and never swallowed the bitter, brown lump. The beer was good after the game. Sometimes vodka. A bottle bobbing around in the pool with us, just fooling around, skinny-dipping after curfew with my roomie Rick, his hair plastered down, paddling softly after the bottle, quiet liquid darkness, a closeness only ballplayers can know, underwater friendship, like the soft sounds of seals playing. When they taught us to slide head-first, they said slide like a seal down a shoot. But I had to go home one summer to get a new mouth and new jaw, a few new teeth and a neat seam across my tongue. They said I deserved it.

I had been resting my chin on the mouth of my beer bottle, and as Pat approached I raised my head. I knew what to say: "Baseball," and the pulsating madness faded with his slow smile.

"Pardon?"

"You play? I mean, your jersey . . ."

"Oh. Just a company softball team. We played tonight."

I could see his skin beneath the red, blue and orange tints flashing on his cheeks. No make-up. No jewelry. No lilt in his walk. I saw the number twenty-one and short hair and ears and simple face and bright mouth and soft eyes, and I cried a little — at least my eyes were wet, obviously with relief.

"I played professional."

"You mean real live hardball? The big money?"

"Well, I played in the minors." Momentarily I was sickened slightly by the mixture of my honesty with the severe lights and confusing music, as though the heat and noise and smoke hovering under the heartbeat strobe were laughing, as though I'd made a long-awaited confession.

"I probably would've made it to the big leagues. I can't actually remember giving up on it. But . . ."

He looked away, scanning the dance floor. "You don't have to explain. Most of us understand."

"You do?"

He turned back toward me. "My name's Pat."

"Gary." We shook hands, more than one shake, then he tapped his brow with a yellow scarf he took from his pocket. "Let's get outta here, okay? Kinda hot tonight. Kinda tight in here."

There was sweat on my neck. I agreed with him. It was too hot in there.

His yellow-shirted partner taking the throw-down at second base is duck-ing, but hasn't run away. The catcher nearly falls down while throwing. The ball flies at the other guy like a big rock thrown anonymously out of an angry mob. Catching it nearly sits him down backwards. But he returns it. Doesn't stall, doesn't lob it high in the air or roll angry grounders. The other guy throws without emotion. Only when he catches, seconds before it reaches his head, do his white teeth show, tight between his lips, set together on edge, and his eyes shut and his head goes down behind the mitt. The ball slams home, pushes the glove back into his face. The catcher is throw-ing zingers. Still rising as they reach second base. And even as the twenty-year-old wiggles out of his drenched yellow shirt, the catcher can't wait, won't slow down, has to keep the rhythm, can't fight momentum. The other guy has his mitt in his teeth, pulling the yellow shirt over his head, and it's stuck there, inside-out on his head with the glove still in his mouth, but the catcher throws anyway. The guy turns his back and catches the ball between his shoulder blades. It doesn't sound like a hand slapping flesh, but it does slap, bites and leaves a red birthmark on his skin. The catcher is sorry for that. But the other guy finishes removing his shirt, turns and faces home plate with his twenty-year-old chest, hairless and shiny wet, heaving in and out. Hopefully anger and not fatigue. The catcher tenses in preparation. The twenty-year-old picks up the ball.

We found a basement under a hospital, down the block from the club, filled with steam from the hospital laundry, but empty, three A.M. I'd walked the night air for over an hour, breathing gallons, cool and damp, and heard Pat's soft footsteps beside me as we talked in late-night voices. The things people talk about: great teams, memorable players, bad trades. I felt him listening carefully. More carefully than he should've, or maybe my imagination. When he spoke, I tried to be interested, but was dis-tracted by the thud of my heart, my deep slow breathing, and his beside me, our footsteps setting the same pace.

Then he said, "See there," pointing to the basement window at ground level, a yellow glow. "Let's go inside."

"Someone's there."

"Not at this hour. They leave the light on. The machines are running."

"How do you know?"

He smiled and took me to the window, easy to open, and he touched my elbow lightly as I put my legs through. It was a drop into the basement, and he followed, wanting me to take his legs and catch him as he came through the window. But I said, "No, jump like I did," and I turned to see where we were.

The machines droned. I already felt slimy from the steam, once again found it hard to breathe. Once again too noisy for common talk. Through cloudy yellow windows in the dryers, I could see hospital sheets tumble. Pat took a pole and shut the window.

"I felt better outside walking."

But, again, Pat only smiled.

I said, "I left with you because . . ." I stopped.

I mumbled, "I never said I . . ."

I whispered, "I don't know."

Pat found a radio. He didn't have to search long. Just walked right over to it and clicked it on.

"No. I'm sick of music."

"I'll put it on low."

"We left there because the music was too loud."

Pat smiled, but not at me. Smiled gently at his hand on the radio dial. He said, "Did we? I forgot." He didn't turn it off. I heard it through the tiny speaker as though the club up the street piped their music here.

"The music gave me a headache."

"This'll be okay."

We waited, the steam and most of the basement between us, until Pat picked a song. Slow but bouncy. He moved his hips. I watched without moving—uninterested or uninvolved or unamazed or disappointed or undecided or dead.

He put his arms over his head, flowing like underwater grass. I didn't move and he came no closer. Our shirts were wet. I saw his, felt mine. He took his off and resumed the dance. I also removed my shirt. He was very thin. There was only one light—the yellow light bulb at the ceiling which we'd seen from the street. It cast shadows under his collar bones, between his ribs. His flat tummy had little hair, but there was some, dark and wet around his navel.

He came no closer throughout the whole dance. He danced alone. The song ended and an advertisement began. Pat turned to change the station or to turn it off. Then changed his mind and left it. He picked up his shirt and came through the steam toward me. Up close, I saw that his skin was slick. So was mine. But neither of us wiped ourselves.

Pat said, "I really don't like that place either."

"Why did you go?"

"Why did you?"

"Someone from work took me. I mean, I followed him . . . in my car. He said I may find it's what I'm looking for, or it may not be after all." I laughed, a strange sound there. "Maybe I already found out, though, a long time ago."

Pat didn't laugh, but he smiled. The smell in the laundry room was like something rotting there. He said, "Gary, let's be honest with each other."

Wish I could say I was surprised, even shocked. "Haven't we been?"

"I love baseball. I'm a real fan."

"Oh yeah?" I said dully.

"Isn't there something mythical or mystic about the game? The legends, the half-truths, the hero worship, the sanctity of the clubhouse, and all that? A whole world you can escape into." The steam seemed to shift. The machines stopped, the sheets made one final flop. Somewhere a fan still swished, though barely a whisper, and the radio was playing music again, thick with boogaloo percussion. Pat said, "I've always wanted to meet a real player."

Caught.

"It's been a long time."

A long time since I was on third base, a triple lashed into left center, then got trapped off the bag with Ricky, bleary-eyed, at the plate: In his sick weakness—only twelve hours after something had happened underwater that I'd thought neither of us could exactly remember—the booze was suddenly to blame. But, if true, he wouldn't've had to smash my face with the bat. Yet, just minutes before they dragged me away, there I was on third base. I loved being twenty-years-old on third base. The last time I was on third. The last time I loved being twenty-years-old.

The catcher has extended to his full motion: crouch for the catch, rise and throw, using arm, legs and body. The ball is like a rope between him and the man on second, twenty years old. The catcher's jaw aches. Probably his teeth are clenched.

The steam began to clear but never left all together. The window dripped. Dawn was gray. Pat danced, then stopped. Resting, breathing heavily. When he bent at the waist, profile to me, I could see how narrow he was just above the belt. He put his hands on his knees and his ribcage expanded and contracted.

I yawned and he laughed. Then he checked his watch. "The morning shift will be here soon, at six-thirty."

"We'd better go."

"We'd better hurry." He turned the radio up. The tiny speaker distorted the music into a mash of electric sounds, nothing soft or bouncy to it. Hard and coarse like sand in my mouth. Pat came toward me again. We stood facing. "How about a game, slugger." He unbuckled his pants, let them drop, wiggled his hips to remove the underwear. His clothes shackled his legs from the knees down. I flexed my jaw without parting my lips. I thought I felt the pin there, for the first time. They told me I'd never feel it.

He was like silk yet the music was nails. I crouched like a catcher, squatted on the floor, held my balance with my fingertips pressing against the cement in front of my feet. At first he shuddered, quivered, then the jolts became a rhythm. Pump, throw, catch, return, and again. Like waves, smooth rollers, in and out. The water swelled but never broke, never crashed white and foamy. I was out beyond the breakers, swimming with a seal, born to slip and slide, glide and dive, run races, play tag, throw and catch, touch each bag with the right toe, never stumbling off stride, never fooled by the pick-off. Trapped off base. Caught. My roomie, Rick, sluggish and mesmerized, still in the box, still at the plate, hypnotized by the rhythm of the rundown, pitcher to third to catcher to short. But *my* reflexes weren't dulled, put my head down and broke for home, past the surprised catcher—out of position too far up the line. I was home free, sliding face first, only my own man waiting at the plate to greet me, to embrace me . . . but he cocks his bat and takes a full swing—

On hands and knees, I bit down. Hard. The scream wasn't mine this time. The scream that ends it. I spit blood and shut my eyes and grabbed my hair, and spit again. We doubled, head-to-head on the floor where he vomited, yellow acid. I spit blood.

Then I left through the window, left him crying on the floor, his cheek lying flat in the yellow slime and saliva-blood, crying.

Everyone had said I deserved it.

Each throw pounds dust from the pocket of the catcher's mitt. He chokes on it, his eyes water, but they don't stop. The catcher keeps digging the ball out of his mitt and the other keeps sending it back. When he blinks, there's grit and dirt in his tears. The other guy is still throwing hard, harder than he did at first, as hard as a twenty-year-old body can. Throws with the strength in his legs and the long muscle down his back. The catcher grunts as he receives it, catches each one near his head, around his eyes, in front of his mouth. He tries to throw back before the other guy can recover from his follow-through. But the other guy is quick—getting quicker—and the catcher's motion is getting awkward. He's throwing harder than is possible for someone who's busy protecting his head, his face, his nose and mouth. Dig and throw and recover and return. They're both yelling, grunting shouts with each throw—not words, the voices of their bodies. Wind-up, release, get set to catch. Someone has to finish it, let the end happen. The boy throws and the catcher shuts his eyes but still sees everything. As though the ball is standing still and he's the one hurling his head toward it, to catch the moment of splintering bones and spurting blood, and teeth that rattle loose. His head snaps back.

Gold Moments and Victory Beer

GORDON WEAVER

The way it happened, Big Edwards just leaned forward in his chair, reached out, and slapped Smitty smack across his tan face. "There," he said, like he'd taken a dare on something. "There" was all he said. I was facing the both of them, chair sideways to the damp table filled with pitchers of victory beer, so I saw it all. I was always seeing everything. Which is one of my troubles.

Ray Botts didn't see it. He was harping about the mess somebody made washing up after the game in the men's toilet. He nodded his round head in the direction of the toilet and said, sullen, "Who was it crudded up the sink for the Christ's sakes?"

Fred Jantke saw. He looked at Edwards, but he wasn't for doing anything about it just yet. "What the hell was that for?" was all he had to say. Ray Botts still didn't notice anything. He looked at me, accusing.

"Tee-bow," he said, "is that you, dirtied up the sink?" I didn't answer, waiting for Smitty to pick it up or leave it.

The way it happened, Big Edwards had said to him: "You know, Smith, I get on the force now, I'm in a position for hanging you if I feel like it."

Smitty didn't smile, not even the cynical ten-dollar smile. He kept his eyes on Edwards, knowing I was watching him, and said, "You're a liar and a eee-lapper, a four-day creeper and a turdsnapper." The Big Edwards peered at him like he didn't see him any better than he heard him. He leaned forward, peered, then slapped him smack in the face.

Well, I thought to myself, what's the difference anyway? I always see everything; I'm always watching. What's the use of anything anyway? I thought. That's about when I was feeling the lowest about everything, right after he slapped Smitty.

Even coming back from Pumping Station Field in Fred Jantke's car, naturally having won, I was pretty sour. Not that there wasn't some good feeling too. Nothing can ever sour everything for me.

We won of course—Edwards is without fail the best fastpitch softball pitcher in the County Fastpitch League, and likely one of the three, four best in the state. And I had a few good moments. Three for four, one double that faster I could've stretched to third—no apology, since my arm from right field and my stick make up for lacking speed. Speed is my short suit; I admit it.

There's undeniable good moments: seeing it from out in right field, the sun bouncing off Edwards' sweated red forehead, that big man shrugging his shoulders to let out his breath as he toes the rubber, and then that big arm comes around, the little flap sound it makes when his hand brushes his pant leg to meet underhand regulations, the sharp *pop* sound when the ball lands in Fred Jantke's glove behind the plate—hearing it almost before I see the batter twist his back trying for the pitch. I hear the infield talk when they whip it around the horn after Edwards fans another batter, a little applause from the stands behind the screen, and then Ray Botts comes off the bench with his clipboard in his hand to wave us out-fielders around to position for the next man up if Edwards hasn't already fanned the entire side.

When I'm sticking too. I like grinding my spikes in deep in the box, and I keep taking practice cuts right up until the pitcher starts his motion. I fox the hell out of them, because I can choke up on the bat to place the ball while it's already coming at me. That kind of fast I have. I can feel it when it's right, the second I hit that six-inch inseam ball. And no denying I like to hear the clapping and the shouts from the stands, and what they say from the bench. On first base, Ray Botts in the coaching box pats me on the fanny and starts putting it to the pitcher to watch me like as if I was likely to steal.

Good, running in to help pick up mitts and bats in the long canvas bag with *Axel's Inn* on the side in white paint that's faded to look almost like chalk after nearly three seasons. Loading up in the cars to get to Axel's, winning team serves the beer, loser's sponsor pays. Undeniable.

In the car heading for the tavern, Fred Jantke spat out the window expertly and said to Ray Botts, our manager-coach-statistician-utility player, "RayBotts, for Christ's sakes, why you don't put in a official protest, them em-pires! they don't see nothing." He grabbed the necker's nob on the wheel and steered around a safety island.

"Quit bitching," Ray Botts said. "Edwards goes into police school now, he'll be pitching for the police department, you'll have something to holler about. Then it's honeymoon all over for us, you'll have something to cry for."

Really? I ask myself. Then I'm sour. That's how I get that way. Fred Jantke cleared his throat to hawk again. Ray Botts was busy in the official scorekeeper's book. It felt like no breeze came in the open car windows. I'm sour as hell.

Big Edwards wants to be a cop, goes to police school, so what? So Axel's Inn doesn't win every Saturday afternoon anymore. So we don't grab off the county trophy every year. We don't grab off a trophy in the regionals, likely the sectionals too, this year. That's so what. And more: where now how there's this fair-to-good chance on the state invitational championship (individual engraved plaques as big as meat platters), without Big Edwards there is positively no chance. Which is also so what.

Without Edwards we're just another tavern team, a few trophies over the bar, tarnishing a little each year. Without Edwards we're just what we are, I'm thinking. That's so what. Christ, I am sour.

"As a team we hit .379 so far the season," Ray Botts said.

"It ain't hitting counts, Ray Botts," Fred Jantke said.

"Tee-bow," Ray Botts said, "you're sticking a wicked .505. That's good for maybe third, fourth in the league." I opened the back window all the way and spat, hoping I didn't streak the rear fender. He was trying to say something cheerful.

"You lose Edwards," I had to say, "you won't care what nobody's sticking."

Some more of my moments: coming into Axel's. I walk behind Edwards, who rides with Voss because Voss has a convertible. I walk in behind him, seeing those shoulders fill the doorway, standing only high enough on him to look at the back of his red neck, and I think how here is the best softball pitcher of maybe an entire state, and I am possibly the third leading percentage hitter in the county league, and I have to hold myself back, slow down so as not to crowd into the back of Edwards' sweaty jersey, white felt letters on green, Axel's Inn, because I feel like I'm glowing and would burn anyone who touches me.

Inside I wave first to Les, the regular bartender, who is in the middle of saying to Edwards, "You put them away, Big Ed?" All unnecessary. I spot Schneider, the beat cop, sitting at the bar, deadheading on duty of course. I clown a bit to work out of what I feel because I can hardly stand it. I yank Schneider's cop's hat off the back of his head and plunk it down on Edwards from behind. "Schneider," I say, "look what's coming on the police force these days."

"For the Christ's sakes," Schneider says, who could care less.

Edwards obliges. He turns the hat sideways, steps to the end of the bar, pounds his fist and snarls at Les, "Everybody outta da pool!"

"Hey Les," says Voss, a middling good first sacker, "this means he gets free drinks and scoff like Schneider, right?"

"Where's my graft?" Edwards snarls.

"That'll be the day I get graft," Schneider slurs.

Edwards sailed the hat back down the bar to him. Ray Botts went behind the bar to see to tapping the victory barrel. "You all set now, Big Ed?" Les asked.

"Week and a half I report to orientation. They got the academy right downtown in the Safety Building annex. Eight hours a day, five days a week, then you go on duty, but on probation," Edwards said. He reached his long arm behind the bar to take a fistful of hard boiled eggs from the wire rack.

"Have fun is all I say," Schneider said, having been lucky enough to become a cop when the standards were lower.

I look up above the bar at the row of gold trophies on the shelf, dusted regularly by Les. All sizes, and the biggest the County Fastpitch League traveler, which remains here permanent, with names engraved, when we win it for the third season in a row this year. Whatever way they list us, alphabetical, batting order, I'll be there: *Thibault, George.* In gold.

I'm looking at the row of gold above the back-bar mirror, seeing my name, gold on gold, and I'm glowing again. Edwards is talking to Les and Schneider, Voss is calling for the Sheepshead cards, Ray Botts swearing at a clumsy beertapper . . . with this year's championship already cinched, forever and forever, my name's in gold at Axel's Inn, and all the regulars and chance stoppers-in will see my name if they look, the names of all of us, which is why I hate thinking it has to end. Ever.

Then Smitty comes.

"Wait, don't tell me, let me guess," he shouts from the doorway. "I got it. You won!" It's his usual. He's looking right at me, and I'm embarrassed, caught dreaming about myself. Then I see I'm standing close next to Edwards, who Smitty considers a crud and a phony, which makes me afraid he classes me with him. The thing is, I admire the both of them.

Smitty steps just inside, into the fanned dark cool, hands on hips, sneering at everything with his stance. He snickers at me, at all of us, at softball games and the victories we celebrate with beer.

From behind him and round him the losing team players filed in now, circles of sweat under their arms, ovals on their chests and backs making their purple jerseys even darker. Hide-Away Bar. We took them 14–0 in seven innings. Their dirty spikes click on the tile floor and leave a trail of bits of grass and dried mud. In contrast to us as we mill at the bar, like sweated horses walking off the heat to keep muscles loose, waiting for the first foamy glasses of beer, Smitty stands still and apart, wearing a colorful flowing aloha shirt hanging out over pressed but faded slacks. He smiles and shows his gold-flecked teeth.

The losing captain, hauling out his sponsor's money to pay Les for the beer, looked at Smitty, then at me, puzzled to see a Negro in this neighborhood.

"RayBotts," Schneider said, "mark your glasses, the leech is here."

"He's the closest thing to a mascot for us since Les's pig died," Ray Botts said, pushing foam off the top of a glass with a wooden tongue depressor.

"Tee-bow," Smitty said, smiling at me, "your father work?"

"Nope," I obliged, "he's a cop." He came up to me at the bar, winked, lifted one finger to Ray Botts to include himself in on beer now being drawn, clear and yellow, in heavy pitchers. Les shoved a glass to him.

"Aaaagh?" Smitty said, rolling his lips dry of beer foam, grinning with his eyes at me. "If you didn't keep on winning, chum, I don't wonder but what I'd have to go to work in order to keep on drinking." Which is exactly what I often thought about myself when the first one was going down. I glowed, felt close to him.

He was a part of what we had there at Axel's Inn, and I wanted to keep him a part of it as much as I wanted to keep Edwards, or Ray Botts, Voss, Schneider, Les, all of us.

The first year we took the county championship—that year we got as far as the state sectionals—we came pouring in out of the sun to drink winner's beer, and there he was. Smitty was at the far end of the bar, smoking a cigarette he must have mooched from Les, chewing cashews from a cellophane sack, nursing a bottled beer. I watched, and he stayed, watching; when the barrel was down below half, most of the losing team gone, nobody to care, Ray Botts handed a glass to Smitty and told him to suck up, it was free.

He came every Saturday after that, arriving just after we'd get back from the Pumping Station to celebrate, probably coming all the way across town from the Negro district to cadge free beer. But not without integrity. Not obliging. I noticed.

He never cringed, never crab-walked sideways up to the bar. He never had to ask for a glass, and I never heard him say thanks for a drop, for anything. And when the Saturday got dark outside, the noise over, the sweat dried and stiff in our jerseys, the half-dozen or so of us left drew up at a table with Smitty. What he did, what he contributed—I doubt he ever so much as held a softball or a bat in his hands—he talked. Just talked. He mocked, needled one or all of us. He told stories, jokes, lies. It's what he did, he said, for a living, being as he never worked, as a matter of pride. He could talk.

As for instance. Once he told us about his ten-dollar smile, the one he used to borrow ten dollars with. Later the same afternoon he borrowed ten dollars from Ray Botts, only reminding us what he'd done after he had the tenner in hand. Ray Botts chased him around the bumper pool table and out the door, but we needled him so hard, all got to laughing, he let Smitty back inside.

And that's what got to me, bothered me, started me sour. His talk. The time half a dozen men and their women came in after a matinee at the Repertory Theater across the street. Les told them he didn't have the makings for Old Fashioneds and Whiskey Sours, but they settled for booze and mix. Ray Botts started the hassle. One of the men, tuxedo jacket and all, turned to his woman and said, "Look at the team."

"Ooew," Ray Botts said loudly, turning to Fred Jantke, drawing his mouth out in a pucker, "Ah dew wish ah had gone to the thee-ahtah this ahft-tah-noon, doe-wen't yew?" The man turned around to face us, rotated his glass on the bar with two thick fingers. Les the regular bartender looked hard at Ray Botts. Fred Jantke's no fighter that I ever knew, but he was beer-tight enough to oblige: "Rah-lay," he said, "ah dew think the theah-tah is grand!"

The man in the tuxedo jacket ran his tongue over his lips and looked us over one by one to see how many were ready to back up our boy. I dropped my eyes—George Thibault is no fighter I can assure you—and discarded the comment I was rehearsing. I stared into my beer, drank deep.

Fred Jantke stood up, cupped one hand to his mouth, pointed to the tuxedo man, and sang out, "Ollie ollie oxen all free, this guy's lookin' bad at me!" I ducked automatically and shoved my chair back to get running room; Smitty sneered at the whole thing and lit up a cigarette mooched from my pack on the table.

That tuxedo guy seemed to stumble, he came so fast. He grabbed Fred Jantke where he stood, handful of jersey, and cocked a punch while bulling him back into the bar. Ray Botts picked up a free chair to crown him with. It could have been right nasty.

It was a miracle, Schneider walking in just then. "Drop the chair, Ray," he said. I was seeing him rest the heel of his hand on the leaded billy he carried in a loop on his cartridge belt, just in front of his service .38.

"Tell this crud to go to the Mint Bar then, this ain't no cocktail lounge!" Ray Botts screamed. But he dropped the lumber. Tuxedo man let loose Fred Jantke's jersey and wiped his hand on his sleeve.

"You started it, RayBotts, admit it," Les said, mostly to Schneider. Schneider made Ray Botts and Fred Jantke leave, talked to Les and the tuxedo people for a second, downed a courtesy shot from Les, nodded hello to Smitty and me on his way out. I don't clown near so often around him since then.

"He sure as hell handled that nice," I said to Smitty.

Smitty wrinkled his nose, showed his inlays, tossed off his beer, said, "Would have served them right if he pinched them for it." Then he went up to the bar to refill our pitcher.

"What the hell," I said when he came back, "are you siding with those people against RayBotts?" The possibility shook me. Smitty was supposed to be one of us. I tried to hold onto it, the games we won, our celebration, that gold above the bar, I felt my glow fade. Smitty laughed. "Tee-bow," he said, helping himself to my cigs again, "I'll tell you something you already know. Ray Botts is a bully. So is Jantke. Neither one's tough, but they got to believe they're bad actors just to live with themselves. Trouble is they get so much beer in them, they know better. Then they need somebody like my man in the suit. And baseball games, and all that kind of crap."

That hurt. "You wouldn't have helped them?" I glanced at the row of trophies over Les's head.

"I'd done just like the man, Tee-bow, tied into the both of them—"

"Either one could cream you easy," I said. No lie. Smitty is maybe five-seven at most, skinnier than me and not near as straight.

"So what?" he said. "Thing is, next time they'd bully somebody else, wouldn't they. Two kinds of people can't take me, Tee-bow. Phonies and bad actors. Phonies because they can't take anyone knows the truth about them, bullies 'cause they only bully people who don't fight back."

Now that was the beginning, when I started losing my moments. They still came, came when I stood out in right field at the Pumping Station and answered the infield chatter with my own pepper, when I dug my spikes in at the plate and took my practice cuts right up to the second the ball left the mound, when we poured sweating into Axel's and huddled up under that row of gold trophies to wait for the barrel to be tapped. But I couldn't stay away from Smitty, because I know the truth when I hear it as good as the next man, even when I was dreaming to myself about how my name was going to be up there forever and ever.

This Saturday, this day it happened, Edwards and Les and Schneider were talking just generally, Edwards telling Schneider about the examination he passed for police academy. "Tee-bow," Smitty said, "cigarette me." I slid my pack down the bar to him and settled in to listen to Edwards. Now he was telling the story again about having known No-Hit Don Larsen of the New York Yankees. "Schneider," he said, "I know Don Larsen very well, played ball with him, and Don said when he signed with the Yankees they took him into the locker room at Yankee Stadium, and they showed him where Ruth had his locker, and they said to him now you're a Yankee. . . ." He told it often, but with enough beer nobody cared. Some of us maybe even believed him.

"When the hell you going to get a job, Tee-bow?" Smitty asks me.

"I got a job."

"Name it."

"Encyclopedia salesman." Partly true, since I'd only recently been canned from that. Smitty laughed.

"I mean a real job."

"Same day you get one."

"That's different," he said. "I know I'm a bum and I don't care, but you do. So when you going to work?" Players from both teams were settling down at tables now to play Sheepshead, which is how Voss supplements his unemployment compensation. The fast drinking was over, the steady strong drinking on the way. Going sour. I ignored Smitty.

Les and Schneider were looking down at Edwards' right arm, which he had laid out, palm up, on the bar like a cut of meat. Edwards looked at his arm with this look, like thinking, could it be true this was really his very own arm? Schneider and Les looked respectful, quiet, like they'd look at somebody's bankroll.

"A million-dollar arm!" Edwards said, shaking his pink head. "A million dollars, and I threw it out on American Legion doubleheaders and fastpitch for beer." Les and Schneider lifted their eyes in sympathy. What we all understood was that nobody was called on to say anything.

"You're a liar," Smitty said, grinning over his free beer, "and a pennywink. You eat cat shit and your breath stinks." Les hustled away to help Ray Botts draw beer. Schneider adjusted his hat and hitched up his cartridge belt, groaning faintly. I watched. Edwards' face showed the shock, as good as if Smitty'd picked up the sunburned arm and thrown it at him.

Smitty kept his eyes steady on him, smiling his you're-a-liar-and-I-know-it smile, with the gold-rimmed edges of his lower teeth showing, the mooched cigarette burning slowly between his brown fingers, the beer glass beading in his other hand.

"You suppose they'll pressure you to pitch for the police department after you start, Big Ed?" I said, just to be saying something.

"May be," he said. He dropped his eyes and walked away from Smitty's laugh to a table where someone asked him did he strike out thirteen or fourteen today.

"You have to do that?" I said.

"What's he to you that you got to wet-nurse him?" Smitty said.

"That isn't it at all, man. What is it with you? You get a kick out of calling people liars and bums and all?"

"But ain't it the damn truth?" he said, and shook another cigarette out of my pack.

"Look at you," I said. "Goddamn leech, sponge my weeds, sponge beer, sponge—"

"Do I deny it?"

"What the hell's that matter!" I yelled. "I sweated two hours in the sun for this beer at least, so did Edwards and the rest of us, you come in, drink up for nothing, and give us your smart mouth to boot—you bastard, Smitty—"

"Tee-bow!" he said so loud I shut up. "How long are you gonna kid yourself this is all a big deal?" He opened his hand and stretched his arm to include everything, the players standing around Ray Botts to get their pitchers filled, the Sheepshead game at the table, Les wiping the bar, everything. The pool table, the jukebox. The trophies.

"What do you know about it," I said. I spoke softly now. "What do you know, leeching crud? See that county league trophy? This season's over, you're gonna see my name up there. All of us, our names up there. Stick in your hat how much you know about it, sponger." He laughed.

"Maybe when you're forty they'll let you be a big-time manager like Ray, huh?" I looked at Ray Botts, the bully, working over the barrel. His paunch hung over his belt. He was balder every time I met him. He was telling someone about a fastpitch team upstate that would doubtless be invited to the regionals . . . but they had no pitching, he was saying with confidence.

Schneider left to finish his beat. The married men left. The men who worked graveyard shift left. It got down to one table of us, Voss playing solitaire, Ray Botts talking about his ideas for publicity when we got our bid to the state invitational this year.

"Soon as we get the official letter," he said, "I'm calling the newspapers and I'm getting those jokers to give us some coverage. Hell, the rest of the entries are big, right? Resort teams with college ringers, like we lost to in the sectionals last year. Hell, we're the only neighborhood tav-ren team's ever been invited two years running—three years with this year."

"Can you see the sports page put Axel's Inn in big print, RayBotts, though?" Voss said. He practiced palming cards. Me, I couldn't listen to that bar talk any more. I watched Smitty and Edwards.

"Didn't you ever fail at anything?" he asked Smitty.

"Plenty of times. Except I never lied about failing at anything is the difference."

"Listen, Smith," he said. He laid his arm out in front of him, clenched his fingers into a fist.

"Why the hell shouldn't we get the same publicity some smelly factory team loaded with ringers gets?" Ray Botts was saying.

Then Smitty called him a liar again, a liar and a eee-lapper. Edwards slapped his mouth. Ray Botts was suddenly hollering about the sink in the men's toilet. Smitty never flinched.

"You want to prove it?" he said.

"Damn right," Edwards said. He got up, a head and a half taller than Smith, seventy pounds heavier easy. Then everyone in the tavern knew what was up, and all the noise was over. In a second, I could see whose side everyone was on. It figured. They needed that state invitational, the mention on the sports page, the names engraved on the trophy. Like me.

"Kick his ass out, Les," Fred Jantke said, "he's got nothing to do with this place. He's a crud drinks free beer."

"You want me to handle your light work, Big Ed?" Ray Botts said, getting up now also.

Smitty put them down. He stood there with that ten-dollar, you're-a-damn-liar smile on his face. "Not in here you don't," Les said. He picked up the cue from the bumper pool table for authority.

"Come on out?" Smitty said to Edwards.

They headed for the door, and I was right behind them. Ray Botts moved too, but I turned on him and shouted in his face, "Yes, goddamn, I washed my funky hands in the sink! Clean it up and shut your damn lip about it!" And by God, he did. Stopped, I mean. Nobody came after us. We stood on the sidewalk in front of the tavern in the dusk. An air conditioner in the window of Les's upstairs apartment hummed and rattled.

When Edwards spoke, I finally understood. "He goes inside," he said, jerking a thumb at me. "Just you and me."

"I'm staying," I said, deciding that if Edwards whipped him—*when* he whipped him—I'd take a turn, lousy fighter that I am and always will be.

"Start something," Edwards said, sagging a little.

"Hobo your way over," Smitty said. "I'll pay your freight back." They mixed and traded punches. Three, maybe four, but I couldn't see exactly, only that it was about an even exchange, no marks on anybody. Just huffs of breath, a quick *thud thud* of sound, and then Smitty slipped, pushed not hit, into the gutter. He struggled to get his footing, and I figured Edwards would catch him off balance there and cream him.

But Edwards quit. He stood high over Smitty on the curb, sagging, put out his hand. "Let's shake, forget it," he whispered like he didn't want me to hear.

Smitty's aloha shirt was pulled open. He took time now to button it, wide open if Edwards laid into him. "Shake?" he said. "Not no, but hell no! Go on," he said, "hit me now while I'm fixing my shirt, hit me when my hands are down."

"Come on, Smitty," Edwards said, voice pleading, "shake and forget it."

"Afraid to hit me now, Big Ed? You afraid I'll get my sandwich while you're having a meal? Admit you're afraid and I'll shake with you, big man." Edwards pulled his hand back and stepped away from the gutter before he spoke.

"You little nigger," he said.

"Is that all you got left, Edwards?" is all Smitty said. Edwards turned around, looked down the street like he needed someplace to crawl in, away from everything. But the tavern was all there was. He walked in Axel's, the neon shining on his forehead. "Tell ' all about it, Big Ed!" Smitty yelled after him.

"That's good enough," I said to him, "you said it enough. He knows. We all know."

"Did you see that, Tee-bow?" he said, smiling.

"I seen it." There must be something to it, I thought, if you can stand up to a man twice your size. Then I remembered how I was ready to take Edwards myself. "Come on," I said, "come on across the street, I'll buy you a beer at the Mint Bar." He winked and made a circle with his thumb and forefinger. "One sec," I said, "I need to get my mitt first."

I went in and picked up my glove from a booth. I didn't see Edwards. Nobody said anything until I was on the way out. "Practice, Tee-bow," Ray Botts said, "Wednesday, six-thirty, Pumping Station, practice."

"If I can make it," I said. "I don't know yet what I'm doing Wednesday." Smitty and I crossed the empty street.

"Make it two," he said. "That's the theater-in-the-round crowd. I never go there unless I got a firm promise of at least two drinks. They don't like serving Ni-grows, so I need two to take the trouble." I laughed with him.

"You come all the way across town for that, don't you, Smitty."

"Why not," he said. "It's my right, isn't it?"

"You're on," I said. I hold the door open for him, follow him inside to buy him a little victory beer. I am glowing.

The Cage

FLOYD SKLOOT

The path to Theo Deane's beach house was overgrown with weeds. Its entrance was hidden somewhere at the end of the gravel road where Mel Niles stopped his panel truck.

At least the man was home this time. Because here's that sleek car of his parked snug against the huckleberries and rhodies and poison oak like it's hiding from the neighbors. A Lexus, an Infiniti, an Eternity, Mel couldn't keep the names of those fancy vehicles straight. Every time you see a rig like that on Highway 101, it's this same slate gray color.

Mel rattled around in the back of his truck for a few minutes. Bracing it on an edge, he dragged a bulky parcel over to the door, hopped out and looked around. He'd been delivering stuff to the man's house for ten months and still was never sure where the entrance to that damned path was. Mr. Deane must erase his tracks like a secret agent or something. Mel scanned the trees for the little wrinkle he'd noticed last week, not much more than a nick in the leaves. Then he looked down where it met the ground and spotted the rock shaped like a dolphin's back. There you go. Now all he had to do was lug the damn parcel two hundred yards through the woods, slip himself around a cluster of salal, cross a little bit of soft sand, heft it up six steps and knock on the door. No sweat.

Except it weighed a good sixty pounds, he thought. What now, a full-size reproduction of Candlestick Park, put it together on the back lawn? Comes with your blustery wind, your piped-in crowd noise, smell of hot dogs. Or how about a set of bats made of brass for warming up the muscles?

Mel lifted the parcel onto his shoulder and groaned. He realized he should have used the dolly, but it was such a chore getting a dolly over the grass and sand. I know, this is a steel workout bench, some assembly required. The man had more equipment than the local gym.

At least Mel had timed it right today, caught the man when he was in. Doesn't like us to leave his parcels on the porch, doesn't want to be driving forty minutes over to the UPS office to pick them up. Bring them anytime Friday afternoon is fine, he says. And the manager actually agrees. So there's a Theo Deane corner in the office now. Some Fridays, Mel had a half-dozen things for him, three or four trips back and forth between the truck and the house like a donkey.

What the hell, it was no big deal, and every once in a while the man gave Mel a little something. Not supposed to take tips, no gifts, but Mr. Deane made it seem more like a favor on Mel's part to take the stuff from him. Two half-court tickets to a Blazers-Lakers game, for example, which was well worth the drive into Portland and back. A nice aluminum baseball bat for the little boy, hit the ball it makes a hollow ping that Mel still can't get used to hearing. A roast chicken, like Mr. Deane had accidentally cooked one too many. Last month, a set of passes to see Free Willy over at the Newport aquarium, a real killer whale that was a movie star, the kid loved it. Mel couldn't think why he'd never taken him there before. Whale swimming around in there, big smile on his face, real name of Keiko but they use a stage name when he does his films.

Mel remembered his first trip to the Deane place. It was last year, early fall, a small enough parcel to carry in one hand, probably nothing more than a housewarming gift. Wasn't long before the weekly shipments filled up a quarter of Mel's truck. That first time, he had left the parcel by the door and was headed back to the truck when the man called out to him. Mel went around back to find him standing halfway between an enormous mound of topsoil and a good two dozen racks of sod, looking back and forth between them like he wasn't sure which one was supposed to go down first. Wind was making the rolling stretch of wild grasses look like they were waving so-long. Mel noticed the few giant coreopsis near the bluff and the occasional dune tansy and he knew exactly what was going through this man's mind. Trade this nice native look for about an eighth acre of thick, closely clipped grass, make a playground out of it. He was surprised when Theo Deane turned around with streaks of tears running down his cheeks.

Slowly, over the course of the next six months, Mel watched the place change as each new piece of equipment was installed like some kind of postmodern sculpture in this blustery garden. His Level Swing machine and his Rapid Wrist Machine, his Rocket Arm and his Pepper Net. He wondered how the man could sleep at night, all those shadows and strange howling noises when the wind blew past.

What's that noise now? Sounds like the waves turned solid back there, smacking into the wood the man has buttressing his slope. You never know what to expect when you come to Theo Deane's. A couple months ago, Mel had found him around to the side of the place. Must take Fridays off there at the law firm in Portland, pretty nice deal. Had on an old-fashioned Chicago White Sox hat with twenty-some stripes running down from the button to the bill so it looked like a bird cage on his head. Had his back next to the wall of the house and dangling from the roof eaves was a baseball attached to a strap that was attached to springs that were attached to the house. He's pretending to throw the ball, concentrating so hard he couldn't hear Mel coming, and from the sweat all over his face it's obvious the man's been at this for a long time. That was his Arm Strong, a unit Mel had brought him just a week before. Didn't weigh too much. Mel had thought the parcel was maybe a collapsible fishing pole or something from the way it felt and sounded inside the packaging.

Now Mel put today's parcel down on the back porch and stretched his back before ringing the bell. House made of glass, just about, what they call solar plexus, passive soul, whatever. Leave it to Theo Deane to come up with a passive soul when he's living right smack on the edge of the land. Got a dream house in a dream place and he's the unhappiest man Mel ever saw. Passive soul, that's right, always hot in those houses. Mel himself was just about sweated through his shirt. Middle of February, it's sixty-six degrees, he thought. Mildest winter we've had in years, must be the ozone melting down. He thought he should have worn his summer uniform, stored now in the kid's closet till June maybe, the brown shorts that made him look like an old man retired to Florida.

Mel waited for Theo Deane to make his way to the front door. Always something. Either he's in the shower, middle of the afternoon, or he's in the back room daydreaming, or he's off somewhere working out. Then it's Just a minute Mel. Name that tune.

Nothing doing. So Mel rang again, then heard the voice riding on the breeze: "I'm out back."

Well, fine and dandy, you're out back. I'm not about to drag this parcel to you, that's one thing I do know. Mel left it leaning against the wall and walked around the house.

Theo Deane was in a cage. A long, low cage, its mesh thick enough to darken what-all was inside. The cage stretched most of the way across his back yard, a good seventy feet long, held in place by three blue metal braces front, rear and middle. At one end, there was a machine spitting baseballs out of a hole dead-center. At the other end, there was Theo Deane—in a shabby gray sweat suit and this time battered old navy blue New York Yankees cap—swatting at the baseballs and grunting each time he swung.

"Just a minute, Mel. There's five," then he shut up while another pitch came and he swung and grunted. "More balls in there before," another pitch, another swing and grunt. "I can get out of here."

Mel. Calls me Mel and wants me to call him Theo. Hard to do that because the man just seems like a Mr. Deane, not a Theo. What kind of name is Theo, anyway, Greek? Theo, the God of Parcels. Apparently, he was once called Teddy, which must have been a very long time ago because he's got about as much Teddy in him now as Mel has Bunny, which used to be his nickname till he got old enough to put a stop to it. Teddy Deane, played a season and a half in the big leagues, a real hotshot, a Yankee in pinstripes, till he took a pitch in the face, busted up his eyesocket good. Mel had looked him up in the boy's Baseball Encyclopedia, one skinny little entry with huge numbers, led the league in this and that, and then he's gone.

He sure hit the last pitch on the sweet spot. Jesus, Mel thought, that one sounded like a gunshot. Sees well enough now.

Theo Deane came out of the cage, wiping his face with a towel that had been dangling from the door. Towel had Brooklyn Dodgers written on it in fancy blue script. Huh, not much loyalty in the man.

"Sorry about that, Mel." Theo smiled and led them back around the front of the house, taking the porch steps two at a time. "Had to finish my hundred swings." Mel followed, just wanting to get the man's John Hancock and get out of there. Plenty of stops to make yet.

"There it is," Theo said as he touched the parcel. "I've been waiting for this."

Man, look at this guy. We're probably the same height and weight but he looks four inches taller and thirty pounds lighter. Not a crease any-where — the face, the neck, even the sweat clothes he's got on and you know he's been working out in them for a while. How's a guy get to look like that?

Mel handed him the brown plastic gizmo and magic pen for a sig-nature. Not supposed to ask customers what's inside a parcel, but curios-ity was killing him. As was his neck, carrying the thing.

Theo finished signing and looked up. He smiled as he read Mel's face. "It's a Solo Socker, Mel. No home's complete without one."

Mel nodded like he knew what the hell the man was talking about, pursing his lips, narrowing his eyes. Then he turned around to leave. "See you next time, Mr. Deane."

"Theo."

"Right. Well, you have a good week, Theo."

Serves me right, Mel thought as he walked past the salal. Serves me fine, wondering what's inside.

A Solo Socker. What the hell is that, some kind of code words? I'm supposed to know what he's talking about? Maybe the man is a spy after all. He sure is a solo socker, Mel thought, no friends that I ever see. Except there was that one lady back in the fall, was here a couple times, had those legs on her so she didn't need no stairs to get up into the man's loft. Ol Theo and this one could look each another in the eye, she must have been a steady six-two. Had that one blue eye and the other brown, the strangest looking woman Mel ever had seen. Peeking out at him from under a thick strand of copper colored hair. Strange, but what's the word he was look-ing for? Alluring, that's it. Just about had Mel hypnotized when she was talking about these scallops she wanted to cook.

But she's gone now. Which is probably why he's out there in the cage. A solo socker, that's how the man struck Mel from the get-go.

The next week, Mel was back there with three parcels, each one as big as the Solo Socker. Pretty soon, the man's going to have to buy the land next door just to house all this equipment. That, or start throwing some of the older stuff over the edge. Maybe he's got one of those underground bunkers somewhere, he stores the stuff he isn't using.

When Mel returned with the final parcel, Theo Deane was waiting with a glass of lemonade. Make that a vat of lemonade. Mel wondered how long he was supposed to hang around there trying to drink the whole thing down.

"Come around back with me a minute," Theo said. "You can help me with something."

Mel walked with him, but hung back a little. Just what he needed, start helping customers assemble the junk he brings them. Take him three days just to deliver one day's worth of parcels. Mel had a full afternoon's work left and couldn't be playing no games here.

"Don't worry, this won't take five minutes."

Damn, the man can read my mind. Spooky. Mel tried to drink and walk at the same time, to keep up with Theo, but he had to stop before any more lemonade ended up on his shirt.

"Come on in here with me," Theo said, unlatching the cage's door, which was just a frame of metal poles strung with the same dark netting as the rest of the cage. Mel thought, he wants me to go in the cage with him?

"Man, I haven't hit a pitched ball in years."

"That's ok, Mel. All I want is for you to adjust the pitching machine while I stand in the box. Can't get the damn thing set right. It hasn't thrown me a strike all day."

"I ain't got no screwdriver on me."

Theo laughed. "Just tilt the head of the thing a notch or two, once we get going."

So Theo stood beside the official home plate he'd nailed at one end of the cage and Mel, putting his drink down on the soft grass and sure it was going to topple over, stood by the pitching machine at the other end.

He did not like the light in here, if you could call this light. Plenty bright enough to see, no doubt about that, but stripped of its warmth or something. Taupe, he thought. The light in here's taupe. Or dead, maybe that's closer.

"They've got machines now that can throw curve balls," Theo said as he waggled the bat toward Mel. "I just ordered one."

Great, Mel thought, and it probably weighs eight hundred pounds.

"Don't worry, it's light as a feather. All right, see if you can move the head on that down about a half-inch."

Mel touched the top of the machine, which moved fractionally and spit out a ball. It looked like Theo was going to swing. Mel threw himself to the ground, remembering the rifle shot sound he'd heard last week.

"Jesus, Mel, I wouldn't hit the ball with you in here. Relax."

You relax, Mel thought. He dusted off some stray grass and took his position again, adjusting the machine according to Theo's directions and watching him like he'd watch a panther in the wild.

"Next week," Theo said, "I should be able to tell. Once I get that new machine."

After his injury, Theo had tried to come back, tried to play again for the Yankees. But he couldn't see well enough to track the ball's flight and got dizzy whenever a pitch curved. He couldn't catch either, the ball caroming off the tip or heel of his mitt. Soon, his left eye began developing an early form of cataracts. He went through a lengthy course of laser surgeries, but his vision simply never came around. For half a year, he couldn't stand up for more than twenty minutes at a time without losing his balance.

It took six months to admit that he was finished as a baseball player. The doctors were the first to say so. Even the Yankees said so before Theo did. One night in May, when the next season was already well underway, he called his brother Conor and said, "I guess I can afford law school now."

In three years, he had established his practice in Portland, a city he loved for its setting and its easy style, what the magazines called livability. The opposite of New York. He even liked its rain. They liked that he was a former ballplayer, but didn't hound him on the streets, reserving that for their beloved basketball players. And it was the right place to practice environmental law. Soon Conor had moved up from San Francisco and they were practicing together. But in the last couple of years, Theo had begun losing focus. He turned more and more work over to Conor and the staff, tried fewer cases, and began to plan his comeback. He hadn't been in court in 17 months. He was 32; it was now or never. Conor told him he was nuts and threatened to move back south.

When they were finished adjusting the machine, Theo led Mel back around to the front of the house. Mel looked at his watch. He would have to drive like a maniac to get back on schedule.

"I won't keep you but a minute longer, Mel. You ever play any ball?"

Oh wonderful, now he wants to reminisce. I could be here till Sunday. Mel didn't think the man really wanted to know about his story, so he said, "Just some high school hoops."

Theo halted as if walking into a wall. "Wait a minute, I recognize that tone of voice."

"What?" Mel played back what he'd just said. "What tone of voice you talking about?"

"'Just some high school hoops.' Come on, tell me more about your high school hoops."

"That." Mel snorted. "Well, it was fun while it lasted. This was in Portland, 83-84. We had a run at the state finals two years straight and I got me some college offers. Took a full ride to Oregon State, man, the Beavers. But then I tore up my knee freshman year, the scholarship went away and I finished up my degree at the community college back home while I worked hauling freight around. All I wanted to do was move out here to the coast. Like I said, just some high school hoop."

"So what did you do with it?"

"Do with what?"

"I don't know, your desire to play, all that energy." Theo waved his arm vaguely in the direction of the ocean. "The drive."

Mel shook his head. "I don't even watch it on TV, hardly. I got a life to live, wife and kids, work. What do I want to do with playing hoops, tear up my knee again and lose my job?"

"You have a court at the house, though, am I right? The nice backboard and a rim with a net."

"What for?"

"You're kidding me."

Mel shook his head again.

"You can just let it go?"

"Let it go? I never had a hold of it. Look, I got to get back to work, Mr. Deane. Thanks for the lemonade."

"Theo," he took the glass from Mel. "Do me a favor and call me Theo, all right? Now what about your son?"

Mel studied the man's face. Don't go near that, Mr. Deane. "What about him?"

"Aren't you going to teach him?"

Mel chuckled. "Lee takes after his mama. Winter, he wants to be a wrestler."

After Mel left, Theo went back into the batting cage and began rounding up balls. He loaded them into the machine's auto-feeder, set the speed ten m.p.h. slower, and trotted to the far end. Picking up the bat, he quickly set himself and crouched.

He hated the way it sounded in here. The slightest wind whistled when it passed through the cage's netting. The occasional sea gull circling above him, bugling for food, sounded like a besotted Bronx heckler. No matter how much oil he slathered on the machine, the gears clacked and clattered as it loaded each ball and he could always tell when the pitch was about to come. This did not make for good practice. The light seemed strange too, as though stained by the sand and pollen that gathered in the netting. He could use some stadium-quality lights, though the neighbors might not appreciate them. Lights and maybe one of those adjustable tees that help you shorten your stroke, and a recording of ballpark sounds — the vendors, the chatter and cheers, throw in a few nasty jeers. *Hey Deane, go back to court, ya bum.*

He was just being too sensitive, having trouble concentrating. Bear down and hit, Deane.

He pulled the first pitch hard into the netting at his right. That would have landed in the dugout, he thought, and scattered the whole team. In the back of the baseball magazines he has been reading, where the equipment and other items for sale are featured, they've got personals ads now too. Russian ladies who want to meet ballplayers or fans or anybody in America who ever ate a peanut. Asian girls who love to please. Hey, baseball is huge in Japan, maybe one of those girls knows how to pitch the split-finger fastball.

Theo waited on the next pitch and lined it into the net to his left. Better. A double over third. His mind was getting clearer now. He hit the next pitch into the screen in front of the pitching machine. Take that, sucker. It wasn't till the sixth ball that he hit one really right, a rising liner into the corner of the cage, a sure gapper, three bases in the old days when he had his speed. Well, he still could run, maybe not as fast but for much longer than when he was playing. He was in better shape now and every bit as strong, he thought.

Right, and I know the law better too. But that and all my practice here is not likely to get me into a Yankee uniform again. Maybe the Devil Rays, though, new team looking for a crowd-pleaser. Theo wondered if he could talk Conor into being his agent, make a couple calls.

When the machine was empty, Theo rounded up the balls, loaded them and shut the machine off. He left the cage, walking toward the house while he slipped off his batting gloves and put them in his rear pocket. His original plan had been to stay in Portland this weekend, since he had a dinner appointment scheduled for Sunday afternoon. It was a lot of driving for just one full day of practice, but he couldn't bear to be away from it anymore. Besides, he didn't mind the road between Portland and the coast, especially this time of year when there was less traffic and the evergreens were a dark tunnel at the summit of the Coast Range.

Theo moved the three parcels into his shed and hefted the big parcel that Mel had brought last week. He carried it around to the back, tore it open and spread the flaps on the grass. Just as he'd thought. Solo Sockers came in about twenty pieces banded together without instructions. That's why he hadn't touched it all week. He started sorting them; they were mostly interlocking tubes and brackets, in schoolhouse red, with one rectangle of mesh about the size of a twin bed sheet, a length of elasticized cord and a cheap baseball. Simple enough. But something was off, he wasn't sure what.

As Theo went inside for a screwdriver, the sudden warmth of the house made him realize what the problem was. Aerodynamics. In the harsh coast winds and storms, he'd need something to anchor his Solo Socker or the whole unit would end up on Highway 101.

He stopped long enough to pour himself a glass of Merlot, took a sip, then left it on the counter as he went to the shed for a bucket. He spent the next ten minutes gathering up small stones, working his way along the path to the gravel lot by the road. In the woods, footsteps crunched over fallen leaves and twigs, probably a hungry raccoon or stray cat.

Theo remembered that he hadn't stopped to pick anything up for dinner. So he would have to go out, driving another twenty minutes each way to the nearest restaurant. Now he realized the afternoon was cooling fast. Things felt like they were beginning to crowd up on him. It would be sunset soon and Theo tried never to miss a coast sunset. Every weekend while he was at the beach, he stopped whatever he was doing, walked to the edge of the bluff, sat with his back against the smooth driftwood lair he'd assembled the first week he'd moved in, and thought of nothing but the slow descent of the sun. Even when it was too cloudy to see the sun, which it often was, Theo went to the bluff and watched anyway. Which meant he'd better hustle.

Coming back behind the house again, he filled the tubes that would comprise the Solo Socker's base with stones before fitting them together and locking them in place with brackets. If this didn't work, he'd fix up some metal clamps and spike them into the ground, holding the thing in place like a tent in an alpine meadow.

It took a while to get the elastic cord attached properly to the top and bottom braces, but when he had it together right the baseball settled in the heart of his strike zone and Theo smiled. Looked pretty good. He could work on his stroke first thing in the morning, practice keeping the swing short. The cases he was working on back in Portland could wait. Hell, the law always waits, at least environmental law does. Motions and countermotions, like the movement of the tides. There was no rush for anything. He slapped the ball once with his hand to test the cord's tension, went inside, picked up his wine and headed for the driftwood.

Mel got home about a half hour late. He'd speeded things up after leaving the man's place, but not enough to break even. He knew Shondra was going to be a bit testy, Friday night and he's holding things up.

His son was sitting on the floor of the living room, back pressed against the sofa, watching television. His hat was on backwards, of course, and he was squeezing two hand grips, strengthening himself up while he watched his show.

Mel followed the sound of clattering cookware and found Shondra in the kitchen, nodding to herself. Great, either she's singing, which is a good sign, or she's agreeing with herself that marrying Mel Niles was as dumb as her daddy always said, which was not such a good sign.

He walked over and slipped his arms around her waist, drawing Shondra close, nuzzling her neck, kissing behind her ear the way she liked. "Sorry, baby, I'm a little late. I'll make it up to you."

Then he left the room before she had a chance to say anything harsh. He wandered into the living room and sat on the sofa so that his legs hung next to Lee's left shoulder.

"How was school, my man?"

Lee actually muted the television. That was a first. Mel hoped the boy wasn't in some kind of trouble.

"No problem," Lee said. "I made weight, so I go varsity tomorrow against Otis."

"I didn't know Otis had a high school."

"Otis Levingston, Pop. Third in state last year."

Mel nodded. "What time you on?"

"Could be five, five thirty."

Mel had missed the last three times his son wrestled. They weren't going to talk about that, exactly, but he knew it would be good for him to be there tomorrow. He wanted to, he really did, and it was a Saturday meet too, pretty rare, a tournament. But he was so damn tired.

Hell with that. Mel went upstairs to change. He would go to sleep early, sleep late, whatever it took, but he'd be there when Lee tangled with this Otis kid. Bank on it.

He took off his watch and dangled its band from the raised, golden arm of the figure on his state basketball championship trophy. He undressed and took a quick shower. Then he came downstairs wearing his old tan chinos and the faded gray tee shirt that said Benson High School Basketball, proud that he could still fit in the thing.

Shondra was setting the kitchen table. Mel took her in his arms again and kissed her lips, taking the silverware out of her hand while he did, and gently nudging her toward the chair that she always sat in for her meals.

"What's with you?" Shondra asked.

Mel smiled at her. He took care to put the knives, forks and spoons just where she liked them, all facing the right way, each utensil where it was supposed to go.

How to Write a True Baseball Story

RICHARD PETERSON

Now you can't look it up, but, if you've read enough baseball fiction, you know it's not that easy to write a true baseball story. I'm sure lots of writers have tried, but when they sit down something strange must possess them. Instead of writing truthful things about baseball, they always end up writing fairy tales, ghost stories, or moral romances, but rarely, if ever, do they write a true baseball story.

I'm not going to lie and tell you I've actually written a true baseball story, but I am going to tell the truth about what happened to me when I tried to write a true baseball story. And maybe my true account will explain why it's so hard to write the truth about baseball.

This is not an easy thing to talk about, but as soon as I started to write a true baseball story, I began hearing voices. Now I admit to reading about the voices in *Shoeless Joe* and I'll even confess to weeping every time I watch the ending of *Field of Dreams*, but this business of hearing voices didn't happen to me in an Iowa cornfield or at a major-league ballpark or at the Hall of Fame. And it didn't happen at midnight in the clear, cool air after a thunderstorm or at noon on a blazing summer day or in some dusk or dawn fog bank. It happened at either ten minutes to ten or ten minutes after ten on an early March Saturday morning or, to be as truthful as I can be, on a March sixth Saturday morning.

I'd like to be more precise about the time, but my wife, depending upon her current outlook on life, sets all the clocks in our house either ten minutes fast or ten minutes slow. But I know it was Saturday morning because that's the only time I have for writing a true baseball story. You see, I'm an English professor, actually a specialist on Irish writers like James Joyce, so during the week I'm too busy playing the academic game. But, on Saturday morning, my wife, the retired school teacher, takes off just before nine for her part-time job as a kennel girl at the local vet's office, my son, the eternal college student, is sleeping off his Friday night poker game with his buddies, and I get to spend some uninterrupted time, or so I thought, writing a true baseball story. And I know the date was March sixth, because I checked the *Play Ball* calendar in my study for a good omen and there it was—March sixth was the birthday of Willie Stargell, one of my favorite players from my childhood team, the Pittsburgh Pirates.

Now, when I finally sat down at my desk, I thought about writing a thinly disguised autobiographical story about playing catch with my ghostly father, or maybe going to my first major-league baseball game with my lovingly remembered father, or just talking baseball about my beloved Pirates with my wise and caring father, but I had a hard time figuring out my first sentence. I considered starting my story with "river run past Three Rivers Stadium," but that seemed entirely too Joycean and "stately, plump" Willie Stargell seemed true but unkind. Finally, I had an inspiration, but when I wrote down "Once upon a green field of the mind when I was a boy of summer," an opening sure to catch the eye of Roger Angell of the *New Yorker* or George Plimpton of the *Paris Review*, I heard a voice say:

"If you stop it, he will come."

Obviously, I was surprised by the voice, but I'd have been more in awe if the voice hadn't been so rude and insulting. Besides, at my advanced age, any indicator that you can still hear is a good sign, even if what you hear is a disembodied voice telling you to stop writing. Since I felt more humiliated than honored, I decided to make sure I wasn't confused by the message. After all, the voice, which, by the way, sounded a lot like David McCullough's, might have said, "if you don't stop it, he will come." So I picked up my pen with the miniature Pirate cap on the clicker and, just to make sure, went back to finishing the sentence I thought I'd begun so gloriously. But just as I added "my father and I" to the sentence, I heard a low moan, then the voice spoke again:

"Ease his pain. Don't finish the sentence."

From the desperate and pleading tone of the voice, I knew I had the advantage as long as I had my pen in hand, so I wrote on my Pirate note pad, "if you don't want me to finish the sentence, then tell me who he is and where I can find him." This time in a tone so angry I thought it would wake the dead, or at least my dead-to-the-world son, the voice thundered out:

"Go the distance. Put down that silly pen, walk out to your son's car, and go the distance to the university library. He'll be in the stacks waiting for you."

As difficult as it is for an English professor to turn his back on a sentence fragment, I got up from my desk, carefully stepped around my cardboard cutout replica of Forbes Field and hurried out to my son's car. I realized, once I headed up Old US Highway 51, that I should have asked the voice for more specific information. Unlike many of my students and more than a few administrators, I know the location of our library, but I didn't have the exact location in the library for my meeting. The voice had also avoided identifying the mysterious "he," who was, I assume, to be my guide to the true baseball story.

Being a critic by profession, I also wondered why I couldn't just meet my guide at the university's baseball field. Our baseball Salukis were off playing at a tournament somewhere in Florida, Abe Martin Field was deserted, and the morning, for early March, was sunny and pleasant. But here I was, driving by a field with green grass, no lights, and uncomfortable bleacher seats, and, instead of meeting Joe Jackson or better yet Honus Wagner or Pie Traynor, I had to go to the library for a workshop on how to write a true baseball story.

When I arrived at Morris Library, I discovered that the baseball field wasn't the only place deserted on a Saturday morning. As I walked through the empty main lobby with all the former university presidents staring down at me from their portraits—and not one of them, I should add, wearing a baseball cap—I figured that whoever "he" was, he'd most likely be waiting for me by the library's stacks of baseball books in the recreation division on the fourth floor. I took the stairs instead of the elevator for fear that no one would hear my own desperate and pleading voice if the elevator broke down, but when I got to the fourth floor there was no one in sight. I walked in and out of the aisles of books willing to instruct me on everything from mountain climbing to scuba diving, but when I got to the shelves of baseball books, there was no ghost writer waiting to instruct me on the art of writing a true baseball story.

It appeared that my guide wasn't to be some baseball writer skilled in the alchemy of turning the exaggerated anecdotes of old-time players into histories of golden ages and legendary heroes, or even some paleontologist, political commentator, or middle-aged poet claiming to know all about baseball and the meaning of life. The only other possibility, and the one I should have thought of as soon as the voice told me to go the distance to the university library, was that my guide to writing a true baseball story was himself a writer of baseball stories. Who else but a writer of fiction would know how to write the truth about baseball.

As soon as I made my way back down to the Humanities Division on the second floor, I found the section for American fiction and started walking alphabetically through the stacks. There was no one lurking anywhere from A to Z in the section for nineteenth-century American fiction, but I didn't think that some dime novelist like the creator of Frank Merriwell and his fabulous double-shoot pitch was likely to be my guide for writing a true baseball story. It wasn't until I began moving past the stacks for twentieth-century American fiction that I finally sensed an emanation, and that emanation, to my horror, appeared to be coming from the aisle for authors from K to L. As I turned into the aisle, I was afraid my baseball dream was about to be transformed into a nightmare, that my guide to the true baseball story was to be none other than W. P. Kinsella, the self-proclaimed hater of all academic critics. It was Kinsella, after all, who had said academic critics have no sex life and get their thrills from hunting sexual symbols in literature. It was the same Kinsella who said academics exceed garbage men in pettiness and small-mindedness, a comment I thought rather offensive to garbage men, and had declared that if you truly wanted to be a writer, you should get as far away from academia as possible. I dreaded to think what Kinsella, who said he had the heart of a critic in a jar on his desk, would say to an academic critic who'd decided he should be the one to write a true baseball story.

True enough, my ghost writer or guiding spirit or whatever he was suppose to be was standing in the aisle right by the Ks, but I knew in a moment that what turned to face me was no Buffalo Bill Kinsella in faded denim. My baseball guide, with his straw boater in hand, was a Dapper Dan, tall, clean-shaven, well groomed, and dressed meticulously in a dark suit and tie slightly embellished, to tell the truth, by a bright-striped shirt with a high starched collar. He was certainly no country rube in appearance, though as fashionable as he looked, his dress was also about eighty years out of date for our meeting.

As I moved down the aisle, I identified myself, but when I reached the Ls and tried to compliment his baseball stories, he stopped me in mid-sentence:

"Let's cut the gab. I know who you are, what you are, and what you've been up to. Why do you think I'm stuck here, staring at my own misbegotten books. And don't give me that hearts-and-flowers routine about my baseball stories. If I hadn't written all that Dear Al stuff, I wouldn't be spending my afterlife traveling through time warps just to baby-sit another rook who thinks he can write a true baseball story. Do you have any idea of how many of you are out there, thinking you know all about baseball, all writing the same lies about your ballplaying youth, all telling the same boring stories about your poor dead fathers, and not knowing enough to fill a knothole about playing baseball or writing fiction?

"Well, don't just stand there looking sheepish and forlorn. I'm not exactly remembered for my kind words or goodness of heart, you know. Besides, I've got more than one rook on my lineup card today and I'm not getting any relief help. If you want to know how to write a true baseball story—and why anyone in his right mind would want to write a true baseball story is beyond me—let's find a corner somewhere so I can set you straight."

I was beginning to feel more haunted than helped and, I confess, more than a little curious about a couple of the complaints from my Hall of Fame writer, but I let things go for the moment. I suggested we walk up the aisles to the Rare Book room, a place rarely visited even on week days. Fortunately, when we entered the reception area there was no one on duty, so we stepped into the small workroom and sat down at one of the tables:

"This place looks like a mausoleum. Just look at all the busts in here. There's D. H. Lawrence and G. B. Shaw and James Joyce, all looking down at you and me, and we're going to talk about writing baseball stories. Why don't you just write something critical about baseball fiction—there's my sorry attempts at short stories, and the copy-cat stuff by Runyon and Thurber, and there's Harris's Horatio Alger stuff, and Kinsella's fairy tales. Why not just write an essay about the way baseball writers keep feeding adolescent hooey to all those Huck Finns and Holden Caulfields out there who never want to grow up. It wasn't Abner Doubleday who invented baseball. It was Peter Pan."

I got up from the table, picked up a scratch sheet from the top of the card catalog, sat back down, and began copying out the unfinished first sentence of my baseball story.

"Alright, I got the message. So let's get this over and done with. First of all, if you want to write a baseball story readers are going to think is true then get your baseball details right and maybe mix in a little history—but lay off the Black Sox stuff because that's been done to death and besides, that fellow Asinof already proved the real story is better than fiction. You maybe can throw in some real-life players just for fun, but then you've still got to think about your main character. You've got nine positions, unless you're dumb enough to write about a manager or worse yet an umpire, but I'd say stay with a pitcher when you're starting out because he's the center of attention anyway. All you need to do is come up with a colorful nickname, maybe something a little better than Lefty or Cannonball, a larger-than-life personality, maybe exaggerate his size or shrink his intelligence, and make him a green rookie trying to prove himself or a washed-up vet trying to show that he still belongs. Pitch your character in the pennant or World Series deciding game, and what do you have—a baseball story."

As I sat there trying hard not to stare at the straw boater on the table and trying even harder not to lose my patience, I realized I had just been fed a lot of hooey. My ghost writer was giving me clichés and formulas instead of telling me how to write a true baseball story. Instead of playing along, I decided to go after him. I challenged him to stop his griping about rook writers and Peter Pan readers and for once in his life, or at least in his afterlife, to tell a true baseball story:

"So you want the truth about baseball and you want it in a story. No boobs or rubes. No naturals or supernaturals. No fields of dreams. No fathers playing catch with sons. No two outs in the bottom of the ninth, bases loaded, three-two counts, no let's win the pennant or World Series for little Bobby or Billy in the hospital. Just the truth. Well, let's see how you handle this one.

"A long time ago, when the game really mattered, there were three boys, let's call them brothers, who loved baseball. Now the first brother had a real passion for playing the game. He wasn't that powerful or that fast, but he was so determined to be the best that he was a demon on the field. Winning was so important to him that he was willing to do anything in a game to give himself the edge. He became feared and even hated, but no one was better at winning a baseball game.

"The second brother was a gifted ballplayer, a natural, but, unlike the first brother who was willing to play anywhere just to win, the second brother always pitched because he knew, if he pitched, he could control the game. He was a great pitcher, but his real passion was for organizing and controlling things. He kept all the equipment, scheduled all the games, and made up all the rules. He insisted on telling everyone when to bat and where to play. He was resented and distrusted, but if anyone complained or wouldn't play by the rules, the second brother would just pick up his bats and balls and threaten to go home.

"The third brother, unlike the other two, wasn't much of a ballplayer, but he loved baseball with a true passion for the game. He admired the skill and talent of his brothers and enjoyed watching them play so much that he invented statistics to keep a record of what they accomplished on the field and even wrote up summaries and stories about each game. He was always the last one picked, if he were picked at all, but he didn't mind as long as he could watch his brothers play the game and keep a record of their glory and their greatness.

"Now, I'd like to tell you that the three brothers lived happily ever after. After all, they loved the game of baseball and each, according to his own passion, became successful and famous. But you wanted a true baseball story, so here's what really happened. To tell the truth, the first brother, who played the game with a fierce and ruthless passion for winning became frustrated and resentful when he realized that the people who started coming out to watch the games didn't really appreciate or enjoy his way of playing baseball. They applauded his daring and cunning, but what truly excited and thrilled them was the long ball. So to win the fans' adulation, he changed into a home-run hitter, but, as the fans cheered his epic slugging, he lost his hunger for playing the game as well as his passion for winning.

"When the second brother saw all the people coming out to watch his first brother's heroics, he decided to start charging admission. Once he realized how much money there was in baseball, he quit playing the game, though he was still in his prime, and became a magnate. Eventually he turned baseball into a business monopoly by making all the equipment and creating his own teams and leagues. He even figured out a way to own all the players and control their salaries, though when he saw the way the fans worshipped the home run he made sure the long-ball hitters were publicly honored and celebrated as heroes though not necessarily well paid as ballplayers.

"The third brother, the one who most truly loved baseball, became disheartened when he saw his first brother's passion for winning become a desire for popularity and fame, and his second brother's passion for success become a lust for money and power. He watched the playing of the game become less skillful and its management more selfish and greedy. As baseball became less enjoyable and interesting as a pastime, he grew bitter and cynical and even took to drinking too much as he watched the games. When he wrote about baseball, he mocked his first brother's larger-than-life reputation and ridiculed his second brother's moral hypocrisy. Finally he became so bored with the game he had loved so much, that he turned his back on baseball, staggered away from the ballpark, and lived unhappily ever after."

My guide to the true baseball story got up from the table, picked up his straw boater, but before he left, he offered me some final advice:

"Now that I've told you a true baseball story, maybe you can see now why it's probably better if you just forget about writing the truth about baseball. Most of us can only take so much of the truth and when it comes to baseball, we usually can't take much truth at all. But you decide. If you ever need to hear from me again, there's always my books out on the shelves. The only thing I ask is that you think about what I've told you before you sit down again with that God awful sentence—'Once upon a green field of the mind when I was a boy of summer, my father and I . . .' What a lot of hooey. You're lucky all you got was a visit from a washed up, cynical baseball writer and not a Judge Kenesaw Mountain Landis ready to ban you forever from writing another word about baseball."

After my ghost writer waved his boater in farewell, he sauntered out of the rare book room and faded into the shelves. Once he was gone, I got up from the table and quickly made my way out of the library to the parking lot. As I drove home, I tried to make some sense out of what I had just seen and heard. There was, of course, the obvious conclusion that after all the years of reading literature, including an unhealthy amount of James Joyce and baseball fiction, I was finally stricken by delusions and needed psychiatric help or, at least, a heavy dose of Russian realism to purge my soul. Yet, there was also a slim possibility that, delusions or not, my voices and spirits had left behind some lingering truth about writing a baseball story, though instead of feeling as if I'd just completed some magical adventure in search of baseball's Golden Fleece or Holy Grail, I felt left behind and disillusioned. I'd encountered a reluctant baseball guide who appeared before me as if he were paying some terrible penance for having used his talent to write baseball stories. I'd listened to his true baseball story turn into a bitter parable about the betrayal of baseball by those most responsible for loving and taking care of the game. And, worst of all, after going the distance, I was told I could ease everyone's pain by forgetting about writing a true baseball story because nobody wants to hear the truth about baseball.

When I got home, I went right to my study and slumped down at my desk. I took out my Pirate pen and, to the sound of a disembodied sigh of relief, I crossed out my unfinished sentence. As I sat there, I looked around at all my baseball artifacts until I came to my *Play Ball* calendar— and there he was. At the end of a long list of ballplayers born on March sixth, including Lefty Grove, my Willie Stargell, and even one-armed Pete Gray, was Ringgold "Ring" Lardner, 1885, *Chicago Tribune* sportswriter. I figured, what the hell, nobody's going to believe me anyway, so I wrote down, to the sound of distant grumblings, the first sentence to a true baseball story:

"Now you can't look it up, but, if you've read enough baseball fiction, you know it's not that easy to write a true baseball story."

Contributors

David Carkeet is the author of five novels, one of which, *The Greatest Slump of All Time*, grew out of the short story in this volume. The others are *Double Negative, I Been There Before, The Full Catastrophe,* and *The Error of Our Ways*. His short stories and essays have appeared in *Carolina Quarterly, Kansas Quarterly,* the *North American Review,* the *Oxford American,* the *San Francisco Review of Books, New York Stories,* the *New York Times Magazine,* and the *Village Voice*. His essays have been cited in *The Best American Essays 1999* and *The Best American Essays 2000*. *The Best American Sports Writing 1997* cited two other essays, one of them a chronicle of his slow-pitch career titled "Sunday Morning Ball at the J." Along with Mark Harris and W. P. Kinsella, he was interviewed about baseball fiction for the spring 1987 issue of *Modern Fiction Studies*. "The Greatest Slump of All Time" won an O. Henry Award in 1981. Carkeet directs the M.F.A. program in creative writing at the University of Missouri in St. Louis and is the editor of its literary journal, *Natural Bridge*.

Ron Carlson is the author of many books, including the story collections *The Hotel Eden, Plan B for the Middle Class,* and *The News of the World*. His most recent collection is *At the Jim Bridger* (2002). His fiction has appeared in the *New Yorker, Harper's, GQ, Playboy, Ploughshares, Story,* and many other publications. Carlson has moved from third to second base; he hits right and bats right. In 1959, he hit eight home runs to tie for the league lead in Edison Boys Baseball, Salt Lake City. He teaches in the M.F.A. program in creative writing at Arizona State University.

Philip F. Deaver is the thirteenth winner of the Flannery O'Connor Award for Short Fiction. His book of short stories is *Silent Retreats*. He has had fellowships from the National Endowment for the Arts and Bread Loaf. His work has appeared in *Prize Stories: The O. Henry Awards* and has been cited in *Best American Short Stories* and the *Pushcart Prize*. He has just completed a novel entitled *Past Tense*. He played shortstop and third base mostly, never pitched, and while he never hit for power, he eventually did hit for a good average. Since 1954, he's been a Cardinals fan and even now hopes to shake Musial's hand one of these days.

Andre Dubus was a peacetime Marine Corps captain, a member of the Iowa Writers' Workshop, and a Guggenheim fellow. His many books include *Broken Vessels*, *The Last Worthless Evening*, *Voices from the Moon*, and *Finding a Girl in America*. His work appeared in such magazines as *Playboy* and *Indiana Review*, and was reprinted in all the major anthologies. Winner of the *Boston Globe*'s first annual Laurence L. Winship Award (1975) and a MacArthur fellowship, Dubus lost his leg when a car hit him in July 1986. Baseball, he'd claimed, helped sustain him. He died in 1999.

Stuart Dybek is the author of three books—a collection of poetry (*Brass Knuckles*) and two collections of fiction (*The Coast of Chicago* and *Childhood and Other Neighborhoods*). His work has appeared in the *New Yorker*, *Harper's*, the *Atlantic*, and numerous literary magazines and anthologies. He has been the recipient of the PEN/Malamud Award, a Lannan Literary Award, a Whiting Writers Award, and fellowships from the National Endowment for the Arts and the Guggenheim Foundation. His baseball career was cut short in his late thirties by an injury, not, alas, on the field of play, but rather at a party at which he was called upon at his own insistence to demonstrate the "demon drop."

Ray Gonzalez is the author of *Memory Fever* (1999), a memoir; *Turtle Pictures* (2000), which received the 2001 Minnesota Book Award for Poetry; and a collection of essays, *The Underground Heart: Essays from*

Hidden Landscapes (2002). He is the author of seven books of poetry, including *The Hawk Temple at Tierra Grande* (2002) and two collections of short stories, *The Ghost of John Wayne* (2001, and winner of a 2002 Western Heritage Award for Best Book of Short Fiction) and *Circling the Tortilla Dragon* (2002). He has served as the poetry editor of the *Bloomsbury Review* for twenty-two years and founded the poetry journal *LUNA*. He is an associate professor in the M.F.A. Creative Writing Program at the University of Minnesota in Minneapolis. The first time he ever heard the name "Alou" was when he went to see the El Paso Sun Kings, who won the Texas League title with Felipe and Matty Alou on the team, years before they went on to major-league fame.

Patricia Highsmith spent most of her adult life in Switzerland and France. Educated at Barnard where she studied English, Latin, and Greek, she had her first novel, *Strangers on a Train,* published in 1950 to great commercial success and filmed by Alfred Hitchcock. Highsmith wrote more than twenty books, including *The Talented Mr. Ripley, The Two Faces of January,* and *People Who Knock on the Door. The Selected Short Stories of Patricia Highsmith* was published in 2001. Her awards include the O. Henry Memorial Award, the Edgar Allan Poe Award, Le Grand Prix de Littérature Policière, and the Award of the Crime Writers Association of Great Britain. She died in Switzerland in 1995.

David Jauss is the author of five books, most recently *Black Maps,* a collection of stories that won the Associated Writing Programs Award for Short Fiction. His stories have appeared in numerous magazines and been reprinted in the *O. Henry Awards, Pushcart Prize,* and *Best American Short Stories* anthologies. He teaches at the University of Arkansas at Little Rock and in the M.F.A. in Writing Program at Vermont College. After an undistinguished career as a high school baseball player, he played outfield and first base for the Montevideo Spartans in Minnesota's Independent League from 1969 to 1976, during which time he set records for hitting and fielding ineptitude that are still standing. He excelled only at the fine art of bench jockeying, a skill that has held him in good stead throughout his career as a creative writing teacher. "All in all," he writes, "baseball has been very, very good to me."

Owen King is a graduate of Bangor High School and Vassar College. He received an M.F.A. from Columbia University and is at work on a collection of stories called *We're All in This Together*. His stories have appeared in *Book Magazine* and the *Bellingham Review*. Mr. King is a long-suffering fan of the Boston Red Sox.

Jerry Klinkowitz has spent many years as a minor-league baseball owner, operator, and consultant. His book *Short Season and Other Stories* was selected by *Sport* magazine as the best baseball fiction of the year. His other book of baseball fiction is *Basepaths*. He's published more than thirty books on literature, art, history, philosophy, air combat, baseball, and jazz.

Kip Kotzen is a literary agent and the coeditor of *With Love and Squalor: 14 Writers Respond to the Work of J. D. Salinger* (2001). When he was twelve, Kip sneaked down into Metropolitan Stadium in Minneapolis and met Reggie Jackson, Billy Martin, and Rod Carew, and was personally cursed at by Thurman Munson.

Cris Mazza is the author of several books, including *Indigenous/ Growing Up Californian*, *Homeland*, *Girl Beside Him*, the PEN/Nelson Algren–winning *How to Leave a Country*, and the critically acclaimed *Is It Sexual Harassment Yet?* Mazza also coedited *Chick-Lit* and *Chick-Lit 2*, controversial anthologies of women's fiction. Mazza now lives in Illinois but still hates the Cubs. She and her San Diego Padres grew up together. She played in her college pep band at San Diego State University while Tony Gwynn set the school record for assists as a basketball player. She keeps a bat signed by Gwynn in her office.

Richard Peterson is the editor of the Writing Baseball series at Southern Illinois University Press. The author of several essays on baseball history and literature, he has also written *Extra Innings: Writing on Baseball*. Peterson grew up in Pittsburgh in the 1950s and rooted for some of the worst teams in sports history. He has written about the experience in *Lessons in Persuasion: Pittsburgh Connections* and *Pittsburgh Sports*.

Leslie Pietrzyk is the author of *Pears on a Willow Tree*. Her fiction has appeared in a number of literary journals, including *TriQuarterly*, *Iowa Review*, and *Shenandoah*. She is an Orioles fan and was thrilled when an entire, tense morning spent listening to busy signals on the phone finally paid off with tickets to see Cal Ripken break Lou Gehrig's consecutive games record.

Kurt Rheinheimer has published fiction in magazines ranging from *Redbook* and *Playgirl* to *Michigan Quarterly Review* and *Carolina Quarterly*. Four stories have appeared in the *New Stories from the South* anthologies. He was born in Baltimore and was eight years old when the Orioles moved to town. He was instantly addicted, and the team's recent seasons have verified that he is fully incurable. His own boyhood baseball fantasies, which reached their apex when he was a high-school late-inning defensive specialist, are these days lived out as coach and pitcher for the Pre-Geezer Wheezer coed slow-pitch softball squad. Rheinheimer lives in Roanoke, Virginia, with his wife and a varying number of their five sons, and serves as an editor of *Blue Ridge Country* magazine, a glossy regional dedicated to the southern Appalachians.

Josh Russell lives in New Orleans. His novel *Yellow Jack* (1999) has been translated into German as *Der Portätrist* (2002), and his short fiction has appeared in *Epoch*, *New Stories from the South*, and the limited-edition *Winter on Fifth Avenue, New York*. He owns a near-mint 1968 Topps #177 Nolan Ryan/Jerry Koosman rookie, printed the year he was born. He teaches at Tulane University.

Jim Shepard is the author of five novels—*Flights*, *Paper Doll*, *Lights Out in the Reptile House*, *Kiss of the Wolf*, and *Nosferatu*—and two collections of short stories: *Batting Against Castro* and *Love and Hydrogen*. His short fiction has appeared, among other places, in *Harper's*, the *New Yorker*, the *Atlantic Monthly*, *Esquire*, the *Paris Review*, *Playboy*, *DoubleTake*, and *Tin House*. He teaches at Williams College and in the Warren Wilson M.F.A. program, and he's been a lifelong wiffle ball player who's only recently developed a truly wicked sinker, along with a rotator cuff injury.

Floyd Skloot is the author of several books, most recently a collection of essays, *In the Shadow of Memory* (2003). He won the Oregon Book Award in Poetry for *The Evening Light* (2001). His work has appeared in the *Atlantic Monthly, Harper's, Poetry, Georgia Review,* and many other magazines. He was born in Brooklyn in 1947 and moved away in 1957, shortly after the Dodgers announced their own departure. At Ebbets Field, during the 1952 World Series, Floyd Skloot watched Andy Pafko catch a Gene Woodling line drive against the right field wall before Pafko fell into the stands. Skloot was five years old. He now lives in Amity, Oregon.

Gordon Weaver is the author of four novels and nine short story collections, the most recent of which is *Long Odds: Stories* (2000). His work has appeared in *Best American Short Stories, Prize Stories: The O. Henry Awards,* and *The Pushcart Prize.* Recognition of his work includes two NEA fellowships, the O. Henry First Prize, the St. Lawrence Award for Fiction, the Sherwood Anderson Prize, and other citations. He gave up playing baseball in his mid-forties after splitting a finger catching an infield pop-up. He lives in Wisconsin.

John McNally is the author of the story collection *Troublemakers*, winner of the John Simmons–Iowa Short Fiction Award (2000) and the Nebraska Book Award (2001). He has edited three other anthologies: *Humor Me: An Anthology of Humor by Writers of Color* (2002); *The Student Body: Short Stories about College Students and Professors* (2001); *High Infidelity: Short Stories about Adultery* (1997). He has been the recipient of the Jenny McKean Moore fellowship at the George Washington University in Washington, D.C., the Carl Djerassi fellowship from the University of Wisconsin's Institute for Creative Writing, a scholarship from the Bread Loaf Writers' Conference, and a James Michener fellowship from the Iowa Writers' Workshop. Though otherwise left-handed, McNally both catches and throws with his right hand, which seriously hinders his on-field performance and frustrates his teammates. He is an assistant professor of English at Wake Forest University in Winston-Salem, North Carolina, where he lives with his wife, Amy, and their many animals.

Other Books in the Writing Baseball Series

Man on Spikes
ELIOT ASINOF
Foreword by Marvin Miller

Off-Season
ELIOT ASINOF

The American Game: Baseball and Ethnicity
Edited by **LAWRENCE BALDASSARO**
and **RICHARD A. JOHNSON**
Foreword by Allan H. (Bud) Selig

The Chicago Cubs
WARREN BROWN
Foreword by Jerome Holtzman

My Baseball Diary
JAMES T. FARRELL
Foreword by Joseph Durso

The Brooklyn Dodgers: An Informal History
FRANK GRAHAM
Foreword by Jack Lang

The New York Giants:
An Informal History of a Great Baseball Club
FRANK GRAHAM
Foreword by Ray Robinson

The New York Yankees: An Informal History
FRANK GRAHAM
Foreword by Leonard Koppett

The Best Seat in Baseball, But You Have to Stand!
The Game as Umpires See It
LEE GUTKIND
Foreword by Eric Rolfe Greenberg